Of This Our Time

OF THIS OUR TIME

A Journalist's Story,
1905–50

Tom Hopkinson

Hutchinson
London Melbourne Sydney Auckland Johannesburg

To the earliest companions,
Jack, Paul, Stephan and Esther

Hutchinson & Co. (Publishers) Ltd

An imprint of the Hutchinson Publishing Group

17–21 Conway Street, London W1P 6JD

Hutchinson Group (Australia) Pty Ltd
30–32 Cremorne Street, Richmond South, Victoria 3121
PO Box 151, Broadway, New South Wales 2007

Hutchinson Group (NZ) Ltd
32–34 View Road, PO Box 40-086, Glenfield, Auckland 10

Hutchinson Group (SA) Pty Ltd
PO Box 337, Bergvlei 2012, South Africa

First published 1982
© Tom Hopkinson 1982

Set in Linotron Bembo by Computape (Pickering) Ltd

Printed in Great Britain by The Anchor Press Ltd
and bound by Wm Brendon & Son Ltd, both of Tiptree, Essex

British Library Cataloguing in Publication Data

Hopkinson, Tom
 Of this our time.
 1. Hopkinson, Tom
 2. Journalists—Great Britain—Biography
 I. Title
 070′.92′4   PN5123.H/

ISBN 0 09 147860 X

Contents

Illustrations

Foreword

Ever since the early 1930s I have kept notebooks. These were not diaries noting the names of people I met for lunch, but books in which I recorded whatever interested me enough for me to write it down. As factual reference therefore they are often lacking. As they were a record of immediacy with no eye to practical use, I have often found – on turning to them for information on some happening in the Second World War or for light on some manoeuvre of post-war political life – that I had noted nothing for that particular day or week except dreams, conversations with my small daughters, or an argument overheard in a pub. However, happenings which impressed themselves on me at the time – such as the constantly fluctuating situation inside the *Picture Post* office – were recorded in detail. Also, since I started keeping the notebooks while still a young man, they contain memories from childhood and early life which I should not now have been able to recapture.

These notebooks, then, with such letters and papers as I have preserved, plus memory, have been my principal sources. For the checking of facts I have made use particularly of B. H. Liddell Hart's *History of the Second World War* (Cassell, London, 1970) and of Paul Addison's *The Road to 1945* (Jonathan Cape, London, 1975).

I am grateful to Penguin Books for permission to quote from the introduction I wrote to *Picture Post 1938–50*, published in 1970 and reprinted in 1979, and to fellow journalist Jim Brennan for permission to make use of pieces I contributed to his magazine *The Media Reporter*. For permission to quote from Al Huggins's unpublished manuscript 'An Alien Clerk's Tale' about life in Pembroke College, Oxford, in the 1920s, I am grateful to his widow and to my friend and contemporary, Bob Martindale. I would like also to thank Harold Harris of Hutchinson for his careful reading of the typescript and for much sage advice.

I have taken my title from that familiar sonnet of Shakespeare's that begins, 'When in the chronicle of wasted time', and, as the title implies, I have tried in writing not so much to give a picture of myself as, through the medium of my own experiences, to reflect the times in which I have lived.

To my sister-in-law Janet, wife of Brigadier Paul Hopkinson MBE, I owe certain insights into our family life at the time when we were all growing up together in a Westmorland village. I thank my daughter Lyndall, Contessa Passerini, for practical help over the completion of this book, and Phyllis Jones, for long a friend of the family, for prompt and accurate typing.

Lastly, for the fact that the book has been written at all, with whatever degree of detachment it can claim – and for far more besides than I shall ever be able to express – I am grateful to Dorothy, my wife.

Penarth
1982

1
Out of Eden

All five children were standing in a row in my mother's drawing room, which was in a part of the house we seldom visited. At the head stood the eldest, Jack, already ten and a year older than myself, looking responsible and slightly troubled; I came second, and then Paul, aged eight, white-headed and pale-faced. Below him was Stephan, two years younger, peering short-sightedly with head thrust forward, giving him a somewhat truculent expression, and last of all Esther, pretty, blue-eyed, only four years of age and hardly aware of what was going on. The occasion was a solemn one. My father was telling us of his intention and, for the first time in our lives, asking approval for what he meant to do. We were going, he said, to say goodbye to our comfortable home and easy way of life where everything, it seemed, was provided by a kindly body called 'the university', which not only supplied our house and food, but service and attendants – maids, a cook and gardener, even pageboys with silver buttons on their blue-striped jackets. Our parents and we were giving all this up because he was now intending to become a clergyman, a calling at which he would earn a great deal less money. Before long we should go to live in a small house where there would be no maids, so that we should all have to help mother with the housework, wash up, make the beds and clean the shoes – all tasks which at present were done for us.

After outlining our future, my father – in his level, earnest voice, and with his gentle, self-effacing smile – asked each of us in turn to give our assent to his proposal. Jack readily gave his and I followed with 'Yes, father,' in my turn, as did we all. Not one of us would have dreamed of questioning a decision arrived at by our parents, and I think it unlikely that we ever even discussed his proposal among ourselves. Father and mother had decided, and it was therefore bound to happen.

Though I had said yes with the rest, inside I was far from agreeing with my father's intention, and looked to the future with foreboding. From quite early in my childhood I had recognized in my parents a disposition for self-sacrifice, and what I considered an exaggerated concern for other people, those 'other people' who were eagerly waiting to eat up the rice pudding I detested and the fish which my delicate brother Paul would push from one side of his plate to the other, hoping it would somehow become less, or even vanish altogether if forked around long enough. What I had learned about 'other people' made me inclined to be on my guard against them rather than make sacrifices on their behalf. Limited sacrifices, such as pennies into a box labelled 'Waifs and Strays', or the buying of a missionary magazine called *African Tidings* and priced reasonably at a halfpenny, I knew I could not avoid. But now it seemed that these other people and their demands were going to invade our well-ordered life, and I foresaw nothing but harm from the intrusion. Nor was I pleased with my father's choice of profession as a clergyman.

Many years later, when I asked him why he, a natural scholar doing the academic work he loved, should have given it up to enter the Church, he said he had been thinking for some time of this change, but what decided him had been a visit to church one Sunday evening. There he had listened to a sermon so distracted and confused that he realized the clergyman delivering it must be overwhelmed with the burden of his work. 'The only thing to do,' my father said, 'was to go and help him.' I felt I could have listened to a great many distracted sermons without feeling the same compulsion, but I had too much respect for my father and for an emotional response on which he had been willing to transform the pattern of his life, to do more than answer 'I see,' which I certainly did not.

The comfortable, now threatened, home in which we had been brought up was named Hulme Hall. It was one of several residential halls for students, forming part of the University of Manchester – of which my grandfather was then vice-chancellor – and in which my father combined wardenship of the hall with the post of lecturer in classical archaeology. Hulme Hall, whose blackened portico, long since swept away, rises in memory with the grandeur of a temple to Poseidon, was an ordinary enough Victorian house, though sufficiently large for the rooms used by my parents to be separated from our children's quarters by a green baize door. Past this, in our early days, we only went on particular occasions, though once every day, at least, we would be taken down to my father's study to say goodnight before being put to bed at six o'clock. At the back of the house, connected to it by a few arches which we called 'the cloisters', was a quadrangle partly surrounded by the students' rooms. In general we were on friendly terms with them until one day in summer, when they had left their ground-floor windows open and we went round throwing handfuls of grass from the lawn-mower through each in turn. From the resulting row we came to consider that students had no sense of humour and so were best avoided.

Hulme Hall, with one or two similar halls, stood inside an estate known as Victoria Park to which access in those days – when traffic consisted mainly of tradesmen's vans, hansom cabs and an occasional lady's carriage – could only be gained by the raising of a wooden barrier, a task performed by an impress-ively sluggish figure in a coachman's coat with big buttons and a hard hat. This dignitary, supported presumably by subscrip-tion from the residents, occupied a wooden hut in which there was just room for him to sit down, and from which he would emerge to nod recognition to householders, salute important figures such as the warden of Hulme Hall and his wife, keep a sharp eye on delivery boys, and warn away characters he didn't like the look of.

Though I had been told many times not to stare 'because it's rude', it was clear that a being so extraordinary as the gatekeeper must be exempted from general instructions, and I would make opportunities to examine him and his way of life as closely as I could, running on ahead of the perambulator to be out of earshot of our governess, Mim, and her sharp instructions; I would linger behind over a bootlace, and then pause to stare inside when I reached the barrier. The gatekeeper fitted so tightly into his container that when he rose to his feet, it seemed the hut must rise up as well. His elbow rested on a shelf on which stood a teapot, a white china cup and saucer and a small brass stove. In the corner behind him was a coachman's whip, no doubt to slash at any errand boys, their baskets covered with white cloths, who might laugh at him or speak with disrespect. On the breast of his long coat were medals hanging from coloured ribbons, gained, we understood, by feats of bravery at a time when I supposed he must have been more active. But the most magical feature about this imposing man, who made an occasional appearance in my dreams, was that in the tiny window of his sentry box stood a china pig out of whose back grew a crop of actual grass.

Hulme Hall was not the first home my parents had occupied during their marriage. My father's earliest academic post had been in Birmingham, as lecturer in Greek at the university, and they had taken a little house in the suburbs to which they both looked back with affection. Here, to judge by my mother's stories, they had enjoyed a more lively, carefree life, in the days before their family expanded. It was in Birmingham that my brother Jack had been born, and I envied him for having known the blissful experience of being the only child and having the full attention of both parents, then in their young and lively prime, concentrated on himself. My parents' carefree days, however, cannot have lasted long – a year or two until Jack made his appearance with perhaps a few months afterwards – for I was born only fourteen months after Jack, and by then we were already living in Victoria Park.

Jack must have regarded my arrival with mixed feelings. He would, no doubt, have been instructed before long to love his baby brother, and was perhaps glad at the prospect of having somebody to play with. Unconsciously too he may have hoped for a childish ally against the pressures which all parents, but especially the conscientious, place upon their children. But there was also a heavy price to pay since he was no longer the only pebble on the beach, and his nature, always serious and dutiful, was soon further burdened with the task of being the eldest and the consequent need for setting an example. The need to set examples – which usually involved going without something we wanted or not doing something we enjoyed – was a recurrent theme throughout our childhood, and it was impressed on us that in this respect we had special responsibilities due to my father's position, our Christian upbringing and our educational advantages. But on none of us was the burden of example-setting laid so heavily as on Jack, since he had those in need of good example always around in the form of three younger brothers and a sister; to add to his difficulties, at least one of those brothers was far from amenable to any example, and especially unwilling to accept guidance or correction from one so close to his own age.

For a time no doubt our relationship was easy and cooperative. My mother, who much enjoyed telling stories about her children, would often describe how in the nursery shared by Jack and myself she had to confine me to my cot with a net to prevent me from scrambling around the room and setting off down the passage on my own. Despite the net, however, on coming in each morning she would find us playing together on the floor, and asked Jack for an explanation.

'Oh, well, you see, mother,' Jack replied. 'I hold the netting down and little Tom jumps out.'

Even at the age of two, little Tom probably looked askance at his elder brother's unnecessary candour and as, year by year, he grew stronger and more talkative, above all as he showed every sign of rivalry and of refusing to recognize a firstborn's rights, Jack must often have wished little Tom securely back under his net.

My own memories do not, I believe, go back very far, and except for a few vivid snapshot images, like the disconnected fragments of a dream, they are shadowy. It is difficult to separate what I remember from what I was later told. I recall walking beside a pram, a brown-painted vehicle with a

15

crisscross of basketwork on its sides and a strange basketwork holster into which Mim or whoever was escorting us could thrust, not a shotgun or bow and arrows, but a rolled umbrella. My head is about level with the white china handlebar, and the thought in my mind is that I am three and a new stage in my life has started. At three, the first great battle of my life was over, and had been lost. Like General de Gaulle, however, I was determined that this should prove to be only a battle and not the whole campaign. That battle, a contest of wills between my mother and myself, had been fought without quarter and with no holds barred.

Of all the tales of childhood to which visitors at our various vicarages were obliged to listen, none was more frequent than my mother's account of how in my infancy she would wheel me screaming round Victoria Park locked in a struggle which would rage nonstop until we got back to the house, to be renewed next day from the moment we set out. What the immediate issue, if there was one, had been – whether I was demanding to sit up or to be allowed to walk – never emerged from these accounts, which focused upon a furious baby, red-faced and howling, bent on having its own way against a strong-willed mother resolved, in her own words, to 'break his will' for the child's future good. Once, it appeared, a passing lady had been so rash as to intervene, asking why the child screamed continually and whether it was good for it to do so. Just what reply she received was not told, but it was evident she did not intervene again.

Proof that this battle of wills was protracted, conscious, and that both sides threw all they had into it was offered by another of my mother's anecdotes describing how she crept softly into the nursery one early morning. By this time I had acquired the power of speech and there was no more playing around on the floor with Jack. Instead I was arming myself for the day's encounter by going carefully over my lines ... 'Thomas never hasn't,' 'Thomas never doesn't,' 'Thomas never *won't*.'

What effect this hard-fought struggle – and the fact that my father took no part in it – may have had on me will perhaps

16

emerge in my story as the years go by, but one early effect was to make me feel that inner feelings must be covered up and not betrayed; that control over one's destiny has to be fought for; and that in the wrestling match of life one cannot count on finding allies.

By the age of four I had learned to read, and it is about this time that something approaching connected memory begins. I learned to read not out of any wish to study books – I have never loved books as objects and have certainly never loved studying – but because I wanted to read the names of streets, and so make sure of my whereabouts in the world. One of my earliest intellectual satisfactions, and it seemed well worth the effort made, was to spell WILMSLOW ROAD, PARK ROAD, OXFORD STREET, and the other names I had heard passing above my head in conversation, and which I could now check for myself. Once two of us could read, my mother, who had been a schoolteacher before her marriage – not in a girls' school, she would emphasize, but in a school for boys – took our education in hand. Seated with her at the table in the dining room, to which we were now admitted every day, Jack and I were soon starting to learn Latin, history, arithmetic and French.

Though our life in Manchester was pleasant, we all looked forward to leaving it behind. Three times a year with blessed certainty a day would come when we would set off for the station in a stuffy cab, with our trunks piled on its roof, and as the wheels crunched the gravel, we children crowded to the window for a final wave to our rocking horse staring out of the nursery window.

Glan Afon, a small house in an obscure corner of the North Wales coast, had been given to my parents, perhaps as a wedding present, by my grandfather, a notable mountain climber, who had been fond of taking his sons on climbing holidays in Wales, the Lake District, and occasionally in Switzerland. The house stood apart from the village of Aber, itself no more than a speck on the map between the mountains of Snowdonia and the sea, five miles or so from Bangor where the road and rail bridges over the Menai Strait link the isle of

Anglesey to the mainland. The position of Glan Afon, facing both sea and mountains, with a river washing its wall, fields surrounding it and a wood behind, enchanted us, and the little house – with its ornamental gables, bow windows, tall chimneys and rustic porch – seemed to us everything a house should be. But from a grown-up point of view it must have had heavy disadvantages.

Our front garden ran directly up to the station platform and the main line, along which the Irish expresses from London hurled themselves with frenzied whistlings day and night. As a result, the only access to the house was by footbridge over the line from the station yard, or else underneath it through a dark tunnel much used by cows, where the mud even in summer sucked our shoes off. The active young could struggle through, but no car or van ever attempted to scrape under the arch and down the lane, which in any case petered out before it reached the shore. Nor was the shore, when reached, any stretch of golden sands but a waste of shallows, not deep enough for bathing even at high tide, and no more than a vast expanse of mud, through which the channels of streams and rivers wandered mazily when the tide was out.

But everything which made the place inconvenient for our elders turned it for children into an earthly paradise. The noisy trains brought recurring drama as we lay in bed listening to their approach, or clung to the palings against the blast of wind as they stormed by, or else stood on the footbridge, watching them grow from a far-off plume of smoke into engines hauling a string of carriages which came rocketing down the track to vanish beneath our feet in a volley of smoke and sparks. So few strangers braved the muddy tunnel to reach the still muddier shore that we had the whole of it to ourselves for paddling, sailing our toy boats, flying kites and wading down the shallow estuaries against the tide to trap shrimps and little flat fish as they squirmed under our feet. Even the cows in the salty meadows seemed to recognize us, hardly bothering to lift their heads as we raced past.

Since we were at Glan Afon only during holidays, there was little attempt at gardening, even by my mother who knew all flowers by their Latin names. The ground between our porch and the putty-coloured station railings was dug over from time to time by a man from the village, but the much larger space behind the house was given over to blackberry bushes and children's games. Here in summer I would lie on my face in the warm grass nibbled short by the rabbits whose dried-up pellets lay scattered everywhere, sniffing the different wild flowers and watching small insects as they toiled up grass stems, waved their feelers in bewilderment as they reached the top, and then turned to climb down again head foremost.

Alongside house and garden ran our river, to whose sound we awoke and fell asleep, and at the bottom of our back garden, beyond the last blackberry bushes and accessible only by crawling through gaps in a fence made from slates planted upright in the ground, was the 'plantation'.

Even our friendly stream became menacing when it entered the plantation. The overhung banks were slippery, and the water silent. Deep in among the trees a bridge had been made out of a single plank, tilting and unsteady, with a hand wire strung between tree trunks for support. Below the bridge the stream was at its deepest, and it was here that, when we became strong enough to wade, we built a dam and fastened the halves of two barrels together into a raft. This we poled around with broom handles and hoes until one night the spring tides came up and carried it away, stranding our vessel far out in the estuary, within sight but beyond recovery.

Over on the far side of the straits the sun seemed to be shining even when we, under the mountains, were in rain or mist. Looking across to Anglesey we would see the line of low blue hills ending in the familiar shape of Puffin Island, like a shallow upturned bowl but with a strange hump of buildings – a ruined signalling station we were told – rising in the middle. Puffin Island, we knew, was the home of thousands of sea birds; the guillemot that had flown into our lighted window one winter's night, killed itself, been stuffed and now stood perpetual guard over our sideboard, must have come from there.

'When can we go to Puffin Island? When shall we see the birds? When will you take us to Puffin Island?' At least once in every holiday we would chorus the demand.

'Oh, hmm,' my father would reply. 'Yes, well, we shall have to see about that. . . . One of these days. . . . We'll think about it next time we come down.'

In winter, when the light faded while we were still having tea, we would stand in the window, the smaller ones kneeling and resting their elbows on the sill, to watch the lights come on in the small port of Beaumaris, and to catch the first blink from the lighthouse standing on a spur of rock between Anglesey and Puffin Island.

As we drifted out among the sooty shrubs and tired grass after giving assent to my father's project, I realized that it was not only our comfortable Manchester life we had signed away, but our earthly paradise as well. True, it remained ours in name and we might even find ourselves there now and then for a week or two in summer. But it did not need much calculation to work out that if from now on we should be much poorer, there would be no thrice-yearly holidays, so that the days when Glan Afon would be our second home, familiar and loved in every season, were already at an end.

2

Change of Scene

It was the late summer of 1914 when my father told us of his intention, and the First World War must have started since the Hall was full of soldiers, red-faced young men in smelly uniforms who played cricket with us on the faded patch we called the lawn, and of nurses in long blue dresses with full white caps and red crosses on their aproned bosoms.

Eighteen months earlier than this, at the beginning of 1913, when Jack was eight and I seven, we had been sent to boarding school, wearing Norfolk suits, uncomfortable stiff collars like those of choirboys, and little bow ties on studs. We each had a trunk with our initials and carried small leather bags which had a medical air as though containing stethoscopes and pills. Our school, known as Lawrence House, stood on the edge of a sandy golf course at St Anne's on Sea, a corner of the Lancashire coast against which the winter gales came whistling down direct from Spitzbergen or the Ural mountains. At least once while we were there the whole stretch of sea between us and the opposite shore of the Ribble estuary froze over to resemble the Antarctic in which, as we all knew, the gallant Captain Scott had lately perished. Even in summertime on our morning walks over the sandhills covered with spiky grass, evening primroses and a straggling wild pansy, the wind would whip up the sand to drive it painfully against our bare knees.

There were forty-four boys in Lawrence House, and we each had a number stitched or inked into our clothes, and a numbered locker in which to keep football boots and slippers.

Over the work Jack and I had few difficulties. Thanks to our mother's instruction we knew as much as any boys in our form, and in Scripture – to which, as a combination of schoolwork with religion, special importance was attached – we knew much more, being ready with instant information on quite obscure Old Testament characters such as Jonadab, Japheth or that Zimri who knew no peace.*

Lawrence House must have been little different from other preparatory schools of its day and was probably better run and more humane than most, but few efforts were made to help newcomers settle in and for our first year or two it seemed a friendless place. The masters conducted classes and kept order; the bigger boys asserted themselves and impressed a sense of insignificance upon the smaller ones; the smaller ones lived for the end of term and a return not so much to the comforts of home as to the warmth and protection of family life. When at home my feelings towards my parents varied, but from the distance of school their presence became a need and their absence actual pain. During the first weeks of every term great waves of homesickness would come over me, particularly when I was in trouble, and I would slip away into a retreat I had discovered behind a door in the half-lit locker room where we kept our boots and shoes. Crawling in behind a row of overcoats, I was within a few feet of boys passing to and fro, shouting, arguing, occasionally fighting, but was invisible myself and would stay in my retreat until confidence returned or the bell went for evening prayers and bedtime.

Such attacks came usually on a Sunday when we had more time to ourselves. We began the morning by writing a weekly letter home, sitting at our desks as though in class, dipping our steel nibs into china inkwells and writing on thick cream notepaper on which the school's name and address had been embossed by our headmaster, Mr Hoare, using a special machine which he alone was privileged to operate. We were given an hour to write the letter, which had then to be handed in together with an addressed envelope. It was over the writing of

*'Had Zimri peace who slew his master?' 2 Kings 9:31.

22

such a letter that one of those events took place, apparently trifling, after which the water flows in a different direction and nothing afterwards is ever quite the same. On the night before I had had a dream. It was a simple dream which comes before me plainly as I write. I was at Aber in summertime, lying on my back in the grass just outside the bow window and gazing up into a clear blue sky. As I gazed, a seagull, white as only a sunlit seagull can be, sailed across to pass out of sight over the house. This was all, but it filled me with a rapture as intense as though I had been given a momentary glimpse of heaven. The sense of joy persisted and next morning at my desk I described the dream to my father and mother as best I could; having finished the letter, I handed it in, and before long we were all sent to get ready for the walk to church.

During the sermon, as I sat there without listening, I found myself thinking of my letter. What would my father and mother think when they received it? This was surely the letter of some inexperienced child. What was the good of telling my parents about my dream of Aber – did I imagine they could come down and carry me off there? I was here, at school, where I had been sent in order to grow up, and I had better make the best of it and keep my feelings or failings – for what was the betrayal of feelings but a failing? – to myself. I blushed for my folly as I sat there in the pew, and the moment we reached school asked for my letter back, saying I wanted to copy it out in better handwriting. It had already been stuck down, but was handed to me without objection and I began again, taking care this time to make it exactly like all the other forty-three letters which would later be carried to the post by the school handyman.

Dear Father and Mother.
I hope you are well. I am quite well and so is Jack. He had a cold but it has gone and so has mine. Yesterday the first eleven played Seafield and won 2–0. . . .

From this time I stamped with firmness on attacks of homesickness and, since they evidently arose when my mind was unoccupied, I decided to keep it fully employed, leaving no room for weakness to creep in. There were a few shelves of books known as the 'Library', from which we could borrow as we pleased. These were chunky books in large print on pages thick as blotting-paper, with heavily embossed covers and a coloured frontispiece showing some dramatic highlight from the story. Many were sea adventures or concerned with exploration in strange places, where the jungles were full of ferocious pygmies and the deserts were ranged over by murderous bands of hooded men on camels. In their pages boys not much older than myself, with names like Jim Masterson or Dick Standish, survived the horrors of shipwreck only to be cast almost lifeless upon barren coasts. Recovering rapidly, they would maintain order among warring tribes until a friendly ship or regiment of white topeed riflemen arrived – just as our brave lad could hold out no longer against the rebel assault. There were no girls in these stories, though here and there there was a white woman to be rescued, and the only part played by parents was to remain out of sight until the final page, when they would listen with admiration to tributes paid to their son by rough seamen or the commanding officers of relieving forces . . . 'What might have happened if anyone but this lad of yours had been in charge, Mrs Standish, does not bear thinking of.' On such fare I now fed, finding a preference for sea stories and particularly for stout-hearted midshipmen in neat blue uniforms.

Perhaps a term or two after I formed my resolution to abolish weakness, this was confirmed and supported by a physical change due, I suppose, to my eyes having learned to focus. It was now the summer term and we played cricket, the smaller boys in a desultory way, stopping often to argue, fight, turn handstands or chase away the fat brown pony, Billy, which was used to draw the heavy lawn-mower. A few whose bent was biological or scientific would vanish from the game entirely, to go bug-hunting for puss moths or poplar hawk caterpillars whose eggs could be found among the group of poplar trees growing with special luxuriance around the cesspit. The bigger boys, of course, played cricket seriously, being coached in the nets by junior masters and occasionally by Mr Hoare, whose battered fingers had reputedly been earned through his having kept wicket for Cambridge in some far-off era. Under his stern blue eye the older boys competed on a field kept closely trimmed and with the creases marked out in whitewash twice a week.

At first I hated this game, for when I was allowed to bat the hard ball was always hitting my ankles before I could see it, and when I had to field it would jump up into my face. On this day, however, I had been ordered to field for the first eleven who were practising in the nets, and one of them hit the ball up in the air. It did not go far, no further than a cricket pitch, but it went quite high, and what was extraordinary was that I followed its flight and held it as it came down. 'Oh, well caught!' someone shouted and I glowed with pride, but I also thought, That wasn't difficult, I believe I could do the same again. And sure enough, only a week or two later when I was fielding during a game and the boy who was batting took a slog, the ball flew straight at me; I put my hands to my chest to protect myself and felt the ball safely in my fingers. He was out – and I had caught him! I went over to the scorer and watched him write laboriously in his book: *Tiddeman c. Hopkinson mi. b. Faulkner 2.*

So in the course of two or three weeks I had discovered in myself a capacity which could ensure me a position in that world of school in which till now I had been living as a stranger. Diligently I set myself to practise games and within a year, having begun to master cricket and taken with much greater enjoyment to football in the winter, the whole focus of my life had shifted from the family to a larger world. Hitherto during term I had been obsessed with thoughts of home and longing for my parents; now I was happy at school, and during holidays found myself thinking of my schoolfriends and occasionally even writing to them. But though I seemed well enough adjusted to my two lives, inside I had split. During term I was a seemingly carefree schoolboy, occupied with games and hobbies such as stamp-collecting and keeping caterpillars, looking for general admiration while cultivating one or two close friends. Back at home I reverted to family life, doing as I was told, going to church regularly, conforming to expected patterns and not speaking out however much I disagreed. Within myself, however, it was the outside world which now seemed to me more real, and home a shell which before long I would discard.

Only on the journey between one life and the other did loneliness and the longing which I had written off as weakness still sometimes overwhelm me. On the journey back to school, as the train travelled slowly with many stops, darkness closing in and rain streaming down the glass, my heart would sink; I would forget friends and prospects of success, my plans to get into a team and acquire the prestige of wearing colours, and long desperately for the train to turn round and carry me back home. Such impressions go deep, and even today a train journey on a wet winter evening brings a sense of choking misery difficult to dispel.

It was possibly this split, and the conflict which arises when one side or another of one's nature must be kept out of sight, which accounts for a description of myself given about this time by a family friend and shrewd observer whom I must accept as an impartial witness. Known to us all as Pen, his full name was Penoyre, and from earliest childhood he was more a part of our lives than any relative outside the immediate family circle. He had been my father's closest, almost his only intimate friend since the turn of the century when they had both lived in Athens, my father on the Craven Fellowship he had won at Oxford, and Pen either as secretary to the Hellenic Society, a position he held throughout his working life, or perhaps in some introductory role which would lead to his becoming secretary later on. Every summer at least Pen joined us at Aber, having walked much of the way from London in an old white sweater and a faded tropical suit, wearing an eyeglass on a cord which seemed to us to imply mysterious visionary powers. Once arrived at Aber, he became one of ourselves in all the mud-paddling, dam-building, boat-sailing and kite-flying which made up our life, and it was he who had provided the inspiration and craftsmanship for the construction of our raft. But though a child in enjoyment he was in other ways far from childish; possessing strong religious feelings and a delicate sense

26

of honour, he would tolerate no form of deception, and was as strict as my parents on anything he considered to be a matter of right and wrong.

Asked – probably by my grandmother – to sum up the characters of each of us children in a sentence, Pen paid tributes to the nature of Jack, Paul and Stephan, all admirable in different ways, but about me would commit himself to no more than 'Tommy's a dark horse.' I was not sure what was meant by a 'dark horse', but I could see it was not the description of a noble animal which could be depended on for a straight race; though I also derived comfort from the expression, since it seemed to imply that my future was unpredictable and so might prove more interesting than one already visible throughout its length.

In September 1914 we went back as usual from Hulme Hall to St Anne's on Sea, but when that term ended returned not to Manchester but to the small East Lancashire town of Colne, where my father was now the junior of two curates assisting the Rev. Dr Duval, DD, a rotund, full-blooded cleric who was rector of the parish church. My father, whom we were used to seeing smartly if quietly dressed, now wore a clerical suit which soon started to show signs of wear, a dog collar and a black shovel hat. For his duties he was paid what we learned was called a stipend of £200 a year, and since this would only just suffice to feed and clothe the family, we should all have had to leave our school but for the generosity of an uncle, Austin Hopkinson, a remarkable eccentric who would from now on play an increasing part in all our lives, but particularly in my own.

Colne, known to its 30,000 inhabitants as 'bonnie Colne among the hills', had developed during the nineteenth century amid what were still wild and open moors because conditions and resources were right for the cotton mills on which, together with a few small engineering works, nine families out of ten depended. Colne was linked to similar nearby towns, Burnley, Blackburn, Accrington, Preston and the rest, by the grubby but reliable Lancashire and Yorkshire Railway; by roads which were still largely cobbled; and by moorland paths, many of them medieval packhorse tracks with paving stones let into the ground and bridges only wide enough for one horse at a time. Our particular delight and excitement, however, was the tram service whose elderly double-deckers ground agonizingly up the hills to rush hurtling down the other side as if fleeing some terrible disaster, and the opportunity for a tram ride when sent out to deliver messages or parish magazines soon became one of the main compensations of our new life.

Colne was a working-class town, whose menfolk washed in the kitchen before going to 't'mill' and whose women tended their small homes, two up and two down and often back-to-back; they whitened the stone front doorstep and frequently also washed the patch of pavement between front door and cobbled street. Where the edges of the town met the moors stood a few larger houses, each with its coach house and shrubbery, which were occupied by the mill owners and their managers, together with a few doctors, solicitors, accountants, retired tradespeople and well-to-do old ladies.

Our new house, a little larger than most but much smaller than those of professional people, was one of a handful which made up Haverholt Road. Here the hillside had been cut into, so that we reached our front door up two or three flights of steps while the back door opened into a paved yard beyond which were the allotments, hen houses and racing-pigeon coops of our neighbours. From the front we looked out over a scruffy field or two grazed over with distaste by farm animals as blackened as the grass. Behind and beyond ran a medley of streets at odd angles just as the original contractors had found it easiest and most profitable to lay them out, with each house a few feet lower than the one above. On the corners were desultory shops, or pubs giving off that heavy smell of tobacco and stale beer at which my mother sniffed indignantly as we trudged past with our load of shopping. Closer to town were the mills with their soaring chimneys and reservoirs of dirty water which steamed in winter and was at times violently coloured – orange, green or purple, according to the dye being used. The mill engines were steam-driven and from the street we could watch the pistons, connecting-rods and massive flywheels, and see the engineer climbing around with his long-snouted oilcan. The mill engine nearest our house gave out a hesitating cough and splutter, as though it were about to choke but managed just in time to clear its throat, a sound which would form the accompaniment to our life over the next two years.

The house in Haverholt Road was tall, which was as well since the rooms were tiny; its height gave us the benefit of attics and a flagged cellar. 'Go down into the cellar if you want to fight and make a noise,' my mother would order, 'Then you won't disturb father in his study.' So the cellar was our battleground, among washing put to dry on clotheshorses, and our bedrooms were the attics – to the dismay of Stephan, the youngest boy. He was sent up to bed at the same time as Esther, but whereas she slept on the first floor near our parents, he was alone under the roof among shadows and strange noises. The stairs to the attic were dark and steep, creaking mournfully underfoot, so that even to climb them unaccompanied brought terror; Stephan would stand at the bottom calling 'Goodnight' to each of us in turn throughout the house in order to delay the moment when they must be faced.

The ground floor room at the front had been chosen as my father's study. There was space for his classical texts and theological works, a sepia reproduction of a Raphael 'Madonna and Child', and his photographs of the Parthenon. On the mantelpiece, with his tobacco jar, pipes and paper spills carefully folded to save matches, stood two handsome lustre vases from the Pilkington works, whose craftsmen had once consulted him about some problem of classical design. The bow window not only let a good light on to his desk, but afforded a glimpse of the many visitors now coming to the house at all hours, so that answering the doorbell became a routine activity for us all, whatever else we might be doing. At this time, there being nothing in the nature of a welfare state, a large part of most clergymen's time was taken up with social service. Parishioners came to the house when they wanted to get children into schools, themselves into hospital, manoeuvre elderly relatives into almshouses, asylums or burial grounds, or tap church funds to help them cope with the varied calamities of life. To our door also came professional tramps and beggars wanting a 'ticket' for the workhouse, or a handout to carry them a few miles on their endless journey, and from the number who came up our steps it appeared that the new curate had already become known as someone who would rather part with his own half-crown than send anyone away empty-handed. It seemed indeed that my father kept a supply of half-crowns always handy, and I was surprised more than once when we were out walking on the moors to see him run after a tramp who had not even accosted him, in order to slip one almost imperceptibly into his hand.

At mealtimes now a whole new language passed above our heads. Talk was no longer of students and scholarships, excavations and discoveries, the theories of professors and their articles in learned journals, but of Mothers' Union meetings, school boards, parish councils and of something called diocesan conferences. Endless discussions – during which we lay low and dug steadily into cottage pie, followed by rice pudding and jam or prunes and custard – now took place as to whether old Mrs Ridehalgh should be got into the almshouse or looked after by her unmarried daughter who had a job she did not want to leave; and how Mr Hodgson and his seven children were to manage while Mrs Hodgson had her operation. My mother's views were always forthright, and she excelled at finding practical solutions; she also believed that people had to make sacrifices and she was quite ready to tell them what sacrifices they should make. My father was hesitant. He did not care for argument or conflict, and we knew when he disagreed only because he had fallen silent and, when pressed for a decision, would concede no more than that he 'would think about it'.

Besides being continuously active as unpaid social servant to the parish, my mother also cleaned the house with a little, erratic, outside help, washed and mended our clothes, baked bread and cooked, made marmalade and jam, and marshalled the family to appear in good order at church on Sundays. To each of us children were assigned weekly duties of table-laying, washing-up, making beds, or cleaning the seven pairs of boots and shoes. These we did not always perform with a good grace, though we were ready enough to be sent out shopping, with the opportunity to gaze into toyshop and sweetshop windows.

Our evenings were spent in the living room whose single window looked out over the back yard. It was even smaller than my father's study and we could with difficulty fit ourselves round the table for meals, when it became our dining room. Here after tea, while my father went about the parish or sat writing in his study, my mother would put a light to the noisy gas mantle and read to us for an hour or two. As she read she would mend a pile of our school stockings or sew a dress for Esther; she had the ability to read and knit at the same time, though by doing so she was wearing out the eyesight she would one day sorely need. While listening, we all had our own tasks to occupy us. Simple sewing for Jack and Paul, while I, who had discovered a talent for drawing, or thought I had, was allowed to make Christmas cards and calendars. Usually, as I look back, she is reading Dickens, *David Copperfield* or *The Old Curiosity Shop*; at other times *Lorna Doone* or *The Children of the New Forest*. It was always stories that my mother read, whereas my father, who read to us only when we were ill in bed, would take a poetry book from a shelf in his study – Wordsworth, Tennyson, Byron (not 'Don Juan' but the one about the Assyrian who came down like a wolf), and above all his favourite Matthew Arnold. 'Sohrab and Rustum' did nothing to alleviate the cough, chickenpox or whatever I was suffering from, but the melancholy cadences of 'The Forsaken Merman', read in my father's mournfully expressive voice, seemed to be telling me of a sadness and loss that was not merely in the poem but an inevitable part of life itself.

> Children dear, was it yesterday
> We heard the sweet bells over the bay?
> In the caverns where we lay,
> Through the surf and through the swell,
> The far-off sound of a silver bell?

At some moment during our two years at Haverholt Road we were all taken to a local photographer for a family group. My father managed to evade this duty and my mother sits in the centre. She is still young, just on the right side of forty, her brown hair parted in the middle and looped to each side of her face, which has already taken on the patient expression of one whose life is entirely made up of work and can foresee no prospect of a change. On her lap sits Esther, a pretty child of six, with curls and a dress with an embroidered collar. On her left stands Paul, still pale and slight, but starting to look up, as though compulsory fish-eating must have an end and he can see the glimmer of manly life ahead. At the back on either side stand Jack and myself, Jack bearing the firstborn's burden of responsibility with visible anxiety, while I wear the assured look of one who is confident his time will come provided he keeps his head down and lies low.

If today any of us could be enticed out of the frame for a few minutes' chat about life in the year 1917, Stephan would probably prove to be the most rewarding. Born with his intellect already in full working order, he had never bothered with children's books except for the purpose of ridicule, but would abstract whatever he fancied from my father's shelves, reading Gibbon's *Decline and Fall of the Roman Empire* and Motley's *Rise of the Dutch Republic* at an age when other children are still finding difficulty with cats that sit on mats. He would occasionally put a polite question to me about football or to Jack about stamp-collecting, but his personal interest lay entirely in serious reading. He read while getting dressed, read in the lavatory from books previously secreted in the airing cupboard, and would dart away from meals to fling himself down on the hearthrug by his already open book.

'Whatever's burning?' cried my mother, rushing in from the kitchen where she was busy over the family dinner. It was the wool of Stephan's jersey starting to sizzle as he crouched closer and closer into the gas fire.

There was a contrast in Stephan, too, between his nature – which was affectionate and tended to close contact, so that he liked to hold hands while walking – and his mind, which was unsentimental and critical, and his tongue sharp as a knife. Back in our Manchester days, when we had once all been required to hand over a favourite toy to be given to 'poor sick children', Stephan had with difficulty been persuaded to part with a cherished present only just received – a model milk cart drawn by two horses covered in real skin. Having handed it over, the thought occurred to him that poor sick children do not need two horses to pull their milk cart, and he could quite well keep one for himself; they would surely never notice the difference. The children might not have noticed it, but mother did, and Stephan's severe telling-off ended with the threat that, if he did not heed the little voice of conscience when it spoke to him, one day that little voice would fall silent for ever.

Stephan listened without reply. Only when mother had gone out of the room did he nudge me and whisper, 'That's the day I'm waiting for.'

'What day?'

'The day when the little voice falls silent.'

But we were now in Colne, not Manchester, and he was no longer six but nine. Incessant reading had given him a precocious command of language, and as I emerged from the stairs into his little attic bedroom to say goodnight, an almost weightless form landed on my back and a voice loud as a gnat's hissed in my ear, 'The miscreant was pinioned in the arms of a burly minion of the law.'

3

Over the Hills

Our stay in Haverholt Road proved to be short. Only two years after we had gone there my father was appointed to a living at the other side of the town on the border between Colne and Nelson, and we moved to Penrith Road, a short street whose lowermost house verged on the tramlines while from the top one, which was ours, you could walk straight up onto the moor, providing the farmer was not around when you scrambled through his fence. The houses in Penrith Road were much smaller than the one we left, so that two had to be knocked into one to accommodate us all. Almost every man in the street except my father, as well as many of the women and girls, worked in the mills, and we were woken every morning by the sound of their clogs as they set off for work, the men wearing mufflers and cloth caps, and the women with shawls over their heads and sometimes cloth caps as well but with hatpins through them. We too had clogs, but either our feet or our vanity did not get used to them and we only put them on when ordered.

If our home at Haverholt Road had seemed generally accessible, our new one resembled a public office. The door of the front room opened on to the street and, as the only clergyman in his parish, my father had far more callers than before, most of them friendly, good-natured folk who asked 'Is thy dad in?' while stepping inside without waiting for a reply. It was dad they asked for but usually mum they got, as she sallied out of the kitchen in her apron, with hands still floury from bread-making, to protect her Henry busy over sermons in his study. Everything she could she took upon herself, living in a constant round of visits to sufferers, and to the schools, hospitals and council offices through which arrangements on their behalf had to be made. One or two boys would be taken along to carry whatever was needed, and we would sit silent in some overheated kitchen while the wife poured out her troubles and my mother, kindly but decided, outlined a solution and the attitude with which all earthly troubles must be faced.

Though few of these visits were enjoyable, there was one house where I was always glad to go. Each house in those days gave out its own special smell, and one I should have recognized blindfold came from a tiny dwelling almost under a railway viaduct, the home of Mrs Baldwin. She was about the size of a large garden gnome and her home consisted of a kitchen in which the three of us could barely sit down together, Mrs Baldwin in her rocking chair as close to the grate as she could squeeze, and my mother and myself in kitchen chairs on the rag rug. In a basket by the grate lay an enormous cat with which a ritual took place so strange that if ever it were omitted I would inquire after the cat's health to give Mrs Baldwin a reminder. Cackling and chuckling, she would snatch up the hearth brush, at which signal the cat jumped out of its basket and lay down on the rug. Then, while the old lady scrubbed its belly fiercely, the cat would sink its claws into the brush handle, slobbering with excitement.

What, I used to wonder, was the meaning of this perform-ance, at which my mother looked with disapproval and I with fascination? Then one day in talking of her childhood Mrs Baldwin let fall what I took to be the clue. In the nearby village of Wycoller where she had been brought up, there had lived a wizard. Everyone knew him to be a wizard, but nothing could be proved until a farmer, seeing an unusually large cat stalking his chickens, let fly with his gun. He shot the intruder in the leg, but it got away – and next morning the wizard was found in bed with a wounded thigh. Mrs Baldwin talked as though she had known both cat and wizard intimately, and her story, which I did not then know to be a universal folk legend, explained everything to me. Mrs Baldwin was a witch and the cat her familiar. After all we were within a few miles of Pendle Hill which had once been full of the Lancashire witches, and where more likely a spot for their descendants to be living than in the old village of Wycoller? Here, in the now ruined hall, had lived the Cunliffe family, distantly connected to our own, and among them a squire with such a passion for cock-fighting that, when too infirm to leave his bed, he had an arrangement of mirrors constructed on his staircase so that he could watch the birds kill each other without stirring from his pillows.*

If Mrs Baldwin were a witch however, she was evidently a white one, since now and then when we had been sent to her with cakes and scones baked by my mother she would fumble in a tin and give us pennies to buy sweets. It was not so much the pennies, though these were welcome since we had no pocket money except for going back to school, but her tact in giving them when we were on our own that we appreciated, since if she had done this in my mother's presence we would either have had to hand them back, to everyone's embarrassment, or waste them on a box labelled 'Waifs and Strays'.

Up on the moors it was not difficult to believe in wizards and witches, but the cause of the expeditions on which we now began to be sent was not any quest for the supernatural, still less a need for exercise; it was economic. The war had lasted for three years, and my mother had difficulty in keeping her large family fed. The little Co-op along the tramlines was often short of supplies, and one of her ways of eking things out was to 'put down' quantities of eggs when they were cheapest, in an earthenware bowl full of a frosty substance known as isinglass. And so in spring, with baskets on our arms, we were sent out in search of eggs. It was no use, we soon learned, calling at nearby farms whose eggs would all be collected for the shops, but up in the hills were others, more remote, where they were glad to sell. Despite the bad-tempered collies, trained to snarl and show their teeth, the bulls in fields we were obliged to cross, the

*There is a reference to the squire's ingenious practice in Mrs Gaskell's *The Life of Charlotte Brontë*.

weight of the baskets as we struggled home, and occasional soakings, we loved these expeditions.

The moors, we soon learned, were the centre of a secret life; this was something exclusively for men, into which boys were only initiated after starting work. They might drop out for a year or two while courting but as soon as the wife had a baby to tie her down, the husband would be back with his mates. Some took their whippets up there to chase hares; others released carrier pigeons out of wicker baskets. There were contests of knur-and-spell, resembling a primitive golf played with a club like a long billiard cue, having a thick piece of wood for its head. The white clay balls, like tiny golf balls, were suspended in miniature gallows, or shot up by a spring for the strikers to aim at, and an array of fielders marked whose ball flew furthest. On all these activities there was betting, and on certain roads we would be turned back because there was a gambling school in one of the quarries. Occasionally too we would be shouted at by an angry loser, a drunk, or a farmer grown cranky with solitude.

For choice on these outings I would go with Paul. I had not yet got over my childish rivalry with Jack, which led to many fights, usually provoked by me. Jack had taken to fishing in the reservoirs and, seeing him set off one day with rod and net, can for bait and basket for his catch, I remarked that he'd got 'everything needed except skill'. He was already at the gate, but in a flash everything was put down and we were at each other. Stephan was still small and his legs got tired, but Paul was growing up strong and active, and there was nothing he enjoyed more than to be out on the hills, over which, when he was only eleven, we once walked thirty miles in a day. Paul had a patient determination and, however tired or however sore his feet, kept walking on.

'How're you doing, Paul?'
'All right.'
'Want to stop for a bit and rest?'
'No. Better push on.'

Now, as the result of our walks, a new excitement came into our lives. At Lawrence House we wore red school caps, whereas the boys in Colne wore cloth caps and so looked on ours as a sign that we thought ourselves superior. In our own neighbourhood we were soon on friendly terms with most of the boys, but away from home was a different matter, and the usual scene of our encounters was a village called Trawden, a few miles away. Trawden was a close community, resentful of strangers, in which boys wearing red caps were as welcome as the outriders of Genghis Khan, so that when sent there with any message – and not many private citizens at this time had telephones – we would arrange for the three eldest of us to go together. As we came down into the main street we would draw close as if preparing to face cavalry.

'It's t'red caps!' a shout would go up as we appeared, and before we had gone 100 yards half a dozen boys had poured out into the street, trying to push us over and snatch our caps, while we landed out in all directions.

'I'm told you've been knocking my choirboys about? Fighting with them in the street – here, just outside the church? Is this *true*?' demanded the clergyman, to whom some minutes later we handed over a letter, strangely crumpled, from my father. A gaunt figure with a high domed forehead, he glared angrily down an unusually long hooked nose.

'Yes,' Jack answered stoutly. 'We had to fight to get here at all. We always do. They just rush out of the houses and attack us.'

'Sure you don't attack them *first*? Aren't *you* the ones who always start it? That's what my boys tell me.'

'No, we don't,' Jack maintained. 'All we do is defend ourselves.'

'Very well then – defend yourself now!' And the clergyman sprang to his feet, seized Jack by the shoulders, thrust him down on the carpet of his study, and began to aim savage blows on the floor at each side of his head.

'*Do* you surrender?' he demanded. 'Surrender – or pay the penalty!'

Delighted to come across a grown-up who behaved like one of ourselves, Paul and I flung ourselves on him, struggling till our host called for peace and offered to negotiate terms with a packet of chocolate from the mantelpiece.

His name, as we knew from the letter, was Canon Dempsey and he had soon become a close friend of us all. Once he took us in a horse carriage to Pendle Hill, home of those witches for whose descendants we looked eagerly around, but saw no more than two or three cats little different from others we regularly chased. Next spring, having asked my mother's permission, Canon Dempsey took my father and us three eldest boys on our first visit to the Lake District. We fell on this scenery of lakes and mountains, not unlike the landscape of our beloved Aber, with a kind of rapture, and all of us, I believe, from that moment looked on the Lake District as our true home from which, in whatever corner of the world we might be living, we just happened for the time to be separated. For Jack indeed it would become his lifelong home, from which he would be absent only during the Second World War.

On this brief visit, lasting no more than the inside of a week, we stayed in a farmhouse on Lake Ullswater and spent our days rowing up and down what was then an almost deserted expanse of water, landing wherever we chose on its shores and islands. My father's pleas that we should spend at least part of the time walking fell on deaf ears. Our host had formed us into a committee to which every decision had to be referred, and he answered all my father's arguments with – 'I know! I *know*! But what *can* we do? We're outnumbered on the committee.'

At the station when we got back my mother was there to meet us. Still living among lakes and mountains, I was too depressed to speak but felt reproached when she, who had been left at home, said sadly, 'I thought you'd be so happy when you got back from your holiday!'

I tried to appear more cheerful, but it was not only the contrast between Ullswater and the noisy streets of Colne which was occupying my mind. During our visit I had come to a decision, meditated for some time past, which I saw would affect the whole of my life, and which before long I must reveal to my mother and father. This was to go into the navy, and since in those days would-be officers entered the Royal

Naval College at Osborne at the age of thirteen, this was a decision which must quite soon become effective. Over the coming weeks I disclosed my plan, which met with no opposition, and for the next year or two I had a ready answer to requests as to what I wanted for birthday or Christmas presents – books about the sea. Before long I had acquired a handful of works which I looked on as the basis of my seagoing library, destined for the shelves of my cabin in some battleship or destroyer.

From the five years we spent in Penrith Road there are three events which stand out in my mind; one of them concerned my mother, one my father, and the third our sister Esther. The one which involved my mother was trivial but haunting, and I see it now as plainly as I saw it over sixty years ago, down to the position of the furniture, the objects on the dressing-table, and the pattern of the wallpaper. My grandmother, my father's mother, had been the daughter of a wealthy solicitor with a passion for collecting precious stones, and she was one of the few in our widespread family of well-built, fresh-faced Hopkinsons who possessed any charm, which she had in abundance. She was beautiful, humorous and self-indulgent, smelled always of perfume, wore silk dresses pleasant to touch and rustling delightfully when she moved – which, apart from her regular carriage drives, was usually no further than between her drawing and dining rooms. She kept her youngest daughter, Phyllis, who remained unmarried, in perpetual attendance by her sofa, but did this as she did everything, with a regal graciousness which made it appear less of a servitude than a mark of special favour.

Fortunately for her grandchildren, one aspect of her indulgence was a love of giving presents and at Christmas the first thought for each of us was to know what grannie had sent. Her giving was not confined to Christmas and birthdays, so that a shower of parcels might descend at any time, welcome as rain in the Kalahari. At this moment such a shower had just fallen; all our presents had been looked at, and I happened to be standing by my mother in her bedroom when she opened the large cardboard box addressed to her, unfolded a succession of tissue wrappings and disclosed what appeared to be a beautiful, shady summer hat. But instead of lifting it out and trying it on in her mirror, my mother went red in the face, slammed the lid back and pushed the box angrily away under the bed.

'What on earth's the good of that to *me*? Does she imagine I can wear a hat like that in Colne?'

Shocked by her ingratitude, I said nothing and walked out of the room. From infancy it had been instilled into us all to be grateful for presents and even if we didn't like what we were given, at least to behave as though we did. So what could such a breach of her own standards imply? Why should she be angry at having been sent a lovely hat? And what did the words 'in Colne' suggest? Could she have worn the hat and enjoyed it if we had still been living in Manchester? To these questions I could give no answer.

It was a matter of conviction with us all, something never questioned, that 'father 'n' mother' thought as one on every issue. Above all, from the way mother had thrown herself into the parish, bustling about in a flurry of good works, I had never questioned her complete agreement with her Henry and his decision to become a clergyman. But now, recalling evenings at Hulme Hall when she had come to say goodnight to us in a flowing dress, wearing jewels and with hair carefully arranged, on her way to a dinner party, concert or theatre, the suggestion floated before my mind that there might exist another Evelyn Mary, less dominating and less fiercely moralistic – but whom the mother familiar to our everyday life had felt compelled, out of loyalty and duty, to pack into a cardboard box and kick under the bed.

It would be agreeable to recall that this perception made me more affectionate and considerate towards my mother, but I think the reverse is true. I considered myself the loser by the repression and instead of trying to make her sacrifice easier, placed myself outside her situation in a state of self-occupied resentment.

The event concerning my father seemed on the face of it equally trivial. One Sunday evening, having taken service, he walked up into the town to visit some parishioner and I offered to go with him; it was a dark blustery night and as we walked home we heard shouting ahead. Quickening our pace, we came up with a drunk wandering along the tramlines, shouting incoherently while a few youths followed, jeering. My father went up to the drunk, put his arm through his and steered him to the pavement, then as we walked along asked where he lived. To my surprise the man did not throw him off or answer with abuse but explained how to find his home, allowing himself to be led while the youths simply disappeared into the darkness.

Over this slight incident I pondered many times. I had never doubted my father's physical courage. As a small boy I had seen him run up and separate two fiercely fighting dogs, yet in the run of everyday life he showed a diffidence, a reluctance to assert himself which at times seemed verging on paralysis. He had, I considered, more understanding and sympathy, a wider judgement than my mother's, and yet allowed her to make decisions with which he manifestly disagreed. I used to long, and suspected that my brothers at times longed silently as well, for him to exert an authority I was certain he possessed. And now, in a situation where there was no need to intervene, he had acted with an assurance which imposed itself both on the drunken man and on the youths. Where had this come from? Was it a power of which he had the secret, but would not use except in crisis? And would it one day be accessible to me if I should need it?

The incident concerning Esther was more deeply charged and involved problems even wider-ranging for a twelve-year-old. Among the sick persons my father regularly visited was a former postman, who now never went out since he suffered from an ulcerous condition of the face which made him unwilling to be seen. He was a studious man, who read much and looked forward to the long talks the two men had together. One day he said as my father was leaving, 'You've been coming to see me for a long time, and it has meant a lot to me. There's little I can do for you in return, but there is one thing. I'm a student of astrology, and if you bring me along the dates and hours of birth with the birth place of two of your children, I'll cast their horoscopes.'

Not wishing presumably to disappoint him – since he was the last person to be moved by idle curiosity – my father took the required information about his eldest and youngest, Jack and Esther. What the man said about Jack made no impression on me, nor I think on Jack, but what he said about Esther was so extraordinary, both as a statement about her and in its implications, as to impress us all. Esther, he wrote, had come into this world following a previous existence of such wickedness that she would spend the whole of this life atoning for it, and had indeed chosen a Christian home and strict upbringing in order to constrain the dark side of her nature. She would never marry, devoting herself wholly to good works and self-sacrifice, and probably in the end would enter some religious order. The idea that our little sister had ever been anything but good and sweet, that she was never going to marry and have children of her own but live a life of ceaseless duty, came to all of us as a shock and as her brothers we resented it on her behalf. But it would have come as much more of a shock had we known that the predictions would come true and that Esther, after teaching in India and working for relief organizations in Europe following the Second World War, would indeed enter a religious order, the Community of the Resurrection, and spend most of her life as a missionary in South Africa and Rhodesia.

On myself, a lasting impression was made by this, my first explicit contact with the idea of reincarnation. Though brought up in the Christian belief that the present is our only life on which an eternity of bliss or wretchedness depends, I had never accepted that aspect of Christianity and now, while remaining Christian and at times experiencing feelings of devotion – particularly around the time of my confirmation – I simply dropped belief in a judgement day and adopted the idea of reincarnation. It was not that I argued myself into reincarnation as a rational belief – indeed I held very little argument within myself on any subject – but rather that I accepted it as something I had known about all along. I also noticed that, while my mother pooh-poohed what the astrologer had written, my father neither condemned nor ridiculed but simply passed the statement on as a matter of interest to us all.

Early in 1918, when my father had been less than two years in his new parish, the pattern of our lives was again disrupted when my father decided to join the army as a private soldier. The war, which seemed to us children to have become a permanent feature of our existence, was going badly. Not only the *Manchester Guardian* which we took at home, but even the *Daily Mail* from which Mr Hoare read extracts to us at school after morning prayers, admitted, if not to defeat, at least to almost continuous 'reverses'. No doubt my father must have talked the matter over with my mother, but he said nothing to us and the first we knew was a letter from her during termtime, telling us the news. Neighbouring clergymen were to share the services, my mother would take charge of the parish welfare, and we were all instructed that, with my father away, we must be particularly good and helpful. But my father was now over forty and the only corps willing to accept him was the RAMC. Their training centre happened to be at Blackpool, within easy walking distance of St Anne's, so that during the summer term he could sometimes come over in a uniform smelling forcefully of disinfectant and take us out to tea. Many boys had fathers or brothers in the army, but they were all officers and we felt proud of our father as a private soldier. On him, as on many others, the army exercised a rejuvenating effect. Having always stooped and carried his head on one side, he now stood up straighter and looked taller. His cheeks grew rosier. Some of his suppressed sense of humour had returned and he appeared to stammer less.

Father was still at Blackpool learning to be a stretcher-bearer when I went back in the autumn for my last term at Lawrence House, Jack having already left for a public school, St Edward's at Oxford. I was looking forward to this term for two reasons. I was to be captain of football and had resolved we should win all our matches, but I should also be taking the first step in my chosen career by going as a naval cadet to Osborne. I already knew much about the Royal Naval College, and that to gain entry I should have to pass examinations and go before a board consisting of three captains. I had no fear of the examinations, having studied the papers set the previous year, and still less of the captains. Their concern must be to find out if a boy genuinely wanted to go into the navy – and I had wanted nothing else for the past two years – and also to decide whether when he got there he would make a good officer. About this too I had no doubts.

One day in November as we were going for our school walk along the front, we saw a small aeroplane coming from the direction of Blackpool. Leaflets came floating down, white against wintry clouds, and we rushed onto the shore to try and catch them. They were small squares of newsprint with a few lines beginning, 'An armistice was signed today between ... ' Neither we nor the master in charge knew just what an armistice was, but we understood that the war was over, our side had won, and peace and happiness would follow before long. This was confirmed when we got back to the school and saw that Mr Hoare, who had worn nothing but a black tie since 4 August 1914, had put on a coloured one, and then learned that we would all be given an extra half-holiday.

Very soon I had less cause to rejoice, for my father on his next visit told me he had 'discussed things' with my mother, and they both wished me to give up any idea of entering the navy; in view of all the suffering war entailed, they did not think it right for one of their sons to devote his life to war as a career. They hoped I would not be too disappointed and suggested I might consider going into the Indian civil service. About having to give up the navy I said little, since I would neither pretend not to be disappointed nor admit to disappointment. The suggestion of the Indian civil service I passed over in silence. I did not like the sound of a civil service, Indian or otherwise, for my mind was set on a quite different kind of life. Moreover I had a special antipathy to India and the Indian people, not through any fault of theirs but because a particularly strict aunt, a sister of my mother's, was spending her life in India as a missionary, and so the whole subcontinent was associated in my mind with Aunt Christine.

As regards my immediate future, my father went on, he had spoken to Mr Hoare asking that I should be entered for a scholarship examination to a public school. Two schools were proposed, St Edward's and Shrewsbury, and of the two I unhesitatingly chose Shrewsbury. At St Edward's I should once again be following Jack, whereas Shrewsbury was connected for me with a cousin, Gerald Sanger, who had been head boy there before going into the army, and whose good looks, lordly manner and deep voice I much admired.

Very soon, however, it appeared that it was by now too late for me to enter for a Shrewsbury scholarship, since the year's examinations had already been held, so that I must, after all, go to St Edward's. As I was the brother of a boy already in the school, they were willing to accept me although this was not the beginning of the school year; and though their regular scholarship examinations had also already taken place, there was a further scholarship available for which I could sit after entering the school. And so, at the beginning of 1919, when most new boys had already been settled in for a term, I arrived with Jack in the city where I should spend the next nine years.

4

Ladder of Learning

The world in which I now found myself was so demanding – and in its way so harsh – that I soon forgot my lost naval career, and after my first term or two I gave it hardly any thought. Sixty years ago St Edward's was a curious place. It had an agreeable red-brick quadrangle, an excellent headmaster known as 'the warden', and the standard of its music and singing was renowned, but otherwise it was more like a penal settlement for young delinquents than a place of education. The war was hardly over, fees were low – only £90 a year – and the masters and staff ill-paid. Our upbringing was not intended to fit us to become industrial magnates or even prosperous professional men, but to survive in imperial outposts and draughty vicarages, and for this it was shrewdly calculated.

I had arrived in the middle of winter and quickly found myself sharing, with the 170 or so boys already in the school, the two concerns of trying to keep warm and trying to keep fed. The first was made almost impossible by the regulations under which we lived. Three thin red blankets only on the bed, and all windows, of which there were many in the dormitories, to be kept open at night. Curtains or blinds did not exist, and if the rain came in you must pull the sheet over, or put the pillow on top of your head instead of underneath. After football we plunged straight into an unheated swimming bath – there were no facilities for washing mud off first – and for physical jerks in the quadrangle we were only allowed to wear singlets ('zephyrs') and football shorts. Inevitably in winter we all suffered from colds and many of us had chilblains from October till March. The food would have provoked a murderous riot in any prison. After four o'clock tea – consisting of a bun and a cup of tea – there was only supper at 6.30, which was more tea with bread and margarine; anything else, even jam, had to be bought from the school shop by those with money to pay for it. Tins of cake and scones which my mother sent every month helped Jack and me along, and we had also a kindly aunt living in Oxford who invited us to her comfortable home, not now and then but every Sunday as a matter of course throughout the term. Without these resources we should have had a hard life indeed.

Prestige in the school attached only to success in games, but even to a thirteen-year-old looking for heroes to worship, our standards were abysmal, so that it was almost as unusual for the school to win three matches in a row as it was for a boy to attain some academic distinction. Our masters wore caps and gowns, handed out work and supervised lessons, but except during teaching periods the discipline of the school did not depend on them. This was in the hands of the eight or ten prefects who had the power to administer beatings, known as 'bummings', though only for the senior prefect was this a serious call on his energy and time. For the benefit of the prefects, a fagging system was in force, and at a shout of 'Lower School' all boys from the junior forms must race towards the sound and form a queue, from which the last arrival would be summoned to polish the prefect's shoes, tidy his study, fetch his books from wherever he had left them, or make toast over a gas ring for his tea.

St Edward's at that time did not follow the conventional pattern of organization into houses, each under its own housemaster, which provides, in theory at least, some personal supervision; instead it was stratified into layers of seniority like a civil service, each layer inhabiting a form room named after a colony to remind us of our imperial heritage: Jamaica, Natal, Canada and so on. As a new boy I was in the lowest form room known as Ceylon, but even at this low level of life we had our code of honour and our victims. Given the choice of writing lines or being beaten, one should choose a beating and endure it, like a Red Indian brave, without a murmur. Should you choose lines you were liable to be written off as a wreck, and for wrecks existence could rapidly become a misery. An inspection of 'new kids' took place in Ceylon shortly after I arrived, and we were lined up by the half-dozen biggest boys. It was a Sunday so we were wearing dusty Eton suits with striped trousers and black jackets, stringy black ties and starched Eton collars.

'What's *your* name?'

'Hopkinson minor.'

'What's your father?'

'A clergyman.' Many other fathers were clergymen too, so this was not held against me.

'Are you a wreck, Hopkinson minor?'

It was the first time I had heard the word, but it sounded uninviting so I answered a determined 'No.'

In the hard world of school, as in other hard worlds, the worst offence was to be weak, or rather to show weakness. Norris, the boy standing next to me, was an only child, with a mother but no father. Unlike the rest of us, this was the first time he had been away from home and he could not stop his lower lip from trembling. In this society he was a foredoomed victim, and if he haunts his tormentors as much as he has haunted me who did nothing to protect him, they will have paid sufficient penalty already. After only a term or two, his mother wisely took him away.

The other side of the picture was that St Edward's was both a musical and a religious school, reflecting in this the character of its warden, W. H. Ferguson, a dignified, awe-inspiring but humorous and warm-hearted man. Twice every day the whole school streamed into chapel, wearing surplices and with polished shoes; there was a prefect watching our feet, and failure to polish brought an inevitable 'bumming'. The choir, under its organist W. K. Stanton, later to become a renowned BBC musical director, had reached a peak of excellence, and to support their efforts the whole school practised hymn-, psalm- and carol-singing every Sunday. I was the least musical of boys and when tested for the choir

49

could emit nothing more than a low buzzing sound.

'You're as bad as your brother,' Stanton remarked, looking for the next name on his list.

But unmusical as I was I could feel my heart lift with the roof-cracking roar which greeted a favourite hymn, such as 'For all the saints' or 'Mine eyes have seen the glory of the coming of the Lord'. Equally I would tremble with happiness when two or three little monsters raised their heavenly voices in the anthem on Sunday evening ... 'Many waters cannot quench love, Neither can the floods drown it ... ' or 'For in the wilderness shall waters break forth ... And streams in the desert ... ' Some of the voluntaries played on the organ as the choir walked slowly out with the whole school standing in their places affected me too, and once, seeing Mr Stanton in the cloisters, I asked 'What's that you were playing, sir, as we came out?'

He looked at me in astonishment.

'Brahms, boy! Brahms, of *course*.'

The name was unfamiliar but I made a note of it.

After only a few weeks of my first term came the scholarship examination. Already I thought of myself as belonging to the school and had no wish to be sent anywhere else; I had also been assured that even if I failed our benevolent uncle Austin would continue paying my school fees. However the scholarship, worth £30 a year, would reduce the family obligation and in any case, once having entered any sort of competition I was always determined on success. All had gone well, I thought, until we came to the Greek exam. Greek had not been taught to us at Lawrence House, and though for my last term or two I had taken Greek as an extra, I had got little further than learning the alphabet and a few simple words and constructions, not supposing the language of Homer would be of much service to me in my battleship. Fortunately we were not required to turn English into Greek, only to translate Greek into English, and I had managed the half-dozen short sentences, but having done this, I found myself faced with fourteen or fifteen lines of solid text, full of unknown words among which I could discover no single clue.

I looked round at my competitors, three or four of them already in the school, plus as many more struggling for admission. I was hoping to see faces as blank as my own, but all except the boy next to me were scribbling busily. He sucked the end of his pen and then muttered, loud enough for me to hear, 'Jerusalem to Jericho . . . Jerusalem to Jericho . . . what the *hell?*'

But he had given me all the clue I needed, and I looked at the text with fresh hope. The words 'Jerusalem to Jericho', I thought, could only occur in one place whatever the language – in the story of the Good Samaritan which I knew by heart from those many Sundays spent in church. All I had to do was to write the story out, taking care not to put 'poured oil into his wounds' where it should be 'set him on his own ass', and the scholarship would be mine – as indeed it was. Securing it was more than money, for it meant that next term I should be in the Upper School, no longer obliged to run at every prefect's shout. I would also enjoy the curious privilege of carrying a cushion, or 'sit-upon', around with me from class to class to mitigate the hardness of the benches – a comfort and dignity from which Lower School boys, quite rightly I now realized, were excluded.

Movement up the ladder of school is mercifully swift, and after two terms I moved out of Ceylon into Field House, away from the main buildings, which had formerly been someone's comfortable villa with garden and tennis court. It stood at the edge of the playing fields and there were only about twenty of us there, with no prefects or seniors and only one master – or 'beak' – in charge.

Here, unlike Ceylon, there was no bullying, and each of us spent time as he thought fit. Two of my companions were farmer's sons from Somerset, heavy and slow-moving, but skilled at slipping out into the fields and setting mole-traps in the ditches. They would skin their prey on a wooden board, curing the skins with salt emptied into envelopes at meal-times, and then sell them for an enviable tenpence each to a tailor for making waistcoats. Though I caught no moles, I too at times would creep out in the twilight through the meadows down by the canal and listen to the corncrakes and nightjars that were then common around Oxford, or else glide into the bushes and along by a hedge in the early morning for a swim in the outdoor baths while the mist was still curling off the water.

It was a sign of growing confidence that in my last term in Field House, a summer term, I took a bold step. The choir, because of all the time they spent in choir practice, were allowed two extra half-holidays each term, and my plan was to enjoy the half-holidays without being in the choir. The only other group entitled to take the special half-holidays was the band, a dozen bugles, four side-drums and a big drum, which led the OTC on route marches. My problem was that I could neither blow a bugle nor play a drum; there was however one other instrument in the band, the cymbals, which I thought might be within my musical capacity. All one had to do, it seemed, was to clash them; no need to vary the note, raise the pitch or employ great musical expertise. The present cymbalist despised his instrument, having ambitions to become a bugler – but could I insinuate myself into his place?

I approached the big drummer, Moody, our school full-back and fast bowler whom I had played against in practice matches, stressing my enthusiasm for cymbal-playing and my respect for so admired a body as our OTC band. My approach succeeded just in time for the first choir half-holiday, and so now every Friday evening I marched round the quad with my fellow-musicians, a cause of derision to our school-fellows and of complaints from the north Oxford householders whose ears were affronted and children kept awake. Before long, Moody in his turn asked a favour of me. A handsome, black-haired youth of seventeen, he was in love with the warden's niece, a radiant beauty glimpsed only once a week in Sunday chapel, with whom he had somehow managed to make contact, and it was now my task to slip letters for her into a pillarbox set into the garden wall of Field House. But one evening, chatting with friends as we walked over, I forgot the letter, and only discovered it in my pocket as I undressed. What should I do? I could post it in the morning and say nothing – but supposing it was urgent? Arranging a meeting, or making up a quarrel? Having waited until it was half dark, I crept downstairs, worked my way through the shrubbery, leaned over the wall to slip the letter in, and thankfully regained the entrance. Tiptoeing upstairs, full of self-satisfaction and good will, I heard the voice of the master in charge, Mr Tilly.

'*What are you doing there, Hopkinson?*'

Too taken aback to think up any lie, I was about to say what came into my mind, 'Creeping around the shubbery, sir,' when without waiting for my answer, Mr Tilly went on, 'I watched you in the house match this afternoon, Hopkinson. How old are you?'

'Fifteen, sir.'

'Well, you'll make a batsman one day, Hopkinson, providing you *give your whole mind to it*. But there's one thing you were getting wrong. Here, let me show you.'

And, going into his study, the master, who was even more impassioned about games than we were, came back with a bat, and in the semi-darkness of the landing was soon showing me how to deal with a well pitched-up ball on the leg side, and the question of what I was doing in the grounds a couple of hours after lights out was allowed to pass unnoticed.

By next term I had left Field House and was in Main School, a senior boy. Here the dormitories were larger, with more than twenty of us together, each with our three blankets, window to be kept open, trunk at the bed foot containing best suit, clean clothing, and a coloured tie which we might wear only on the last day of term. Down the middle of the dormitory ran a double row of wash stands holding basins of cold water for our morning wash. The floor was of bare boards with a strip of matting by each bed. At night we undressed in silence; the prefect lolling in the corner might appear to be reading, but would detect the slightest whisper.

'Prayers!' he would shout, and in a second we were all on our knees to our Creator and must remain there motionless until he shouted 'Time!'

A religious prefect such as Mortimer, later to become Bishop of Exeter, might keep us at our devotions for a whole two minutes and became highly unpopular by doing so; others, less devout, would call 'Time! almost before they had finished saying 'Prayers!' A quarter of an hour exactly was allowed for getting into bed, and every head must be on the pillow as the chapel clock, which also sounded quarters, finished striking 9.30. But by now discipline had become part of me and I conformed automatically, like a circus horse.

Though the general level of teaching was low, there were those among the masters from whom much could be learned, though not always in the subjects they were teaching. In the fifth form I came under a Welshman, Griffiths. Appreciating our ignorance and lack of interest in anything except sport and the trivialities of school life, he would often at the start of the morning's work read out some passage from his newspaper. Germany, our defeated enemy, was to be made to pay 'until the pips squeak'. Did we agree with this? Indeed we did! But how could the country pay unless its industries were restarted? And if they were, wouldn't Germany become industrially dominant again – which was partly what had caused war in the first place?

A League of Nations had been launched to make certain there were no more wars. A good idea, we all agreed. But how, he asked, was it to function? Would it have armed forces of its own? And if so, who would provide and pay for them? Eagerly we would argue on one side or the other, but before long would always ask; 'Please, sir, which side's *right*? Should the Germans be made to pay – or shouldn't they?'

'That's for you to think out,' he would reply. 'And now get out your Virgils – the unhappy Dido has just been deserted by the prig Aeneas, you recall. Let's hear you translate the next ten lines, Hopkinson minor.' I, at least, learned far more from Mr Griffiths's refusal to tell us what we ought to think than I did from our official lessons.

At sixteen I was moved up into the sixth form, and here for the first time enountered scholarship, an attitude of mind for which I was still far from ready, if indeed I ever should be. Our sixth-form master, Goldie, was a kindly, ineffective man with a sidelong walk, the face of a bright-eyed trusting bird, and a mind filled with a burning passion for the classics. He spoke of

Greek and Latin writers with the reverence with which preachers in chapel spoke about St Paul, or we of our athletic heroes, and he credited us young barbarians with at least part of his own devotion. When I showed up a piece of so-called Latin, scrambled hastily together the previous evening, he would lay my exercise book before him hopefully as though expecting to find nuggets of erudition in a river of smooth-flowing prose. My mistakes he would mark apologetically at first, and would clearly much rather have overlooked them if he could. But as he crossed out, underlined and rewrote, his brow grew dark and I realized that this week's production must be shameful even by my standards. Now my eye, running on ahead, detected a monumental howler, a masculine adjective which had some-how attached itself disgracefully to a feminine noun. If only he would leave the room for a moment, I could alter it before he came back. But when Mr Goldie arrived at it he paused, head on one side like a bird examining a strange insect.

'Ha! So you fancy you have me there, do you? I was not aware of a masculine form for the noun *mensa*. Certainly the feminine is more generally accepted. Let us see what authority you depend on!' Reaching for the heaviest dictionary, he traced all uses of the word down to the latest Silver Latin authors.

'No, no!' he declared at last. 'No authority at all! We cannot allow you to create your own!'

It must have been evident soon, even to his kindly eye, that he had no hope of making me a scholar, but he also appreciated my passion for poetry and for the only language I have ever really understood, my own. Soon, at our weekly sessions in his study, he was getting the blue pencilling over as quickly as he could, in order to show me passages by Pope and Dryden, or read from poets whose names I had never even heard, Darley, Quarles and Beddoes. In his eagerness to encourage, he would pull volumes off his shelves and heap them on me, so that now I rushed through my proper work even more hastily than before in order to submerge myself in a tide of rolling language.

'What's *that* you're reading?' demanded the master in charge of preparation, stationing himself suspiciously behind my desk, a position from which he was known to deliver a sharp left and right to each side of the head.

'Something Mr Goldie told me to read, sir,' I answered blandly, adding 'English literature, sir,' as though that must explain everything.

The master moved away, unconvinced but unwilling to involve himself with a colleague, and at least I was keeping quiet.

A letter from my father gives the picture of himself, of our relationship and perhaps also of me at this stage. Sixteen years old, I was now in or on the edge of the school rugby and cricket teams, and in later life when I looked back, I would always date my impression of myself as having ceased to be a child from this time. It was the spring term and we had just started to play hockey; if the school were to form a team, I should be in it and had written for permission to buy a hockey stick.

Father answered in his neat handwriting, making the minimum mark necessary to represent each letter, with words evenly spaced and the lines at equal distances apart.

It would be right to get a hockey stick – get a good one but don't spend money on fancy woods or splicing.

I hope that work goes well. Put all that you know into your classical work. 'A Grammarian's Funeral'* is right – and hard slogging at grammar and determination to get at the real meaning of language opens out the view into the big things of life – it is worth the grind and the renouncing of other things. Don't try to reap too soon. Ploughing and sowing are life's job.

It's a dreadful thing to have a father who slips too easily into the pulpit.

All love from mother and from your father

Henry.

I acquitted my father of tending to slip 'too easily' into writing as he had, being aware that even a short letter would have cost him a full hour or more. However, I did not borrow Mr

---

*Just what lines in Robert Browning's verses my father was referring to I can only guess, but perhaps they were – 'That before living he'd learn how to live – No end to learning.'

Goldie's copy of 'A Grammarian's Funeral' in order to find out what Browning had written about the importance of studying grammar so as to 'get at the real meaning of language'. I was not a boy who accepted criticism readily; on the contrary I resented it all too quickly. But neither was I one who pursued an argument to the end if doing so would result in conflict which I might avoid. I could see that my father felt I ought to be giving less time to games and more to my schoolwork, but since he did not say this in so many words I felt free to overlook the implication; after all, I assured myself, I was in the sixth form at an early age and my end-of-term reports were good. What I mainly derived from his letter was a sense of the wide gap between the ways in which the two of us looked at the incidental problems of daily life. I had written to him to know if our family could afford for me to buy a hockey stick, and he had answered that it would be 'right' for me to buy one, adding advice as to the kind of stick to buy – a matter on which I felt my judgement likely to be better than his. And in fact, having secured approval, I did not buy a hockey stick at all, since for some reason the school decided not to form a team.

While games were absorbing my attention, Jack was hard at work preparing for university. The summer term would be his last, and it was expected that he would go to Oxford. Shortly before Jack, as Hopkinson maximus, moved off the St Edward's scene, Stephan had made his appearance on it in the undignified guise of Hopkinson minimus. He at once established a position for himself by his good temper, obligingness and ready wit. He had secured from somewhere a toy theatre in which he put on performances, using the pantomime figures supplied by the makers as basis for an ironic running commentary on school life and its personalities. These were so successful that he was actually able to charge a small sum for admission and would come home at the end of term with more money than he started; career masters had at that time not yet been invented, otherwise he would certainly have found himself guided in the direction of banking and finance.

Paul, besides growing stronger year by year, was developing a taste for lawless adventure. With a companion's help he had discovered a metal box near the railway line in which the platelayers kept their fog signals, prised it open and removed the contents. Having done this two or three times, he could enliven the tedium of Sunday afternoons by fixing a number of fog signals to the line and hiding down the embankment or in a culvert to enjoy their effect. Ingenuity at times carried him and his imitators to greater lengths. The main line into Oxford from the north runs alongside Port Meadow in a straight line for several miles, and here through the early-morning haze the driver of an express witnessed a frightening scene – two smallish men in overcoats were wrestling furiously regardless of the express bearing down on them. Suddenly one drew a large knife, raised his arm and stabbed the other, who fell prostrate across the track. The driver slammed on his brakes, but as he struggled to stop, the mortally wounded man scrambled to his feet and made off across the fields in pursuit of his attacker.... The days when in our walks at Aber I would look back on a slight, pale-faced figure, lagging far behind the rest of us under a huge sailor hat with the lettering 'HMS *Indefatigable*' on the ribbon, were gone for good.

We were all in different ways adapting ourselves to the present and preparing for the future, a future which had already taken two or three long strides into the present, for, at the head of the notepaper on which my father had written his letter of advice to me, a printed address in Manchester had been crossed out and a fresh one written in. We no longer lived in Colne. A brief spell in a Manchester parish had come to an end as well, and our new home was on the edge of that Lake District where we had all so passionately longed to be.

5

In Our Own Shire

Two years after he got back from the war, my father had been offered a living in Manchester, a part of the city called Greenheys, sprawling away behind the university at which he had formerly lectured. It was a large parish, neither industrial nor residential but full of cheap boarding houses, struggling shops and decaying one-man businesses. Only the churches and pubs raised their heads above the squalor of a district which has since been totally demolished and for which there must be very few regrets. Here my father's work was arduous and never ending, so that after little more than a year his health broke down; doctors ordered him to move somewhere less exacting, and my mother, who missed the warm acceptance and good humour she had met in Colne, was equally insistent on a change. Kindly providence, responding perhaps to the unspoken prayers of five children, led us now to Burneside, a village on the very edge of that Lake District which we had continued to dream of as our rightful home.

No sooner did we learn of the prospective move – this was back in the summer of 1921 – than Jack and I, determined cyclists, set out to pay Burneside a visit. As we saw the grey stone vicarage with the hills rising beyond and heard the rooks cawing in the churchyard, we stared at one another in happy disbelief. The previous vicar and his family had already left, so we went into the garden. Along its foot and embracing a wide meadow ran a river fringed with trees, from one of which as we watched a kingfisher flashed past. Only three or four months later, after one more term at school, we came back for the first holidays in our new home. Inside, the house was roomy as well as pleasant, and for the first time Jack and I had each a room of our own.

Our arrival in Burneside put fresh life into us all. Paul immediately learned to ride a bike and, as soon as he could partially control it, pushed it a dozen times in a morning to the top of a little-used farm road for the excitement of flying down between the hedges with a spill at every third run. Stephan, who had previously to be chased out each day like a reluctant domestic animal, now took to bicycling and walking with Esther on long expeditions. Though small for his age, which was now thirteen, Stephan covered the ground in strides with a kind of rolling swagger as though on his way to rejoin a tea clipper at Deptford. He still read as persistently as ever, and when sent by my father with a letter to the post office barely 100 yards away, would take a bicycle 'to save time' and a book on the handlebars 'so as not to become bored'. Esther, who now set off every morning for the girls' high school at Kendal, had transformed herself in a few months from a child into a demure schoolgirl with a green blazer and hat, long black legs, and prep to be done when she got home, for which she must have silence.

My mother, besides the general work of the parish, had taken on a stimulating new activity. Finding that our village – which included several hamlets as well as a number of outlying farms – had no district nurse, she at once set herself to raise the money to provide one and, having succeeded, went on to raise more money to provide the new nurse with a car. My father, heartened by the sight of the hills and the smell of mountain air, showed for a time a welcome assertiveness. He told me off when I failed to shovel into the coal cellar a large load deposited directly onto the back doorstep by the coalman. He also one morning at breakfast did something none of us had ever heard him do before, and I at least never would hear him do again – he complained about something given him to eat. In a spirit of adventure or perhaps for reasons of economy, my mother had put out a new kind of cereal – small bolsters make of spikes like those on gorse bushes or the notorious 'wait-a-bit' thorn of

Africa. The packet described these as a specially nourishing form of rice, and we boys chewed our way through a bolster each with no more than a sidelong glance to make sure the others were doing their duty equally. But when my father had taken his first mouthful, he pushed the plate away. 'I cannot see what advantage this stuff has over chopped barbed wire,' he said, reaching for the marmalade.

After this we were hardly surprised when he bought a car. This was an extraordinary vehicle called a Trojan. It cost £100, was almost impossible to start, and dangerous both to those inside and outside it when in motion. It had solid tyres like a pony trap, and only two gears; in top gear the car could be worked up to a dizzying 30 m.p.h. at which speed the man at the wheel enjoyed the same sensations as drivers tearing round the Indianapolis circuit at 200 m.p.h. – only he did not enjoy them for so long. On reaching a hill, and Westmorland was full of hills, the Trojan must drop down into second gear in which the top speed was a grinding 6 m.p.h. But none of this mattered to us; what was important was that we were now, for the first time and far beyond our expectations, a car-owning family.

It was the effect of our move on my elder brother, however, which surprised me most. There was hardly anything which required more circumspection in our family than to spend money on oneself and not for some charitable purpose. Only the summer before I had been sharply rebuked for buying an evening paper to learn how my beloved Lancashire was faring at Old Trafford, when I had only to wait patiently till next day to read all about it in my father's *Manchester Guardian*. But Jack, in general the most dutiful of us all, would occasionally take some action which no other of us would have dared, carrying it off with a bland assurance that somehow bypassed criticism. No sooner had we arrived in Burneside than Jack told Paul and me he was buying an air rifle.

'I don't mean a toy. A proper rifle.'

'But, good Lord, Jack,' I asked, 'd'you really imagine you'll get away with that?'

'"Get away with it?" What d'you mean? I've got the money.'

'*Where* have you got it? Don't tell me you've managed to

save up three quid!'

'Those savings certificates grandfather gave us. I've never cashed any. There's more than enough to buy a rifle.'

'But they're supposed to be for your old age. They're to keep you from the workhouse when you're paralysed and all your teeth have fallen out. . . . You'll never be allowed to lash out the certificates on a deadly weapon.'

'And how *can* you cash them anyway?' asked Paul, with his practical sense. 'Father's probably got them stowed away in his bank.'

'No, he hasn't. I had them, and I've cashed them already at the post office. Had to, to send up for the rifle.'

'Did you ask father and mother if you could?'

'No,' Jack answered easily. 'I just told them I'd done it. There's a piece of land on the hill that's simply crawling with rabbits. I shall be off up there as soon as I get my BSA.'

Paul and I gazed at him with the awe due to a man who has seized control over his own savings certificates.

But I too had a plan to put into effect. During the previous term I had gained a place in the school rugby team and Mr Tilly, our coach, had urged me to get some games during the holidays. 'I don't want you forgetting everything you've learned. It's easy to slip back if you don't stick at it. I'll give you a letter in case there's the chance of a few matches in the north.'

Kendal, as I already knew, had a strong rugby team and I soon learned from the telephone book – for we were now also a telephone-owning family – the address of the club chairman. Then, with Paul to support me, I walked into Kendal, presented myself at his business office, and handed in my letter. The chairman looked me up and down, saw that I was not particularly large or strong, and said he'd 'let me know if anything turns up'. This seemed to me rather offhand, so I said I'd be glad if in the meantime he would lend me one of the club footballs so that I could keep in practice just in case anything did. This possibly impressed him, because a couple of days later he phoned to ask if I could go to Ilkley on Saturday with the Kendal team whose regular full-back was injured. Thrilled at sixteen to be playing for a man's club, I walked into Kendal early on the Saturday to meet my new clubmates at the station.

The journey to Ilkley passed quietly as I sat in a corner of the saloon marked 'Reserved for Kendal RUFC', reading my book and answering when spoken to; they seemed a powerfully built lot, and I felt glad we were all going to be on the same side. The game was a rough-and-tumble affair in a high wind, after which in the darkness of a December evening came the journey back. One or two of the older players had evidently been told to look after the Burneside parson's son, but, after kindly seeing that I got some food, they also found time to take in a few pints before we reached the station. There was also a buffet on the platform, from which a good supply of bottles was carried into our saloon, and soon everyone was singing, swaying from side to side and with eyes half-closed:

> The boys of Old Kendal, Old Kendal, Old Kendal,
> The buggers do not work at all.
> They get up quite early, quite early, quite early,
> And piss through a hole in the wall.

As the songs became more anatomical, our scrum-half, the only small man in the team, whose name seemed to be Wank, got up onto the luggage rack to see if he could climb all round the saloon without touching ground; as he passed over my head a lurch of the train dislodged him so that he fell almost on my feet. Just in front was a cup of tea, brought me by a kindly footballer since I wasn't sharing in the beer; in a flash Wank had snatched this up and flung cup, saucer and spoon over his shoulder with drunken accuracy straight through the only open window. Thrusting his sweaty face in mine, he explained – 'In case of men working on the line' – and climbed back onto the rack.

By the time I reached the vicarage, having walked the few miles out from Kendal on a wet and windy night carrying a case packed with my muddy clothes and boots, everyone except father was in bed. He was putting the finishing touches to tomorrow's sermon, but he quickly made tea, found something for me to eat, and sat down with me by the kitchen fire. He described what had happened during the day and then, as I

63

rose to go up to bed, inquired: 'Well, Tom, and how did you get on today? Are the Kendal team a nice quiet set of lads?'

'Yes, thank you, father,' I replied, 'a *very* nice quiet set of lads.'

A year after we arrived in Burneside Jack went up to Oxford, having won an exhibition, or scholarship, at St Edmund Hall. As a good-looking, unattached young man he was soon in demand for parties and dances, of which there were plenty at neighbouring country houses. On Windermere too, only a few miles away, there was a yacht club, so that during the summer he could fill in time spared from study with sailing and playing tennis by day and dancing at night.

To the passion for games which Paul and I shared, Kendal offered a perfect outlet. There was an enthusiastic following for rugby; hundreds would turn out to watch local matches, and in the spring when there was enough daylight we would sometimes play two matches in the same day, afternoon and evening, with only a hot bath and a cup of tea between. In the summer we played village cricket, or tennis at one of the nearby houses. Arduous exercise at this period was as necessary to me as food and I suffered if a whole day went by without at least a couple of hours of walking; even mental activity produced a physical response, so that if on a wet afternoon I read a book that excited me, I would soon stop reading, change and set out for a long run in the rain.

As I look back over our life in Burneside, the same five or six impressions project themselves again and again on to the screen. In time they spread over several years, but all centre round the place and belong to the period of our growing up.

A few months after Jack had bought his air rifle I was seized with such a passion for shooting that one morning after breakfast, having noticed a flock of starlings feeding on the berries of a mountain ash, I concealed myself against its trunk and in a few minutes had shot nine. Each time one of their number fluttered brokenly to the ground the rest would fly up a few feet, only to be drawn back instantly to the feast of berries. I was describing this achievement to Paul when my father chanced to overhear. He looked at me, and uttered only one word, '*Why?*' But that was enough. From now on I shot only what was edible and could therefore, I considered, be classified as 'game', and my shooting of it as 'sport'.

The best place for such shooting was a stretch of moorland a couple of miles above the village. Its name was Ratherheath, known locally as Rad'reth, and it belonged to the squire who, with much kindness since he himself enjoyed rough shooting, allowed us to range over it and shoot anything we could – rabbits and an occasional wild duck. There was a lake up there with a boathouse in which at times two of us would sleep on a heap of bracken, waking up cold in the dawn to watch the herons fishing and to shoot a rabbit or two as they nibbled the early-morning grass.

Here one day, when I was alone and not trying to kill anything, I had one of those momentary experiences in which nothing apparently happens but of which a lifelong impression remains, as though one had looked into another world or had a glimpse of this one as it really is. There was nothing special about the circumstances. I was moving quietly to avoid disturbing the life of birds and insects, and came out onto a grassy track where I stood still, looking at the wood in front of me into which the track I was following slid away. As I looked, my self seemed to melt away; viewer and the scene blended into one. Time stopped or had never existed, and for a few seconds I was part of the universe. . . .

That momentary experience, which many people must have known and some perhaps many times, has never been repeated for me. Quite soon after this though, and at almost the same spot, I had one which impressed me equally, though it was purely visual and not on what had appeared to be some inner plane.

I was walking along the road from Ratherheath to the village with an empty mind. There was no one in sight and the road ran downhill, so that for a minute or two I was not so much walking as allowing my legs to swing one after the other and my body to be carried with them. In this abstracted state I happened to look over a low stone wall at a scene I had passed many times before – a rocky mound out of which were growing three wind-twisted trees, their branches green against a summer sky, and beneath them three reddish cows grazing in line with lowered heads, swishing their tails to keep away the flies.

That was all, but I saw it with a clarity with which I have never seen anything before or since, as though I were looking directly into the scene itself, unobscured by the self-preoccupation through which we habitually look at everything, so that what we see is never the object or person, but as it were a cloudy reproduction taken through our own out-of-focus, distorting lens.

And now I am sitting in a bus coming back from Windermere. I am by myself, the bus almost empty except for a few women shoppers, and the conductor is Dicky Pickthall, a fellow member of the Kendal football team. In intervals between handing out tickets, ringing his bell and exchanging ribaldries with the driver through a glass partition, he drops into the empty place beside me. It is getting near to the end of summer and we discuss the club's and our own prospects for the season. After one such chat, as he moves away, something I had forgotten to say comes into my mind and I turn to call after him, 'Dicky!'

But the word is never spoken, for just behind on the other side of the bus is a girl who must, I suppose, have got on at the last stop. She has a bright scarf over black hair curling to her shoulders, and her gypsy colouring makes even Dicky's ruddy cheeks look pasty. She is perhaps sixteen, a couple of years younger than myself at this time, and she sits in her place, wearing a thin printed dress with the top button undone, in delighted enjoyment of her bodily attraction. Her black eyes are full of mischief, and catching the eagerness in mine, she smiles at nothing, lifts her bundle from the seat on to her knees – and turns to gaze out of the window.

The next move must be with me, but I look away, and a painful blush rises up my neck and spreads over my face. Imprisoned in my upbringing and the inhibitions of my nature, I could more easily run to the back of the bus and throw myself into the road than do what I am longing to do, take a couple of strides and drop into the empty place beside her. When I next dare to look round she is laughing at me, and at Staveley where she gets down, no doubt to sell clothes pegs or whatever she has in her bundle, she turns, sees me gazing through the window after her, and gives a derisive wave.

The next scene that comes up is during a spell of iron winter. With Jack and Paul I have set off for the day; we have walked all morning and are now far up in the hills. There is a powdering of snow on the tussocks of rough grass, frozen so hard that it crackles like glass under our boots. We come unexpectedly upon a little tarn, dull and black as though turned into solid ice. Not more than twenty yards or so out from shore is an islet, a deformed tree whose roots grasp a heap of rounded stones. After testing the ice, Paul makes his way over and Jack follows. The ice crackles, and a little water oozes up around the reeds inshore, but it holds, so I take a run and launch out, meaning to slide rapidly across before the ice knows what is happening. Halfway, however, there is a sound like gunshot and I drop straight through up to my neck before I can even check myself with outstretched arms. There is no bottom beneath my feet, but for the moment I am not worried since I have only to swim over to the islet, which looks closer than trying to swim back. But the ice, though cracked, remains sufficiently solid to prevent swimming, although every time I try to haul myself up on to its surface, it gives way beneath me. My heavy walking boots are now full of water and my trousers soon fill with water too, so that after each breakthrough it grows harder to lever myself out – and the idea is growing that I can very well drown in six or seven feet of water almost within arm's length of safety. Desperately I look towards the islet, which seems to have receded since I first fell in – to see Jack and Paul dissolved with laughter at my futile threshings. Pride comes to my rescue and I refuse to let myself drown while being laughed at. So I make a fresh effort – and another – and another, breaking through the surface and plunging back each time into icy water. But at the last attempt I feel the hard stones of the bottom underneath my boots.

Once together on the islet our problem is how to get back to the shore. But we try one at a time in different directions and soon have all crossed safely over.

There is a sequel to this scene. At church next Sunday we notice a plump elderly man in a well-cut tweed suit whom we have seen before only rarely, though we know that he lives in a comfortable house on the hillside with a housekeeper and a manservant or two. He has evidently heard of the incident because he comes up after the service and, having inquired which one of us had fallen in, rebukes me for lack of consideration. How would he have felt, he asks me to consider, if someone known to him however slightly had drowned in a tarn which formed part of his property and for which, therefore, he might be held responsible? People, he concludes, ought to pay more regard to the feelings of others and less to their own selfish enjoyment.

The scene which next projects itself is also set in the depth of winter. For two days snow has been falling over the whole countryside, a fall so heavy as to create twilight at midday, with the sky a muddy yellow into which the treetops disappear. In the afternoon we get out our toboggans and join with friends to plan out a run. It is a difficult, exciting course, much too steep, and full of hazards from tree roots and concealed edges of rock beneath the snow. Our toboggans are not wooden ones on runners which would break the surface, but are made from strips of corrugated iron by the blacksmith from the mill. They have a turned-up prow of iron and handles to hold on by, and as they speed over the snow with the roar of an express train, they flatten the snow out so that every run becomes faster than the one before. Clinging tight, and all swerving to avoid obstacles, three of us at a time go flying down the long hill to bury ourselves and the toboggan in the heavy snowdrifts at its foot.

All afternoon has been spent like this, and now night has come down and with it a cracking frost. The snow has stopped; the planets are blazing in the sky as though they had just been put there, and the air is sharp and still as if we were inside an iceberg. It is Christmas Eve, and the idea seizes us to toboggan by starlight and go on and on till it is Christmas Day. So now we are again climbing up beside the run, hauling our battered toboggans and carrying an armful of candles. These we plant upright in the snow to indicate danger spots, where they burn steadily, each one in its place, hardly flickering as we go flying by time after time until at last, long before midnight, even we have had enough. As we turn downhill, calling a last goodnight to those whose home is at the top, I think to myself, 'This is how it will always be, year after year. Snow over Christmas, a hard frost and tobogganing all day with friends. Candles burning upright in the snow, the sound of carols from the village, and voices faintly calling out "Goodnight"....'

At the last scene I was not present, but it impressed itself no less deeply on my mind. Going in and out of Kendal two or three times a week, I often passed an aged couple walking into town to do their shopping. They moved always in the same way, the man stumping aggressively forward on his stick some yards ahead of his wife, who trudged after with bent head and a bag in either hand. I knew where they lived – in a remote cottage up towards Ratherheath; no road led to it, but almost at the front door was a small lake or tarn. I had stopped there once when we had been shooting in order to leave a rabbit, but there was no one in.

One holiday I did not see them and asked my father whether they were ill. 'Not exactly,' he said, and told me that on a morning not long since the woman had woken to find her old man gone. He had left no message, but she had no doubt where to find him. To the village policeman when at last he got there, she explained: 'You'll find 'im in t'tarn. 'E wouldn't want for me to die an' no one to look after 'im. Seein' as I won't last much longer, 'e jus' walked in an' drowned 'isself – like 'e allus said 'e would.'

And as indeed he had.

A school life given up to games and holidays spent in games and exercise now blended happily together so that I hardly cared where I was since both gave me what I wanted. But as I was approaching my last year at St Edward's a question not easy to answer loomed ahead – what was I going to do when this year ended? With, behind that and connected to it, the still more oppressive question of how did I intend to earn my living?

Jack's future was already decided, even, it seemed, assured. He wanted to live on in Westmorland where he had made many friends and, as it happened, there was an opening with a firm of solicitors in Kendal. After taking his degree at Oxford he would qualify in law before joining this firm and in due course, it might be hoped, become a partner. Even Paul, a year younger than myself, had a clearer idea about what he meant to be, for a couple of years previously while we were still living in Colne, our Uncle Austin had invited him, Jack and myself to stay at Ryecroft Hall, his imposing house in Audenshaw, in order to spend a couple of weeks working in his engineering firm. We would learn to operate a lathe, or at least begin to learn to do so, and incidentally find out whether any of us had an aptitude for engineering. Whether Paul showed much aptitude or not, he had at least shown more than either of his brothers and so his plan was, on leaving school, to serve two or three years' apprenticeship with a Kendal engineering firm and then go into lodgings in Manchester and serve the rest of his time in Austin's firm, where in due course he could expect to achieve a position in management.

About Stephan none of us had any doubt; with his wide reading, phenomenal memory and rapid grasp of any new subject, he must be destined to become a university professor. In this way, confidently if not always accurately, the future of my brothers was foreseen, and Esther's had been forecast for her long ago by the astrologer postman. But what was I to do? Like Jack I loved Westmorland and would have been happy to go on living there – but in what capacity? Apart from a few lawyers, doctors, dentists, and those engaged in local government, the choice of livelihood seemed to lie between becoming a parson or a farm worker, and I was ill qualified for either. I had over the years developed some slight ability to draw and paint which led me now and then to fancy that I might become an artist, and my father, with his love of painting and sculpture, did not discourage me. From the time we could walk he had taken us round the pictures in the Whitworth Institute and the Manchester City Art Gallery. He was on the latter's purchasing committee and had once persuaded his fellow members to buy one of Rodin's statues. Now and then he would go through some book of paintings with me, or show me the stack of reproductions of Greek and Roman statues he had accumulated for use in lectures, his voice taking on a special tone over works he particularly revered. He admired the Pre-Raphaelites and would have been happy if I had turned out to be Burne-Jones or Holman Hunt – since I showed no signs of being Titian or Bellini – but content enough were I only to develop into a careful interpreter of nature and a respected member of the Royal Watercolour Society. However, it was his affectionate interest which convinced me I should never make an artist.

One Christmas he gave me a book on anatomy and, as I studied the plates and diagrams – realizing that to master all this might be only one stage in the long process of learning to draw as a basis for one day learning to paint – I saw instantly that this was an effort I was never going to make, in which case it was foolish to imagine I might become an artist. Immediately afterwards the thought crossed my mind that if it had been a question, not of learning to draw but of how to write, I was ready to make all the efforts needed. The thought crossed my mind, but – as often with me – I did not absorb it nor derive any conclusions from it, and the next proposal was that I might become an architect. There was said to be a good school of architecture at Liverpool University, with which my father from his years at Manchester had established some connection. I might, it was suggested, go to Liverpool, embark on the course, and 'see how I got on'. My mother liked the idea because I should not be far away, and I neither supported nor opposed, having little idea of what 'being an architect' involved. However, there was still a year before any decision need be reached, and in this year a small incident occurred to alter my direction.

In the sixth form with me was a boy called Patrick. Like myself he was a clergyman's son, and his father, unfortunately for him, had once come to preach in the school chapel.

The sermon had been an emotional one and was consequently disapproved of by his audience, but the preacher had redeemed himself with a final sentence which would be remembered with gratitude long after everything else about him was forgotten. He had been speaking with passion and intensity of the heavenly home to which we are all journeying, and ended with a heartfelt cry, 'If I forget thee, O Jerusalem, may my right hand cleave to the roof of my mouth!'

Either in order to help him live this down or because he had literary ambitions, Patrick decided to produce a magazine for sale inside the school. We already had an official *St Edward's School Chronicle*, produced by one of the masters, recording the names of boys who had come and gone, saying kind words about masters who had retired, and providing accounts of school matches which I at least read eagerly, but this was not at all what Patrick had in mind. He visualized a magazine of literary quality, made up mainly of stories and poetry, and under pressure I had contributed some verses to the first number. This had sold sufficiently well for him to venture on a second, and in this he offered a prize of ten shillings for the best essay received on any subject. It was halfway through term, I was out of money, and I made up my mind to secure that ten shillings. The essay I wrote was no more than a political argument based on an election speech I had heard my Uncle Austin deliver. In it I ridiculed socialist doctrines on the ground that, so far from improving social conditions, they would – by undermining independence and freedom of enterprise – inevitably produce the opposite result from the one they claimed to seek, leading in the long run not to an earthly paradise but to poverty and general misery.

Either it was a powerful piece or the opposition was slight, because I won the award. It took me some time to extort the money out of Patrick, who was having trouble paying his printer's bill, but I managed in the end, and from now on I began to look on writing as a possible way to earn money, though I had not formed any intention to become a journalist.

Now, during my final two terms at school, I began, as senior prefect, to see a good deal of the warden, W. H. Ferguson. He would come into the hall at lunchtime and sit with the prefects on a dais, chatting with us naturally and humorously. Once or twice when in difficulty over some school problem, I would go to talk with him in his study; on one of these visits he asked what I intended to do on leaving school, and I told him of the plan that I should go to Liverpool and study architecture.

He replied, as though deciding the matter then and there, 'But you must go to Oxford.'

I said I would be happy indeed to do so but that it would only be possible if I were to win a scholarship.

'Then we must see that you *do* win one,' he said. 'I shall put your name down for as many colleges as possible. Most of them hold group examinations, three or four colleges together. I'll talk to Mr Goldie about your doing special work – and if you get anywhere near winning one, I may be able to put a useful word in for you.'

I thanked him and wrote to my father who agreed that if I could indeed obtain a scholarship, I should go to Oxford, and we could talk about my career after I'd been there a year or two. And so at intervals during the early months of the year I would go down and sit for two or three days in some college hall, answering papers which I could see had been set to test a knowledge of the classics much wider and deeper than my own. I had also only to listen to the conversation of the other candidates when we came out to see that they were at a level of scholarship far above my head.

My final chance came during the summer term towards the end of the academic year, when my last hope of a scholarship rested on the exams to be held by Pembroke College. These took place in its own hall, and not only did the college have for me an agreeable, friendly look but – much to my surprise after previous experiences – my fellow candidates seemed a friendly lot as well. Less obsessed with learning and more disposed, I thought, to an enjoyable existence, they chatted with me on subjects such as cricket on which I could hold my own. However, the papers proved no easier here than elsewhere, and by the time we reached the last, I saw my hope of a few enjoyable years at Oxford slipping from me. This was an

English essay and we were given our choice of several subjects, one of which was the single word 'Romance'. On seeing this I thought: 'I've nothing to lose. I've got nowhere so far. I'll forget this is an examination and write something to surprise them.' In the two or three hours allowed I put in all I'd got, the results of my desultory reading when I ought to have been studying, my thoughts about what I had read and what might prove to be its relationship to life.

Among the examiners, as it happened, was a very unusual man. Robin Collingwood was not only a fellow of Pembroke, but the author of half a dozen works on philosophy and due before long to become Professor of Metaphysical Philosophy in the university. He was also one of the leading authorities on Roman Britain and a man of the widest European culture. Later I got to know him well, but it was not until after I left the university that I learned what had happened on this occasion.

In the discussion over the candidate's papers, it was soon agreed by the other examiners that the ones I had submitted, though interesting in places, were not up to the general standard required. At this point Collingwood intervened, saying that he had by now served on a good many examining bodies, and that the English essay I had written was the best he had ever come across, and that if scholarships were not to be awarded for outstanding work on the rare occasions when it turned up, he could not see the point of continuing to hold scholarship examinations at all. They did nothing but serve to indicate how competently certain schoolmasters had prepared their pupils, and how dutifully the pupils had attended to their instruction. . . . After a good deal of argument, his insistence eventually gained the day. Few candidates can ever have been more astonished than I when I received the offer of a Pembroke scholarship, and few schoolmasters more delighted than Warden Ferguson.

My final term at school had now come to an end, and in the interval before I went up to the university our uncle Austin paid a rare visit to Burneside. A tall lean man of military appearance, dressed always in a dark suit and bow tie, he had a dry sardonic wit, was accustomed wherever he went to hold the floor, and most of his stories dealt with the discomfiture of those who had crossed his path in the House of Commons and elsewhere. . . . Approached by a reporter from a Manchester newspaper on a project to establish greyhound racing tracks, he had – he told us – carefully dissociated himself from the bishops, civic worthies and fellow MPs who condemned the scheme, saying that in his opinion 'a fool and his money are soon parted, and anything which speeds up this process must be for the general economic good'.

Again, having appealed to the Prime Minister to rid the Conservative Party – which in general he supported, though as an independent owing it no allegiance – of the 'moneylenders' touts and rotten company promoters' with which it was infested, giving their names, he claimed afterwards when the inevitable storm arose to have been misrepresented. Asked in what way his words had been misreported, he said that two of the names he included had been left out of the report and demanded to have the omission rectified.

During this stay I got to know him better than in the past, though he would always remain a remote, intimidating figure. When my mother told me to take him in an early-morning cup of tea, I found him already sitting up in bed smoking his pipe and reading. When I asked if he always smoked a pipe before breakfast, he said, 'Certainly. I sit in bed smoking my pipe last thing at night, d'you see, then I put it down by me so that it's all ready to light up the minute I wake.'

'You always used to smoke cigars.'

'Yes. I like cigars. But I found, d'you see, that I was spending two hundred pounds a year on them – enough to support a whole working family – so I stopped. And now I smoke a pipe.'

During the course of his stay we went for one or two walks. He did not walk as we did, as though we were setting off for a whole day and wanted to cover as much ground as possible in the first hour or two, but upright, hands in coat pockets, with a measured tread as though pacing the corridors of the House of Commons. I asked him if he had always wanted to go into politics.

'When I was a boy,' he said, 'the only thing I wanted in life was to go into the army. I never thought of any other career. So when I became ill and had to have one of my kidneys taken out – so that I couldn't ever become a soldier – I just didn't know what to do with myself. But in the end, d'you see, I've had a lot more fighting than most generals ever get.'

He had, in fact, served in the cavalry in the South African war, and again in the First World War as an officer in the Royal Dragoons from 1914 to 1916. Invalided out on account of the missing kidney – he had covered the scar with his hand at the original medical examination – he joined up again in 1918 as a trooper in the same regiment. In the Second World War, at the age of sixty, he would be commissioned in the Fleet Air Arm.

When his first choice of career, like my own, had been thwarted, what he chose was to become a student at the Slade School in London, but abandoned this almost at once, declaring, 'One week of my life is enough to waste in that place.' Asked by his parents what he intended to do next, he said he would become an engineer, and joined the firm of Mather and Platt with which the Hopkinson family, rich in engineers, had longstanding connections. How had he spent his time there, I inquired.

'Making drawings showing factories which didn't exist, turning out machines that weren't yet in production – to see if there'd be a market for 'em if we made 'em.'

This sounded improbable even to my ignorant ears, but what was factual was that before long he had managed to add a knowledge of engineering practice to his talent for draughtsmanship and strong inventive streak. Then, having designed a new type of coal-cutting machinery, he started to get this manufactured on his own and, as the demand increased, established the Delta Works at Audenshaw, the profits from which had now made him a rich man. Riches, however, did not interest him, and by the time he stayed with us at Burneside he had already given away Ryecroft Hall, the handsome Victorian mansion in which we had all stayed a few years earlier, to the Audenshaw Council, together with a number of houses built to his own plans, as a contribution to the housing shortage after the First World War. He himself had now gone to live in an old barn converted into a small bungalow which, he explained, was slowly lapsing into the canal by which it stood.

His handing over of Ryecroft, like my father's renunciation of our comfortable life, did not accord with my ideas of what was reasonable, and I asked whether he missed the place at all. He did not reply directly.

'D'you see, Tom, the important thing in life is to *have* everything – but not want any of it. If you've never had it, you're bound to miss it. Besides, you don't know whether you could have got it, if you'd tried.... But then, d'you see, if you've *got* everything but still go on wanting it, you're no better off than you were in the first place, since you may lose the lot at any time.... But if you've got everything and *don't* want it, you're a free man!'

Before he left I managed to get in a word of thanks for the support he had given me at school and for his further kindness in making up the money I should need to go to Oxford, and asked what he expected me to get out of these next four years.

'Learn to be arrogant! That's the purpose of going to university. It's what you can get nowhere else, d'you see. It's the hallmark they stamp on anyone who's been there.'

'You didn't go to university,' I suggested, 'but you seem to have managed reasonably well without ... '

'No, no! That's different! I'm not arrogant – I'm just rude. You must learn to go one better.'

And so at the beginning of October, with a new blue suit bought readymade for me in Kendal by my mother, and a cheque to cover expenses for the next few months, I set off to become an Oxford undergraduate.

6

Elysian Fields

One of the smallest of Oxford colleges, Pembroke in 1923 housed rather over 100 students and a mere handful of dons or fellows, of whom not more than half a dozen took any perceptible part in college life. Overshadowed physically by the majestic buildings of Christ Church, we were known to the outside world chiefly for our association with the mighty Dr Johnson, who had been in fact a far from model student. 'He skipped tutorials in order to go skating, he was impertinent to the fellows, and he hung about the college gateway fomenting trouble.'* Neither academically nor in sport was ours then an outstanding college and it still carried the nickname 'Drunken Pemmy' acquired in an earlier decade, but it had a recognized position of its own so that we could always state confidently where we came from among men from other colleges.

For scholars it was the custom to spend two years living in college, while commoners were allowed only one year before having to move out to lodgings in the city. A 'room' in college was in fact a small suite, usually a large study and smaller bedroom, plus a cubbyhole for the servant or 'scout' who kept the rooms clean. Each servant had charge of a staircase with eight sets of rooms, and would also act as waiter in hall and for any private lunch parties given by one of his students. Among his many talents, William, on the staircase in which I had

*From Dr J. D. Fleeman, 'Johnson at Pembroke', in the *Pembroke College Record*, 1978.

78

rooms, knew twenty-six different ways to fold a napkin.

Life in college at this period was a mixture of lordliness and discomfort more appropriate to an earlier century. It seemed to me lordly to have my breakfast carried across the quadrangle under covers and set out in front of a coal fire which William had already laid and lit. It was lordly to sit down in the evening to dine in an imposing hall under portraits of kings and queens, bishops and benefactors, with even our drinking water served in round-bottomed tumblers of solid silver. The scholars of each year, some ten or twelve of us, sat together at the same table along one side of the hall, moving with each succeeding year a stage nearer to High Table where the fellows ate and drank in state, and we took it in turns to read the sonorous Latin grace, as also to read lessons in chapel for a week at a time. We wore flowing black gowns, and the commoners, who filled the body of the hall, wore short gowns without sleeves. Gowns had also to be worn for lectures and tutorials and in calling on any don; they must also be worn, or at least carried, in the streets of Oxford after nine at night. Dons in general were dignified, somewhat remote, beings whose conversation with students, at least until some acquaintance had grown up, was on formal terms – 'Pray be seated, Mr Hopkinson,' or genially sarcastic – 'I can only make things *clear*, Mr Hopkinson, I cannot make you understand them.'

But if some aspects of our life were lordly, others were primitive. There were no baths in college when I first went up and no lavatories on the staircases, only in one corner of each quadrangle. The college, it was said, was still recovering from its extravagance of a year or two earlier when 'the electric light' had been installed. A bath house was at last built before my second year, to which we would splash across through the rain, barelegged and in dressing-gowns or raincoats, carrying the clothes we intended to put on. With a dozen baths ranged round the walls, as well as three or four showers, it was a cheerful place after a match. But until this innovation we took our baths after football much as, I suppose, Byron or William Pitt took theirs, in front of our study fire, using an enamel tip-up bath which the scout somehow contrived to empty without pouring the soapy water over the carpet. Hot water was obtained by leaving a large metal jug in front of a banked-up fire, and if on coming up the stairs you could smell the paint burning, you were sure of a satisfying bath.

After the restrictive discipline of school what impressed me about my new life was the delicious sense of freedom and of being my own master, but what would probably impress a present-day student would be the exact opposite – the number of restrictions accepted without question, and the sense that a particular pattern of manners and behaviour, including dress and appearance, was required. The college gate was closed soon after nine when the bell in Tom Quad across the road at Christ Church had sounded its 101st resounding stroke; until midnight it would still be opened by the porter, but latecomers were noted in his book and a small fine, increasing with each hour, was imposed. Anyone back after midnight – unless he could contrive to scramble in over the high walls – must appear before the dean, who was both disciplinary authority and chaplain, and the wrongdoer might well be sent down for the remainder of that term. All ladies must be out of college before dinner in the evening, and women as distinct from ladies were presumed never to appear inside our walls at any hour.

It was a closed society, to some extent a monastic one, in which all emphasis was on behaviour and little on hard work. Attendance in chapel a certain number of times each week was compulsory, and attendance for dinner in hall expected. You might 'take your name off the books' two nights a week, but beyond that would be charged for dinner whether you appeared in hall or not. If, in comparison with present-day students, our freedom was much less, there were compensations in belonging to a group with a strong communal feeling in which we all soon came to know one another. It was never necessary, for instance, to lock any door, and in neither of the sets of rooms I occupied did I even look to see whether a key existed. Certainly if it did I never made use of it, and our possessions, papers, and correspondence lay around on tables or in desks where anyone could see them.

This was also the last experience I would have of living in a society where money was unimportant, an experience I would fully appreciate only after it was over and I started work in London. My scholarship was worth £80 a year, deducted in instalments after each term ended from the amount owing to the college; and before term started I was given a cheque for £45, so that I had an income of £215 to live on during termtime and to cover my out-of-pocket expenses during vacations, when I lived at home for nothing. What anyone else might have to live on, apart from my close friend and scholar of the same year, Raymond Pocock, I never knew or asked. Most, I imagine, had rather – and some few a great deal – more, and a small number must have managed on a few pounds less, £200 a year being accepted as the minimum on which one could get by. After my first year I would eke this out by tutoring during vacations to pay for clothes or travel, but I never suffered any sense of being less well-off than others, and was able to belong – with only one exception – to all the clubs and societies I wished. Games cost nothing and for the ones I most enjoyed, rugby and cricket, I already had the necessary clothes and gear, but I played soccer in a shirt someone lent me and hockey with a stick found for me by the hockey captain; only half a dozen students in the college owned cars, so that it was usually necessary to include a few car-owners in any team. As for entertaining, most of this was done through various college societies and clubs, each requiring a small subscription, but occasionally those with a lot of money would give drinking parties attended by others who had much less, and this was looked upon as a natural contribution by our hosts to the general enjoyment.

If, in comparison with present-day students, we had much less liberty in our personal lives, we were a great deal freer over the way we spent our time. In the course of half a century the importance which once attached to conformity of behaviour has shifted to diligence in study. In those days it was possible for a commoner of ordinary intelligence to go through his three years at the university and emerge with a degree on the basis of a mere two or three months' study before his intermediate, and again before his final exams. The penalty for idling was usually no more than a reproof, and rarely indeed was any undergraduate sent down for not working hard enough. Students who did get sent down were those penalized for some lapse of conduct such as behaving uproariously when drunk and insulting one of the fellows, or for missing the last train back from London ('the Fornicator') and being caught climbing in over the wall. Scholars, of course, were subject to stricter requirements in the matter of study since if we failed to meet obligations the college could deprive us of our scholarship, but, though known to happen, this was an extreme step seldom taken.

Our freedom from pressure to work hard did not necessarily result in idleness, any more than today's freedom from restrictions produces debauchery. I myself, having done little while at school, learned for the first time the meaning of hard mental work while at the university. There were others who devoted much time to acting, poetry, or reading a language, such as French or German, which they were not officially studying at all; in my own college shortly after my time one undergraduate* spent much of his last year painting the inside of his room – walls, doors and ceiling – with a masterly study in perspective. In order to paint the ceiling he was obliged to lie on his back on a table balanced on another table, and when he went down leaving his task unfinished he was invited back by the college to complete the work.

An American student who went up to Pembroke in the same year as myself wrote an account which is illuminating on this question of the importance assigned to behaviour as compared with work; it also shows the mixture of the formal and juvenile both in our conduct and in college discipline. His name was Al Huggins, and with a fellow American, Bob Martindale, he had been observed by the dean throwing snowballs in the street.

He opened his window (which was immediately above the college gateway) stuck his head out and commented on ungentlemanly foreign behaviour. Before he finished another snowball from Bob caught him squarely. Within minutes the porter told us the Dean sent his compliments and wished to see us in his study. I was ready to pack

---

*This was John Churchill, later to become well-known as an artist, and particularly as a portrait painter.

for home but Bob said not to worry; he could handle the Dean. When we were ushered into the Dean's presence he burst out: 'Sir, we have just learned that in England you do not celebrate First-Snowfall custom.' The Dean asked him to explain. According to Bob, everyone in the United States, regardless of age or station, threw snowballs at everyone else during First-Snowfall. The dean accepted this as tradition and we heard no more about it, but some of the English boys were less lucky. Leo Seccombe (later the BBC Boxing commentator) was Oxford Heavyweight that year, as well as a Rugger Blue. One night he filled a chamber pot with snow and dumped the content on the dean, explaining that he was starting First-Snowfall Custom in Britain. We all thought he would be sent down. But Leo's father was Thomas Seccombe, Lecturer in English at Sandhurst and an avid collector of Samuel Johnson memorabilia. The College seemed anxious to inherit some part of his extensive collection, particularly the desk on which Johnson wrote his Dictionary. We were told that some arrangement was now made between Leo's father and the College. Certainly, Leo was not sent down and when we visited the College in 1953 the Porter proudly showed the Johnson desk.

Huggins adds:

The most rewarding instruction at the University was not from lectures but from debates in the Oxford Union Society and the equally brilliant but more frivolous Pembroke College Debating Society where argument was between contemporaries of widely different backgrounds: Italian, Chinese, Japanese, Indian, North and South American, and African.

There was a wonderfully pleasant group at Pembroke, and as it was one of the smaller colleges we all knew one another.... At Lehigh* 'Bull sessions' concerned either athletics or girls. World trouble spots did not much interest us. But at Oxford it was different and in retrospect I think I learned more from the nightly Pembroke discussions than I learned in any more formal or more organized academic year.'†

Huggins refers above to 'English boys', and though we should have resented the description it was doubtless in general fair.

*Lehigh University in California where Huggins had previously been a student.
†From Al Huggins, 'An Alien Clerk's Tale'. This extract from an unpublished autobiography is taken from the *Pembroke College Record*, 1975.

The American students, of whom we had a good number in Pembroke, were several years older than the rest of us; having already taken American degrees they were what today would be called postgraduates, and I enjoyed their company and their greater experience of life. Bob Martindale besides having taken a degree had played leading parts at the American Theatre in Paris. Don Gillies, whom years later I would bring in to plan the advertising for a forthcoming *Picture Post*, had already worked with an advertising agency in Hawaii. Ray Jack, a Rhodes scholar from Pennsylvania, was a well-known athlete. Bill Fulbright from Arkansas, later to become Senator Fulbright – renowned chairman of the Senate Foreign Relations Committee and founder of the Fulbright Fellowships – had worked in his father's publishing concern. All these, with half a dozen others, brought a welcome breath of the outside world. The debating society of which Huggins wrote enthusiastically was an easy-going affair open to everyone in college. Coffee was provided free, thus ensuring a full house for the start of any debate, and it was then up to the speakers; one who spoke wittily held everyone in his place, whereas a bore soon became inaudible in the rattle of coffee cups being set down as his audience disappeared into the night.

'Who was that who just spoke?' I asked a friend after a particularly entertaining speech.

He leaned across to consult the secretary. 'Seems he's a freshman. Name's Miles – Bernard Miles.'

There was always notepaper in the common room so while the debate continued I wrote a note asking Mr Miles to come to breakfast with me next morning. Later, when he got one of his first parts in London as a walking-on soldier in Balliol Holloway's production of *Macbeth*, we would share a flat in Westminster for an enjoyable year or two before his career moved on to greater things.

The four-year programme of work on which I and my fellow classical scholars had embarked, modestly called Greats, was divided in two parts. During our first five terms we studied Greek and Latin authors, mainly poets and historians, and produced regular compositions in these languages. At the end of that time, after taking an intermediate exam, called Honour Mods, we were assumed to be able to read Greek and Latin with facility, so that we could concentrate on the meaning of what we read. During our last seven terms we were chiefly studying the ancient philosophers, Plato and Aristotle, followed by the Europeans such as Descartes, Kant and Hegel, plus our home-grown philosophers, starting with Hobbes, Berkeley, Locke and Hume. I had worked comparatively hard during my first five terms, overawed by obligation to the college and by the personality of my tutor, H. L. Drake. Tall, silver-haired, dressed always in black, he had an exquisite handwriting and a manner which I found chilling, though those who knew him better considered him kindly and even – when sufficiently moistened with port, on which he was an authority – a genial man.

Having got through the first part of our course more creditably than expected, I now had as tutor Robin Collingwood, the only fellow of the college at that time with a reputation extending beyond the university into the outside world. He was at this time in his thirties, a rotund figure with a springy step, gold-rimmed glasses, scant brown hair and a beaming smile. His thick tweed suits looked like the product of some cottage industry, and from the far side of the quadrangle he might be supposed to have walked out of an illustration by Edward Lear. Across a desk, however, there was no mistaking the precision and quality of his mind, and though his voice was high-pitched, he had an actor's range and control over it. His breadth of knowledge was the subject of many anecdotes, a knowledge by no means confined to academic subjects. In discussion he could explain a point by making a quick drawing, taking a musical instrument down and playing it, or with a reference to the morning's newspapers. This wide range of knowledge, his capacity for relating abstract speculation to everyday happenings, and his wit – which was not contrived but a matter of immediate response – had made Collingwood's lectures so popular that they could no longer he held in Pembroke and had been transferred to a college with a larger hall, where they were attended by many who were not studying philosophy but came simply for enjoyment.

It was the start of my second summer term when I called on Collingwood to talk over the work I should now be doing. After congratulating me politely on my modest success to date, he asked whether I was finding the work for Greats difficult.

'Very difficult indeed, sir.'

'Oh?' he asked with immediate interest, 'why is that?'

'Because I've never been used to mental effort. I was at a school where we thought winter a time for playing football and summer a time for playing cricket.'

'Indeed? Yours must have been an *unusually* broadminded school! I went to Rugby, where we thought winter a time for playing football – and summer a time for thinking about playing football.'

I did not see my new tutor again for several weeks. An attack of jaundice put me in bed, and I only got better after a fortnight's stay in the home of the same generous aunt who had looked after Jack and myself while at St Edward's. When I called on him after recovery, he observed that jaundice is always more serious than it seems, and advised me to take work easily for the rest of the term and not begin the task of reading until the long vacation. He listed a few books, such as Coleridge's *Biographia Literaria*, to read for enjoyment, and said he would propose a subject each week for us to talk over at tutorials instead of my having to write formal essays.

I did not need telling twice to abandon serious study for a term. Owing to some lapse from the strict moral code, our cricket captain had been sent down, retiring before the season's first ball had been bowled. As secretary, I was due to take his place and had already missed half a dozen matches through ill health. My chief friends, Raymond Pocock and a freshman, James Sinclair, were as ardent cricketers as I was, and with only six weeks left of term I would have been happy to have spent them entirely on the cricket field, but I had also a private resolution to carry out.

During the previous vacation I had acted as tutor to a boy who wanted to get into Cambridge; his name was Geoffrey Acland and he was the younger brother of a friend and contemporary of mine, Richard Acland, later to become known as that rare commodity, a politician with strong principles. Their father was a Liberal MP and the family owned big estates in Devonshire together with a fine country mansion, Killerton, which Richard in due course would inherit and hand over to the county. Theirs was a hospitable home and fine spring weather had helped to make my working stay enjoyable, but I had also undergone an experience upsetting to my vanity, and one which I was resolved should never be repeated. Geoffrey and I did our studying in the mornings so that the afternoons were free, and on one of them it was proposed that we should all go riding. I remarked that I had never ridden anything in my life, but the others all said I should find no difficulty; the ponies were small, and they would be around to keep an eye on me.

My pony indeed was of no great size, but it was short of exercise and big enough to know whether it had a competent rider on its back or not. Before the others had even mounted it was off across the park at a trot which soon swelled into a gallop. I let go of the reins to cling on to the saddle and the pony, swerving away across a hillside, ran under some trees, whereupon a low bough picked me neatly out of the saddle and flung me down on my back. The consequences to my backbone, though not particularly serious, would continue up to the present, but the consequences to my pride were painful and immediate. Among the onlookers were not only my hosts and pupil but a young girl I would have been happy to impress. Bitterly I blamed myself for not having foreseen that a day was bound to come when I would need to be able to control a horse, and, still sitting on the ground and struggling to get my breath, I swore that before the next vacation I would somehow learn to ride. Now jaundice and Collingwood had handed me my opportunity. Riding lessons, however, cost money, so my problem was – how could I learn to ride without having to pay for it? There was in the university an officers' training corps, and I found out that it had a cavalry as well as an infantry arm. This was mainly for those going into the army, including indeed a nucleus of future Guards officers who used hunters of their own as 'chargers', but it also admitted ordinary undergraduates like myself, most of whom were hoping to join one or other of the colonial civil services. The uniform was free and so, or nearly so, were the riding lessons, and in no time I had joined.

Our training started in the riding school and our horses were the worst to be got from local stables, too lazy or full of tricks for hire to paying customers. I was put onto one named Jack, which had developed a professional stumble every fifteen or twenty paces in the hope of getting rid of its rider. But if I began by being frightened of the horses I soon learned to be much more frightened of our instructor, Sergeant Ward. As some dozen recruits went shambling round with the dust from the tan rising cloudily over our heads in the early-morning sunshine, his bellow would ring out, 'Sit yer 'orse prop'ly, Mr 'Oskisson. You've got room for a woman between knee an' saddle.' When, having made some progress, we were allowed out to the wide expanses of Park Meadow, he would shake a warning finger. 'None o' that split-arse gallopin' from you, Mr 'Oskisson! You go arse-over-tip – and I'll 'ave you walk that 'orse back to the ridin' school.'

As confidence increased, there developed in me a love of riding which would give me pleasure for many years, and the enjoyment I was evidently finding induced a number of Pembroke friends to join the cavalry too, some having even less natural ability and no emotional reason for learning to control a horse. Unwittingly I had acted as a recruiting officer in reverse, and the ranks of the Oxford cavalry were soon diluted with a high proportion of unmilitary amateurs. A year or so later we all went with our unit to a camp on Salisbury Plain where, on the final day, a mock battle took place in which we were ordered to draw swords and charge over a piece of rough country, no easy manoeuvre for experienced horsemen. In our case we were lucky to escape falling on our swords or running one another through, breaking one or two horses' legs or slashing off several of their ears.

It took time for us to reassemble, as no doubt it did for the gallant Scots Greys after their charge at Waterloo, but at last we were all drawn up dismounted in a square, to be addressed by the visiting general. His voice was clear and carried well. After commenting disparagingly on our military potential, and trusting the country would never have to call upon us in its hour of need, he went on, 'However, gentlemen, I have been informed that a number of you joined the corps, not with any view to military service, but in order to learn to ride.' There was a silence, and he added, 'Gentlemen, you deceive yourselves.'

Seeking to console Sergeant Ward and his colleagues, we entertained them that night in the canteen, where he did not so much drink whisky as take it aboard like a tanker. He had just remarked quite lucidly, 'A cavalryman knows only two pleasures. On his 'orse's back – or in a woman's arms,' I was turning to ask which in general cavalrymen preferred and to hand him another drink – but the sergeant was no longer there. He was flat on his back on the grassy floor of the marquee, far beyond speech or movement. His fellow instructors carried him to his tent, but at five next morning he was down at the station supervising the safe loading of seventy horses into railway wagons.

7

What Next?

Now that I had begun to find new interests and to make new friends, the focus of my life shifted from home to Oxford, where the atmosphere was much freer. Three terms of only eight weeks each seemed far too short, and I felt increasingly out of place at home where my father, I thought, was becoming more abstracted and withdrawn – an inner withdrawal which took practical shape around lunchtime every day.

'Where's Henry?' my mother would ask, bustling in from the kitchen with the dish she had been preparing. 'Why must he always disappear just when I've got his meal ready? He knows we have lunch at one. Go across and fetch him, Tom – he'll be over in church as usual.'

So I would walk across and find him attending to some detail in the vestry. 'Yes, yes! I shall not be long. Just one or two things to see too. I'll be over in a minute. Tell mother not to wait for me.'

I would convey the message, and my mother, as we sat down and she served us all, would continue to expostulate, 'Just when I've got everything nice and hot! He's been sitting in his study all morning writing, and could have gone over to church any time he pleased. Why must he always vanish just when we're all sitting down to eat?'

Why indeed – unless it was because we *were* all just sitting down to eat? At the table would be Jack, just back from his Kendal office. He went to and fro on a Douglas motorcycle whose running was a cause of anxiety to him, so that always on reaching home he would start it up two or three times and let it splutter for a few minutes by the back door to ensure being able to get away on time. Paul too came home from his engineering works on a motorbike, an Ariel, which apparently did not need to be started up and stopped; being anxious to get lunch inside him and be back at work, he spoke hardly at all, but his silence contributed to the sense of pressure. Stephan's sharp tongue and flow of wit, delivered half under his breath into his plate, cannot always have been welcome, and Tom's reserve and preoccupation with his own interests cast a chill down one side of the table. My mother's concern was to get her sons fed and out of the house, and Esther – for whom and from whom my father felt a special sympathy – did not come home for lunch. At this distance from our family table it is not hard to imagine why my father found such regular occasion for not being present; indeed there must have been days when he would have been glad to remain in his vestry altogether, and others when not far below the surface lay the wish that he had never involved himself in the cares of a parish and the pressures of family life, but had remained an archaeologist and scholar occupied with the less demanding interests of the past.

Ever since my last year or so at school it had been his custom to ask me into his study for a talk before I went away again. Inevitably on these occasions he would be led on, perhaps from some inquiry about my reading, to advice about life in general, stressing the need to live in accordance with established principles and the part in everyday life which our Christian religion ought to play. Defensively I would argue that fixed principles do not always help when each situation calls for a varying response; about Christianity I would want to know why after 2000 years it has had so little effect on our relationships with one another, then – turning the knife unconsciously in the wound – would suggest that existence must have been altogether more humane, enjoyable and dignified in ancient Athens. Rising from his chair to lean against the mantelpiece, my father would draw a number of times on his pipe, knock it out on his heel into the grate, and start slowly to refill it. Then, instead of lighting it, he would lay it down beside one of his favourite Pilkington vases, clasp his hands as though in agony, look up to the ceiling and after long hesitation would reply . . . to which I would answer . . . to which he would slowly and painfully suggest . . . until at last, late at night and no nearer an understanding, we would embrace. Afterwards I would go up to bed with the feeling of having taken part in a slow-motion wrestling match, in which the chief care on both sides had been to avoid a too painful confrontation.

Regularly when I got home after each term I would propose that he take, at some convenient time, a whole day off. We would start early, carry sandwiches with us, leave the Trojan in a farmyard and spend the day walking in the mountains. Cheerfully he would agree that we must surely do this – not indeed during the next few days when he was particularly busy, but certainly before a fresh term started. As the weeks slipped by I would continue asking until, with term approaching, I would urge him to specify a day and keep it free. How about Monday, when his sermons would be over? . . . Well Tuesday then, perhaps? . . . Or Wednesday, when he would have got back from wherever he had to go on Tuesday? But our day in the mountains never came, and I had long since given up my boyish attempts to persuade him to come into Kendal and watch one of my football matches.

His sermons too had undergone a change. There was less persuasion, pleading, exhortation – and fewer and fewer of his own words. More and more they were compounded of quotations, partly from the gospels and partly from his favourite authors, beautifully chosen and spoken in his earnest tones, head bent lower and lower to one side, ending with verses from some poem, carol or hymn. At times too there would come into his voice a note almost of desperation as though he would compel himself as well as his listeners to believe. Having spoken of Christ's sacrifice and the power of his example to us all, he ended with a passionate assertion that if God were not indeed like that, then one would be forced to reject God altogether.

Once, following a Sunday morning service in which the congregation mouthed its way through the Apostles' Creed,

I asked, 'What do we mean when we go on repeating every week in church – "I believe in the resurrection of the body"? What kind of a bodily resurrection does the Church believe in?'

With one of his rare flashes of decisiveness, my father replied, 'I can't answer for what the Church as a whole means by "I believe in the resurrection of the body" – but what I personally mean when I say those words is "I do *not* believe in the resurrection of the body."'

At the time I enjoyed his reply for what I regarded as its humour and eighteenth-century freedom of expression. But looking back half a century later, it is not hard to understand why my father felt no eagerness to believe in bodily resurrection for himself and his large, ever-present, family.

During my last two years at Oxford I began to apply myself to writing. I could see that my tutor, Collingwood, did not expect academic achievement from me. Whatever work I might be going to do would not be affected by the sort of degree I would obtain. And as for any prestige which might accrue to him personally from the successes of his students, he was not so much indifferent to it as beyond the consideration altogether. All work done for him, whether as an essay or in the preparation of a theme for group discussion, had to be properly researched and effectively set out, but once having examined it, he was ready to talk about plays, novels, religion, love, or any other subject. On pretentiousness and undergraduate superiority he was severe, though without ever abandoning his attitude of urbane inquiry. At one of our group discussions he mentioned having seen in the paper that Henry Ford was in London, suggesting that he must be someone well worth meeting. He looked at me as though expecting comment, and I replied that I thought it unlikely Mr Ford would have anything at all interesting to say.

'Really – is *that* your opinion?' Collingwood inquired blandly. 'A man who has changed the whole pattern of industry and developed an invention which is transforming social life – and will completely alter the relationship between town and country which has lasted with comparatively little change for centuries . . . but for you he has no interest. Kindly explain your point of view!'

His own range of interests seemed boundless, a philosopher with special emphasis on the practical. Once when I called on him he was repairing his son's mechanical toy with a soldering iron, and at another visit I noticed he was reading Dante.

'I didn't know you spoke Italian, sir.'

'Speak Italian?' He looked up in astonishment. 'Certainly not! Whoever can have told you that?'

'But you're reading it,' I pointed out, 'and without a dictionary.'

'Anyone who knows some Latin can read Italian. Or Spanish too for that matter. And I don't need a dictionary because I've read Dante many times before. But talking's another thing altogether. Is there something you want – or have you just looked in for a chat?'

I explained that I had been asked to play rugby for my county in the north. If I were to go up for this match they could reasonably expect me to travel up for others, which could involve four or five weekends away from college at a time when I was working for my finals.

'And you're asking my opinion as to whether you should accept or not?'

'Yes.'

'Well – it's for you to decide. But I think you'd be foolish to miss the chance of playing.'

Apart from my essays, I had now begun to write for one or two undergraduate magazines and so to come in contact with men from other colleges who were also interested in writing. Inevitably we decided to form our own society; this was to meet in the rooms of each member in turn over two or three bottles of port, and everyone must bring something written since the previous meeting to read out aloud. Three of our members came from the same college, Wadham. Cecil Day-Lewis was handsome and elegant, with a fine speaking and singing voice. He had already published poetry and his intention in life was simply to be a poet, an ambition he planned to subsidize by schoolmastering. His close friend, Rex Warner, tall, pale-faced and black-haired, had a passion for games equal to my own but was also a scholar with a wide knowledge of the classics; his was a special kind of wit combining the flippant and pedantic. 'In a future radiant with the purple of fame and the rose-pink of innocuous love,' he wrote in a letter, 'gleams the brown and green of one pound sterling which I hope shortly to repay.' The third of the trio was Charles Fenby, later to become a well-known journalist. Unlike the others he was completely careless of appearance, and indeed always looked so ill that every time I met him I was surprised he should be walking about at all. His face was white and his weak eyes rimmed with red, he suffered continually and painfully from boils, and at twenty was already going bald. Since I would know him for the next fifty years, I was able to observe how he reversed the normal process of decay, changing from a sickly youth with one foot in the grave into a large, rosy-faced elderly man.

A tall young man from Christ Church named Lennox-Boyd attended one or two meetings, but soon withdrew to become president of the Union, being more interested in politics, to which he would devote his life, holding various ministerial posts and becoming in due course Lord Boyd of Merton. From the same college came another public figure whose financial wizardry would procure him a vast fortune, followed by exposure and humiliation.

Naming ou society caused us trouble, but it was finally decided that it should be called The Jawbone, after the object used by Samson to disrupt the Philistines, and one of our number, Leslie Nye, who had been appointed secretary, was instructed to obtain a donkey's jawbone in time for our next meeting.

'But Leslie,' I asked when the others had left, 'how the hell are you going to do this? You can't just walk round till you see a donkey – and remove its jaw. And it's no use turning up at a slaughterhouse and asking. If they *do* slaughter donkeys they won't admit it.'

'And if that's all you can think of, it's a good thing you're not secretary,' Leslie replied coolly, and a few days later he handed me a letter.

Dear Sir,
    We acknowledge receipt of your esteemed order for one donkey's jawbone. This has now been obtained and is being cleaned. It will be forwarded to you on receipt of your cheque for three guineas (£3. 3s. 0d.).

The noteheading was Selfridge's, which at that time used to advertise that they would supply anything 'from a pin to an elephant'. Before long the jawbone arrived, and, placed on a cushion in a place of honour, presided at our meetings. There were not many meetings to preside at because The Jawbone lasted no longer than other undergraduate societies. Unfortunately it did not die until our group had produced a magazine, *The Broad*,* named after Oxford's Broad Street, which must rank as the feeblest and most affected undergraduate journal ever printed – despite the talent of some of its contributors.
    For myself the importance of what I wrote at this time lay not in any value it possessed, but in the fact that through writing I was slowly arriving at what I thought. A story I contributed, not to *The Broad* but to a better-established magazine, *The Cherwell*, had as its theme the operation of an imaginary Soul Salvation Company. The dean of Pembroke, whom I liked and who had shown me much personal kindness, reproached me for this blasphemous invention. Since I attended chapel regularly he was justified in looking on me as a Christian, and at the time I said little in reply. Nor did I sit down and argue the matter out in my own mind, since it was not my way to face issues squarely but rather to put them on one side and as it were edge round them by degrees. But a few days later as I was walking across the quadrangle, the thought came to me, 'I am now twenty-one. I can decide my opinions for myself. If there is a conflict between being a Christian and being free to write what I want to write, then from this moment I stop being a Christian.'
    With the freedom I had now given myself, I had soon

*The two copies I still possess are, I trust, the only ones remaining in existence.

embarked on writing my first book, despite this being my final year when I should be applying myself to getting a good degree. In this, which I managed to complete though never to submit to any publisher, all action takes place after Judgement Day is over. As complaints mount among the saintly, who had expected something in heaven altogether more luxurious than has been provided for them, and as God becomes increasingly bored with their tedious compliments and the smugness of their conversation, he decides that the populations of heaven and hell should be exchanged. The damned, now established in heaven, are delighted and appreciative, and the saved, stimulated by the challenge hell provides, buckle to in making the best of their new surroundings, with the devil's full encouragement for the way his property is being improved.

As the last year of my university life slid by, I began to be more and more divided over what I was to do when it should end. I was determined to launch out immediately and not hang about at home, but when I asked what I was to launch out *into*, I came face to face with the opposing aspects of myself – the conforming and the nonconforming, the practical and the side that wished to be creative.

I was drawn to writing and felt I might become a writer, but if I chose this course how was I to make a living? I had no illusions that I could write bestsellers, and the thought of a regular literary life – manufacturing a book a year and padding the spaces in between with literary criticism – filled me with dismay. I was trying to learn to write for the time when I might have something I wanted urgently to say, not because I at all liked the thought of sitting at a desk. While in this uncertain state a friend suggested I might go into the Sudan Political Service. I made inquiries and the picture I was given appealed to me – good pay; an outdoor life involving travel, often on horseback, over a vast country; and I could expect two months' home leave in every year. When I called to see the Appointments Committee, they informed me that, having combined work and games in the way I had, I was 'just the kind of man' the commission making the selection would be looking for; interviews would take place shortly, and they were eager to put my name down. I went so far as to write to my old headmaster, Ferguson, who by now had become warden of Radley, for a testimonial. He responded handsomely, assuring the commissioners that I was 'cut out' for their kind of life, as I had plainly shown from the first day I arrived in St Edward's School.

I felt grateful for his generous words, but unsure whether the sterling character he described was really me – and so now, as on other occasions before and since, having carefully prepared the way, I started to draw back. Granted that one side of me was willing to conform to the requirements of authority; what about the other? How would I adapt to a society made up of political administrators, police and army officers and their wives? Being so uncertain of my own direction, how could I assume authority over the lives of other people, perhaps within a few years over many thousands of them? For such a position full confidence would be needed, not only in my own judgement but in our country's civilizing mission, in our idea of justice, our method of government, form of education, and of the benefits these would bring to primitive peoples. What did I know about primitive peoples, their values or their way of life? Nothing – and by the time I did know I should be committed. What would be my position if, after five or ten years' service, I realized that I was in the wrong place, doing the wrong job? I should then have to start afresh at an age when it would be more difficult to find another open door, and with a failure behind me to account for.

Slowly I came to the conclusion that if I chose the Sudan the advantages would be immediate but my problem only postponed. If I were to go, I must expect eventually to be faced with the need either to conform to a pattern I could not accept, or else walk out of a career just when it should become effective. Fearful of being persuaded against my judgement, I called off my appointment to appear before the commissioners.

So I came back to the thought of a writing career, but now with the intention of joining a newspaper and becoming a journalist. But how *did* one become a journalist? At the Appointments Committee they told me flatly that they had never placed anyone in journalism, never received from a newspaper any application for recruits, and had no contacts of any sort with the journalistic world. So far as they knew, the only way to enter journalism was to get to know an editor and persuade him to take you on his staff. I knew no editors, and the ones I wrote to showed no wish to get to know me; however I began to talk about my intention to anyone I knew, and before long an opportunity came my way.

The cousin I admired, Gerald Sanger, had on leaving the university taken a job as secretary to Esmond Harmsworth, son of Lord Rothermere, whose position in the newspaper world Esmond must one day inherit. Gerry now wrote that he had heard of my wish to enter journalism and suggested I come up to London for a talk. There he explained that there was more work to be done for his employer – a young Conservative MP with social and business interests – than he could handle on his own. If I would join him as assistant secretary, I should have a well-paid, interesting job, from which in a few years' time it should not be difficult to step over into newspapers with a proprietor's powerful support; he himself was expecting before long to move over into newsreel work.*

I thanked him, but said I must think the matter over and would write in the next few days. It seemed on the surface a tempting offer, but once again, the more I considered it the less I could see the proposal working out. I did not want to slide into journalism halfway up with leverage from the top; I wanted to go in at the bottom and learn from the beginning. Accordingly I wrote, as I had really known from the first I must, refusing my cousin's kindly offer as gently as I could. A second time he wrote urging me to reconsider, and a second time I said no.

And now, having thrown away this lifebelt, I looked round for another. The only man I knew who had actually got into journalism was Charles Fenby, who had gone down a year before I did, worked for some months on a paper in the north, and was now in London as a reporter on the *Westminster Gazette*. This had been possible because his uncle, Sir Charles Starmer,

---

*Gerald Sanger became editor of British Movietone News in 1929, and a director in 1936. He was appointed administrative director of Associated Newspapers in 1954, retiring in 1963.

proprietor of the Starmer Press, owned a number of provincial newspapers of which the *WG* was the flagship. I had kept determinedly in touch with Charles since he left the university, and now began to tighten my grip around his neck. I went to see him in London and, in the spring of 1927 just before my final term, worked on his kindness to arrange an interview with his editor, Hobman. We got on well, and Hobman agreed that I should join the paper as a reporter in the autumn. It was necessary, however, for him to agree the matter with his news editor and, though he rang through twice to speak to him, the news editor was always busy. He would have a word with him, he said, in the next day or two, and later on I could make the financial arrangements with his news editor direct. I was greatly elated, having found, as I thought, an open door.

My last term ended and, after the camp on Salisbury Plain and the Oxford cavalry's heroic charge, I went for a happy stay in Bath with my friend James Sinclair and his family, before going on to Aber for what would be the family's last holiday together. Rain fell almost continuously, and as weeks went by without any word from the *Westminster Gazette* I started to grow more anxious and bad-tempered. I wrote two or three times, as often as I thought wise, to the news editor who never answered. At this distance it is easy to see that he was angry at having someone pushed on to his staff by the editor when he had just had someone pushed on to him by the proprietor, and realized that if he simply took no action he might well manage to avoid this fresh intrusion. Until one has lived and worked in offices, however, one is unaware of such undercurrents and the important part played by prestige and manoeuvrings for position. Puzzled and at a loss, I finally wrote to Charles asking his advice, and he replied that the only thing to do was to come to Fleet Street and try to see the man concerned.

When I told my father my intention, he opposed my going to London 'with nowhere to live' and said it would be best for me to stay at home 'till the position becomes clearer'; his own idea for my future was that I should become a master in a public school and do my writing during holidays. But when I insisted that I intended to become a journalist and had made up my mind to get, by some means or other, onto a newspaper, he gave me £25 – he had already given me an extra £25 in the previous term to buy clothes for my start in life – and said that when that had been used up I was welcome to come home, and we would then work out some practical arrangement for my future.

And so, at the beginning of September 1927 and at the age of twenty-two, I set off for London to make my living as a journalist, intending later to become a writer when I should have found something I urgently wished to say.

8

First Steps on a Long Road

Charles Fenby had found himself a room in Queen's Road, Bayswater, almost opposite Whiteley's, at the top of a tall house, one of a row of old brick buildings now long since demolished or collapsed. His room at the front cost £1 a week, and there was another much smaller one at the back which I could have for the same rent. I eagerly accepted. The house was a warren of rooms let separately; on all its five storeys there was no bathroom, not even a washbasin, and only a single lavatory under the stairs on the ground floor. Cold water could be collected from a tap on one of the landings.

My room looked out over the tops of trees and down into yards in which a few plants struggled to survive. On a windy day, with the curtain blowing and the treetops waving, I could imagine that I was not entirely surrounded by brick walls. The room was painted in yellow and purple, a gas cooker filled most of the space left by the bed, and on this, with all jets burning, it was possible to heat an aluminuim bath which was kept hanging on the door, should I want the luxury of a soak in my own apartment and have coins enough for gas. There were also public baths just up the road where one could boil oneself pink for a shilling, with a large towel and disinfectant soap thrown in.

Every morning at around 10 a.m. Charles left for his work as a reporter, earning eight guineas a week, which seemed to us both enviable riches. From time to time he would ask his news editor to spare half a minute to meet his friend who just happened to be waiting downstairs, to which the news editor replied 'some other time', and every few days I would try to 'phone him and be told he was too busy to speak to me now but I might call back next week. Meanwhile I wrote paragraphs for the various diaries and columns, which Charles would do his best to insert into the paper and for each of which at the month's end I would collect ten shillings; after a while one of these paragraphs must have caught the eye of the editor, Hobman, because he told Charles to bring me in to see him.

The *Westminster Gazette* was produced in a building not unlike the one we lived in in Queen's Road, a tall brick house, or perhaps two houses in one, in Shoe Lane, just across a narrow street from where the *Daily Express* building now stands. If our Queen's Road house was a warren, this was a beehive; it was unbelievable that the staff of any newspaper could be got into the building, let alone a dispatch department and printing presses, and when these were running the place rattled and shook so that it seemed all the floors must fall through at any minute. On entering I would half close my ears, as I had done when going into the cotton mills in Colne, and on leaving step out with relief into the comparative quiet of Fleet Street. When at last I got in to see him, Hobman was friendly. He said nothing about any job, but told me he enjoyed one or two of my paragraphs and had an idea which I could try out if I liked. What he wanted, he said, was an occasional filler for the leader page made up of half a dozen very short news items with a humorous comment about each. He had thought of the perfect title, 'Folly As It Flies', but had never found anyone to do the job. If I made a go of it, he would use the filler three or four times a week, for each of which I would be paid half a guinea.

This was my first commission – and I feared it would prove impossible. Hobman had explained that he wanted something on the lines of 'Charivaria' in the opening pages of *Punch*, but on *Punch* I imagined they would have contributions from all the staff, plus suggestions sent by readers of papers all over the country. Next afternoon, however, as I looked through the evening papers – there were three in London in those days and you could get the lot for threepence – I thought, Surely in all this there must be half a dozen pieces on which I can write a comment? So for a couple of hours I worked away, attaching a supposedly witty comment to each paragraph, copied it all out painstakingly by hand since I had no typewriter, and took a bus to Fleet Street. Next morning it was in the paper.

At last, I felt, my foot is in the door.

To live in London I needed a minimum of £4 a week, one for rent, two for food, and a pound for tubes, buses, newspapers, stamps, phone calls, drink and general dissipation. Now I felt assured of half the amount, plus the odd bits and pieces wangled in for me by Charles, which was becoming easier now that the columnists accepted me as a source. In addition during my first couple of months I had managed to get one or two short stories – they were little more than worked-up anecdotes with a literary flavour – accepted by the *Manchester Guardian* for its back page, which kept a special column for such items. They paid three guineas, and it seemed reasonable to hope that I might land one a month on them.

But at this moment came a setback to the domestic harmony of Queen's Road. My father, in the course of a short stay with my grandmother in Holland Park, walked over to have a look at my new home. Unfortunately I was out, and something about the look of the place must have aroused his suspicion. Could it have been one or two of the cards stuck against the row of antiquated bell pulls by our front door? Did it cross his mind that Baroness Flogge on the first floor might be indicating a speciality, rather than displaying a hereditary title from some German principality? Did the names of Joy Love and Captain Hugo Gondolphus sound not wholly convincing? Some breath of suspicion, coupled with concern for his son's welfare, evidently caused him to make inquiries, dressed in that clergyman's uniform which gave my fellow tenants as much cause for suspicion as their supposed activities gave him. Exactly what inquiries he made and from whom he made them I never learned, but when I got home in the evening the house was in uproar, and Charles, returning before I did, had faced general indignation – which he rapidly passed on to me.

I could sympathize with all parties, particularly with Charles who had taken me in out of kindness and had his own peace rudely interrupted as a result. I could sympathize with our co-tenants, who shared our single lavatory and cold tap in a cooperative spirit, and would no more have dreamed of thrusting their professional activities on us than we of soliciting them for a year's subscription to the *Westminster Gazette*. I could sympathize with my father's anxiety, but was also angry at his interference. By degrees the storm, like other storms, died down – but the consequence of this one proved to be beneficial. My father, little reassured by his investigation, must have gone over to see my uncle Austin, who had a pleasant eighteenth-century house in Great Smith Street, Westminster, for a few weeks later Austin asked me over and told me there was more space in his house than he could use. The ground floor served as his London office, and he had living quarters on the first floor for times when the House was sitting. But the second floor had so far been unoccupied; it contained a good-sized living room, a bedroom and bathroom, with an attic and small kitchen up a short flight of stairs. If we cared to put in whatever furniture we needed, we could have the flat for the same rent we were paying now – a pound a head.

Charles was unwilling to move. He said I could go if I wanted, but he preferred his freedom and did not intend to come under the general supervision of the Hopkinson family, one experience of which had been quite enough. I assured him we should get no supervision from Austin beyond an occasional sarcastic comment, and that if he meant to reject the place he'd better come over and see just what he was rejecting. This he did, and was at once struck by its central position – he could walk home from Fleet Street or a theatre in twenty minutes – and its convenience, since he could enjoy the luxury of a hot bath without walking 100 yards up the road. He hesitated, but finally accepted.

So at the end of November we moved into our new quarters, and my contributor's account for December 1927, preserved ever since with pride, shows my having received from the *Westminster Gazette* no less than £23. 10s. 0d., almost £6 a week from this source alone, so that I was looking forward with confidence to 1928. We had not yet done with 1927, however, and on its last night I took a girl to a cinema, to find when I got back that Charles was pacing grimly up and down the room. Still in overcoat and muffler, he had forgotten to light the gas fire, always the first thing he did on coming in.

'What's the matter, Charles, have I been sacked?'

'We both have.'

The *Westminster Gazette*, he told me, had been swallowed up that very day by another liberal newspaper, the *Daily News*, which before long would amalgamate with the *Daily Chronicle* to become the *News Chronicle*. Charles, under his uncle's protection, was being taken over by the new management, who were not even making use of the disaster to chisel off two or three of his eight guineas. The *Daily News*, however, was not interested in 'Folly As It Flies' nor in occcasional notes and short literary pieces, so that my income had ended at a stroke; my record contributor's account would be my last, and I was back where I had been in September. Fleet Street, evidently, was not to be taken by direct assault.

Over the next few months I experienced something of the feel of unemployment – the slow dwindling of resources, the disappointment which becomes routine, the attempts to find help where one knows none is to be found and yet must look for it, the fear that one is becoming less fit to be employed, and the envy of everyone who has managed to get inside while oneself is still scratching at the door.

I wrote to newspapers up and down the country, magnifying my experience and qualifications, sending samples of my work and asking for an interview. There were almost no replies. Postage costs mounted while editorial wastepaper baskets filled with selections from 'Folly As It Flies' and cuttings from the *Guardian* back page. I also pestered the few people I knew who had written or were writing for any newspaper or magazine to give me some kind of introduction, only to discover that they, naturally enough, were not going to encourage one more hungry rat into a larder they had themselves perhaps penetrated only with much effort. Just three times, during the weeks in which my remnant of capital ran out, did I come within sight of what might have been employment. One of my applications was actually answered by the *Yorkshire Post* – a paper I have thought highly of ever since, and I was so elated by the sight of its letterhead as to feel I was already on its staff. All I needed to do was to go along and meet the editor in his Fleet Street office and be prepared, I presumed, to live in Leeds – a step I had already taken in my mind. However, there proved to be one preliminary.

The editor, a courteous man, required me to write a short humorous editorial on any subject of my choice in the course of the next hour. I had never written an editorial, but had read plenty and sat down with a confidence which oozed slowly away during the next sixty minutes. It was a fair test and I failed dismally; even I could not suppose what I had written would draw shouts of happy laughter from the citizens of Leeds, and there was no need for the editor even to comment on what I handed in.

A few weeks later hope sprang up again when I was asked to call in and see the *Morning Post*. Far to the right of the *Daily Telegraph*, if so remote a prospect can be envisaged, this was not a paper whose politics attracted me, but if they were prepared to offer regular employment – at something in the region of £4 a week – they would find me ready to support king, constitution and other articles of their faith. The interview was for 2.30, and I sat waiting in a sort of box made from one end of a corridor partitioned off. Soon after three, two red-faced men came in, genially helping one another over the threshold, and looked at me with amazement.

'You trying to become a *journalist?*'

'Yes. That's what I'm hoping. In fact, I've already done a bit, and I thought perhaps ... '

'Much better not! Much better try something else.'

He shook a warning head. There was silence for a moment, and then the other one asked, 'Know anything about horse-racing?'

'Not a lot. But I suppose ... that is to say ... '

They looked at one another. 'Knows nothing about horse-racing,' said one.

'Obviously not,' said the other. The interview was over.

I owed my third contact to Austin. Aware of my difficulties, he invited me to dinner at the House of Commons to meet a man from *The Times* and another from the *Scotsman*. During dinner we all got on well until the moment when the host explained to his guests that his nephew intended to become a journalist, had indeed got started, but the horse onto whose back he had scrambled had been shot from under him, so that he was now looking for a way to start afresh. What could they propose? The man from *The Times* immediately explained that *The Times* was not like other newspapers. It did not take on young men and teach them their journalistic ABCs; it looked round at all the other papers in the country and selected what it required from among those who had already made their mark. This, he added, accounted for its unique position in the country and indeed in the world at large.

I realized, I said, the unique position of *The Times*, but wondered whether from his long experience and many contacts he could help me to approach some paper in the provinces on which I might obtain just such a start as he had been describing. He replied that he would give this his consideration and, already knowing better than to expect results from such assurances, I turned my attention to the *Scotsman*.

'How's your shorthand?' he inquired.

I had to admit that the effort to teach myself shorthand in the evenings had not yet taken me very far. If I had been honest I should have confessed to having surrendered at about page seven.

The *Scotsman* shook his head.

'No shorthand,' he said, 'no chance! With 150 words a minute I might have done something for you. Take myself now – I've a natural *genius* for shorthand. Born with it, I suppose. If I hadn't had, I'd never have got where I am now.'

I had one other bizarre encounter during my search for employment. One of the first things I had done on coming to London was to join the Richmond Rugby Club, and since the season began had been playing regularly for the A team, which mainly went round to public schools; fares and meals were paid for so that no expense was involved. Now someone had dropped out of the first team and I had been given his place. One Saturday, probably because there was an international match in the afternoon, we were to play our own game, an important club match, in the morning and I was told by the captain that if I went along to his city office early enough he would give me a lift down to Richmond in his car. The office was of a kind I had never seen before. With its carpeted floors, bowls of flowers, comfortable chairs and elegant high-heeled secretaries, it looked like a suite in a luxury hotel. In the course of driving down in his Rolls-Royce, the captain asked me what I did for a living and I explained my situation.

'You mean you want to get onto a newspaper?'

'Yes, indeed.'

'Any newspaper in particular?'

'No. Just *any* newspaper – anywhere in the country.'

'What about the *Daily Telegraph* or *Sunday Times*?'

'That would be wonderful, but ... '

'My dear fellow – why didn't you tell me before? *Nothing* could be easier! I know the Berrys very well indeed. Come to my office one afternoon next week, and I'll fix you up.'

He was a tall, handsome man with blond hair and a well-cared-for gold moustache. Could he be Mercury, the messenger of the gods? Or was he even more innocent than myself – but if so, how had he come by a carpeted, flower-decked office in the City, an elegant perfumed secretary and an acquaintance with newspaper tycoons?

When I called on the Tuesday afternoon he did not at first seem to remember why I had come, but on being reminded told his secretary, 'Get me Bill Berry at his office!' We chatted till the telephone rang.

'That you, Bill? ... Jimmy here ... How did the weekend go? ... Good! Well I've got a friend here who's anxious to get on to one of your papers – first-rate journalist, bags of talent, all sorts of experience! Think you can find a place for him?'

There was a pause. 'You say you've got a waiting list as long as your arm? All with talent and experience? Well, old boy, do me a favour! Put a pencil through that lot and stick my friend's name down at the top. . . .' There was another pause before my genial acquaintance rang off and turned to me.

'He says to write in, giving all particulars. Not to him personally, just to the newspaper. Do that – and you'll be hearing from them before long! So long, old boy! Glad to have been of help. See you on the ground next Saturday.'

Walking back to Westminster from this unfruitful encounter I met my old Oxford friend, Leslie Nye, looking as disconsolate as I felt.

'I'd like to buy you a drink, Leslie, but as it so happens . . . '

'I understand. But have you half a crown?'

'Just about.'

'Don't worry – I'm not going to borrow it. At least not permanently. But if you give me the loan of it for five minutes, I can get both of us a drink.'

I handed over, and he led me up one of the lanes to a pawnbroker where, with the help of my half-crown, he recovered his silver cigarette case.

'I'm glad you got your case back, Leslie. All the same . . . '

Leslie silenced me and turned up another alley to a second pawnbroker, from whom he received five shillings on his case. Returning my original half-crown, he led me to a pub.

'They don't teach these things at the university – but somewhere in the transaction you've just witnessed, Tom,' he said, 'lies the secret of great wealth. Once I've mastered that secret, I shall be on my way.'

After three months, with my money gone plus most of a further £10 for which I had written to my father, I went down to Oxford to see the Appointments Committee again. I had made up my mind to take anything I could find that would keep me alive, if possible in London, while I continued trying to get a toehold in journalism. They offered just one suggestion. An advertising agency, W. S. Crawford, had a possible vacancy for a trainee copywriter; it was doubtful what salary, if any, would be paid to a beginner, but they gave me the address to follow up if I wished.

Having written for an appointment to Sir William Crawford,

I turned up at 233 High Holborn at 9.30 one Monday morning. There was another young man waiting in the office, evidently in quest of the same job. We both sat there until 12.30 when a secretary came in and told us it was no good our waiting any longer as Sir William was going out to lunch. We had the same experience next morning, until at 11.30 I decided I had waited long enough; my companion had already told me that he had sat in the same office for three days also in the previous week, and I did not mean to keep him company any longer. So I got into the lift and told the liftman I wanted Sir William's secretary. He took me to the third floor and pointed to a door along the corridor. To the secretary I said that I had now been waiting five hours, having come to the office at times chosen by Sir William, that I had matters of my own I must attend to, and that if Sir William was too busy to see me now, would she kindly give me an appointment for some time when he would be free.

She motioned me to sit down and when the noise of argument in the inner room died down, went to the door, said I was there and had waited all morning, could he spare me five minutes? I was shown in. A thick-set figure with a heavily-jowled red face was seated at an enormous desk. His small angry eyes glared at me while I answered a volley of questions fired at me in a strong Scottish accent.

What did I want? Why had I come to Crawford's? Did I know any of their advertising campaigns? What made me think I would be any good at advertising? Did I *believe* in advertising? How many languages did I speak? How much travel had I done? Why had I been to university? What was the use of universities? What had I learned there – and what was I learning now? If I joined his staff, what contribution was I going to make?

He fired questions off so rapidly that I was able to miss out those I found too difficult. I did not know any of Crawford's advertising campaigns. I did not know any foreign languages – apart from Greek and Latin which I thought it wiser not to mention – and I was pretty sure I did not believe in advertising. But I managed to get across two points – that I thought I could write, having had a fair amount of my work published, and that if I came to Crawfords I should need to be paid enough to live on.

'How much d'you need to live on?'

'£4 a week.'

The answer did not seem to distress him. He told me to go away, write something and send it to him.

'Write anything you like! I want to see what your mind is like. Put your mind down on two sheets of paper – and sent it me! Now you can go.'

My friend Raymond Pocock had joined the Shell organization and was at present in Spain, learning to speak exquisite Spanish before going to spend a great part of his life in Chile. To him I wrote an imaginary letter, giving an account of my interview with Sir William and the impression of his firm I had gained from the waiting room, and posted this to Crawford's with a covering note. I got back a letter offering me a start. It was a strange mixture of kindliness, shrewd perception – 'Trade will become in your lifetime international so languages are essential' – and bombast – 'Keep faith with the people as their esteem means good will.' It was a letter as revealing of the writer as my own – offhand but subtly flattering, seemingly detached but shrewdly calculated – was of me. Both our letters were in handwriting. What I did not know then, but learned after I joined the firm, was that Sir William's devoted secretary had trained herself to write an imitation of his bold, upward-sloping scrawl so exact that even he often did not know which of them had written something he apparently had signed.

And so now on a Monday in March 1928 I turned up at Crawford's for my first day as a copywriter, on a regular income of £4 a week, brought round to me on Fridays in a pay packet.

During my period of unemployment one event had happened which would make a lasting impression on me, though it was in no way connected with my efforts to become a journalist – I had been asked by an elderly couple living on Campden Hill to go to their house for tea; the husband held some educational post, and they had either been staying at Burneside or met my parents in

Evelyn Mary Hopkinson, the author's
mother. She had been a mistress in a boys'
school, and herself taught her five children
to read, write and spell correctly – and
some French and Latin – before they were
sent away to school at seven or eight years
old. Her father, like her husband, had been
a clergyman

John Henry Hopkinson, the author's
father. An archaeologist and a university
lecturer, he gave up his career to enter the
church. During the First World War he
joined the army as a private soldier. Later
he became Archdeacon of Westmorland.
He and his wife died within a few months
of each other

Stephan and Esther, the two youngest in the family, on the shore at the family's country refuge at Aber in North Wales

The author at his preparatory school, Lawrence House at St Annes-on-Sea on the Lancashire coast

Above The line-up of the little Hopkinsons,
preparing to set out into the world. At the back on
the left the eldest, Jack. Beside him, Tom,
described by a family friend as 'a dark horse'. Front
row, from left, Stephan, Esther and Paul

Left The author in his first term at Pembroke
College, Oxford, where he was from 1923 to 1927

The author with the painter John Tunnard, sailing
on the Helston river, Cornwall

some way. As I came in through the door of their comfortable home I thought, This is exactly the sort of gathering I've come to London to avoid. I must get out as quickly as I can. It was a Sunday afternoon tea-fight, too many people packed into a couple of rooms too full of furniture, everyone standing up, squealing with artificial laughter and spilling tea on one another and the carpet. There was no one I knew or wished to talk to, and after exchanging a few politenesses with host and hostess I was about to get away when a white-bearded man, the guest of honour to whom I had been briefly introduced, came over and said he would like to talk to me if I would spare him a few minutes. When I said I would be happy, he waved his hand dismissingly at the party. 'No, no! Not here. This is impossible. I find somewhere quiet.'

He led me to a room at the back, evidently the study belonging to our host, who was too wise to allow it to be invaded by his guests, and we both sat down.

'You are a young journalist?'

I nodded.

'And you know who am I?'

'Your name is Dr Lutoslawski.'

'And you know who that is?'

'You are perhaps some relation of the great Lutoslawski who wrote the standard work on Plato?'

'I am not some relation. That is myself. I am seeing you here today for the first time – and you are the person in this gathering I am wishing to talk to. . . .' He launched into a long exposition.

I listened with a double fascination, first for what he was saying and second for the man himself. The copy of his book in my possession – interleaved with comments in my father's neat handwriting, since it had belonged to him when he too was at the university – had an air of antiquity, its pages yellowed and the leather binding worn. I had supposed it to be a more recent edition of a work written in some Polish or Silesian university a century ago. In lectures, I had frequently heard the author's name spoken with the respect given to those whose authority is beyond question and who, as a rule, are long since dead, so that to find this bearded professor talking to me now was almost as strange as if Plato himself had turned up in Campden Hill and asked if I could spare five minutes for a chat.

Stranger still was the subject of his talk. He began by outlining the theory of preexistence and reincarnation, of which I had had my first glimpse over my little sister's horoscope. He explained how past lives continually influence us and what happens to us in the present. This is not a matter of saying 'I was Julius Caesar,' but of being alert to our impressions of the people we meet and the places where we feel happy or uneasy, since through these impressions much valuable information can be conveyed if we are conscious enough to take it in. The people to whom we find ourselves attracted, the men and women we naturally trust or for whom we feel what we call an 'instinctive' dislike, are almost always those of whom we have had some experience in a previous incarnation – possibly hundreds or even thousands of years ago; he seemed to go so far as to be saying that almost all those we come across in everyday life have crossed our paths before, and are persons to whom we have some debt to repay, or with whom we have some grudge to settle.

He talked as though what he was telling me was of crucial importance and he had far too little time in which to say it; he talked not as though outlining a theory but as though passing on information to be memorized and stored away. I listened to him without a word.

Three points which he emphasized surprised me particularly. He said that contrary to general belief there is no contradiction between Christianity and the acceptance of reincarnation, a point which, he claimed, he had succeeded in establishing with high ecclesiastical authority – I gathered that he was a Catholic – though this would not be publicly admitted for a long time to come.

Second, he spoke of God not as static and changeless, but as increasing in consciousness as the universe expands and man's knowledge of it grows. He spoke of the 'self-development' of God, as though God's consciousness and man's are continually interacting on each other.

Finally – and here at least I had no difficulty in understanding what he said – he declared that his own country 'has a Messianic destiny'. If it had formerly been expedient that one man should die for the nation, it was now destined that one nation should suffer for the whole world. That nation was Poland, and I should see the truth of what he was telling me during my own lifetime.

After what I suppose was an hour of intense concentration, our host or someone must have come to fetch the chief guest, and I left the house in a stupor as though I had been closeted with a visitor from beyond the grave.

Afterwards for a year or two I continued in a desultory way to correspond with Dr Lutoslawski, before allowing myself to be submerged in the tide of everyday activity.

9

A Manic World

By joining W. S. Crawford's I had become part of a manic world.

The post-war boom was at its height and no underground tremors foretold the approaching economic catastrophe as the firm was borne along on recurrent waves of excitement and success. Sir William and those around him had got hold of a basic idea – to apply the principles of modern art to the business of selling goods through advertising. The 1914–18 war had started to sweep away the laboured pictorialism of advertising based on nineteenth-century art, replacing it with a simpler language of dynamic forms which everyone could take in at a glance. Developed in the Soviet Union to help publicize the revolution's aims to a people largely illiterate, restructured and given a sophisticated gloss in the ferment of post-war Germany, this was a language of symbols perfectly adapted to poster display or to diverting a reader's eye from the crowded make-up of a newspaper. A wheel or a winged helmet stood for speed, a jazz trumpeter for enjoyment, a flower or a bird for the outdoor world and a bent figure for suffering.

Out of such dramatic forms and symbols Crawford's created advertising which both invested their clients' products with a glamour of modernity and at the same time hammered home their essential selling points. And around this basic idea a whole philosophy of advertising had been built up which brought the Crawford's organization into a much closer relationship with their clients than merely filling space for them in newspapers. Advertisements were useless unless they formed part of a planned campaign, and a campaign was valueless unless the image it expressed was carried through all the firm's contacts with the public. As a result, firms which had come for 'a few advertisements to tide us over', ended by having their stationery and letter-headings redesigned, their packaging transformed, offices refurnished and sometimes their products reconstructed and their sales managers replaced.

A group of enthusiasts some of whom had originally come down from Glasgow with Sir William, with others who had joined the firm in London or from its branch offices in Paris and Berlin, made up the driving force. They had attracted to the staff an American designer of outstanding talent, E. McKnight Kauffer, whose influence quickly spread throughout the firm, and there were others already there, such as Ashley Havinden and Terence Prentis, whose style and abilities harmonized with his. From them, from the chief copywriter Saxon Mills, and from creative executives such as Margaret Havinden, Ashley's wife, came a flow of ideas to be translated into campaigns for motor-car and petrol firms, fashion houses, beauty products, brands of beer and cigarettes, or patent medicines.

With the exception of Kauffer, who seemed always as cool as his office was elegantly clinical, the firm's directing nucleus lived in a constant ferment, partly genuine but frequently contrived as a means of sustaining their head of steam. Saxon Mills, a small brusque man in his early thirties, but already going bald from the strain of his life and the effort of keeping his fervour at full pressure, would rush in on a Monday morning waving a piece of paper with a few pencilled words on it. He had been working nonstop over the weekend, he declared, until at last his creative effort had crystallized into a slogan – 'Great Stuff – This Bass!' or 'Eno's – First Thing Every Morning'. This would be acclaimed, argued over, and finally approved as the theme for the new campaign to be presented to the client in a couple of weeks' time. The great men at the top worked out the main advertisements in a variety of sizes, the space-buyers planned their schedules, and the subordinate workers – hack artists, lettering men and second-grade copywriters – toiled to produce leaflets, redesign packages, write advertisements for the trade and produce the impressive folders in which the completed campaign would be put over on the client. Finally the day would come and the advertising be presented.

It was a point of honour with the team to get their proposals through unaltered. Inevitably, to show their independence, managing directors and advertising managers would find something they wanted changing, even if it was of no particular importance. They might as well have asked for St Paul's to be shifted a few yards to the east. Battered with arguments, overwhelmed with advertising philosophy, they would usually, as lunchtime approached, concede defeat with dignity. Another Crawford's triumph! Just occasionally a campaign would be rejected, to general gloom and disappointment – quickly dispelled when some new client came along and the process began afresh.

It was now 1928 and Crawford's success, built up almost entirely in the last ten years, demanded a suitably impressive setting through which the power of advertising would itself be advertised. A design for the offices in High Holborn had been prepared by Frederick Etchells, an exponent in Britain of Corbusier's principles, and his new building was already being constructed on the site while we continued working in the old. We operated amid an uproar of automatic drills, hammering on metal, bellowing of instructions up and down the lift shaft, and under a rain of falling plaster. Rushing down a corridor with a proof, you would be met by a workman wheeling a barrowful of wet cement or find the passage you came along an hour ago roped off and its surface being blasted away.

As a would-be copywriter, I worked with other juniors – both men and girls, for the firm had no prejudice against women – under a kindly 'schoolmaster', David Symon, who might himself have been a copywriting star but for continual ill health. It was through him that the inspired ideas of Mills had to be carried out in detail; and he toiled over our crude efforts with the same patience Mr Goldie had once shown over my Latin prose. Mills had perfected a form of advertisement writing well adapted to the displays which Kauffer and Havinden designed.

Anything like argument was out and grammar at a discount.
The text, crushed into a tight panel and set in one of the newly
designed sans-serif typefaces, had to be terse and explosive –
'Chrysler! Its flashing acceleration! Its lightning speed! Its
dramatic flow of power!'

During the four years I spent in Crawford's, two and a half as
copywriter and the rest as an account executive, I never lost the
feeling that I was serving a prison sentence and praying for the
day of liberation. There were compensations. Two of the firm's
junior artists, Douglas England and Tom Gentleman, with his
charming wife Winifred, became friends, sharing my rebellious
attitude. Both men, a few years older than myself, had served in
the First World War and despite all its horrors looked back on it
as a golden age of carefree comradeship. I listened with
admiration to their stories and they would encourage me under
the attacks of the unpredictable Sir William, who was by turns
oppressive and ebullient. When I met him in a corridor or lift,
he would demand, 'Are y'happy in your work? Are y'giving it
everything you've got? Are y'*dreaming* advertising? Are y'a
hundred per cent Crawford's man?'

'No – thank God!' was my never spoken answer, but from
Crawford it was necessary to put up with a good deal. It was *his*
firm, my livelihood depended on him, and his enthusiasm was
at least partially sincere; in addition I was intimidated by his
bull-like presence and undirected emotional horsepower. With
some of the others I could not be so compliant. Once, having
written copy for one of our campaigns, I took it in for Mills's
inspection. He looked up from his desk,

'Well? What's it like? What am I supposed to think of it? Will
it bowl me over?'

'It'll do the job, I think.'

He flung his pencil down. 'How the hell d'you expect me to
be impressed if you talk like that? Don't you know that you
have to *sell* the stuff you write! *Put it across* – as though it's a
message of salvation!'

'Good God!' I said. 'Are we supposed to play that game with
one another?'

He looked at me with well-deserved mistrust.

Indeed I did not believe in the mission of advertising. I could appreciate that it had a part to play in the world of industry and trade, but I did not feel happy to use what writing ability I had in selling patent medicines or making commonplace goods seem better that they were. All consciences, however, require some degree of stifling if life is to go on at all, and I could, I felt, have got through my work with efficiency and reasonable contentment were it not for the pretentious claptrap with which our activities had to be invested. Over this we, the firm's underlings, were in two camps – those who believed in our mission and those like myself who found it impossible to swallow. Three of the youthful believers, whose names were Colman, Prentis and Varley, would one day leave the firm, launch out on their own and become for a while the advertising world's front-runners. Others, like Tom Gentleman, Douglas England and myself, waited for a bomb to fall and the prison walls to break. But the bomb which eventually fell was not the kind we were expecting.

Before long the economic slump which had started in the USA had spread to Britain and firms looking round for ways to trim their budgets were soon reducing or cancelling their advertising. By 1931, Crawford's was experiencing its first serious setback, and there was a shake-out of staff. Douglas England was handed a letter inviting him 'to accept a freelance post', which he rightly interpreted as informing him that he was sacked. Fortunately he soon got a job making drawings for *Punch*, where he was a lot happier than he had been in advertising. A few others were dismissed and the rest of us invited to accept a 10 per cent cut in salary. It was, we were assured, not compulsory, but if further reductions had to be made later, then those with the firm's interest at heart must naturally enjoy a better chance of staying on. I myself, neither a success nor totally a failure – I had progressed in the course of three years to a salary of £12 a week (now less 10 per cent) – was made an executive with a few minor accounts to handle since there was not enough work for all the copywriters.

Throughout these years, whatever my ups and downs, I continued to devote all the time I could to my own writing. I had managed to produce a novel, and to get it published. It was a wild and whirling affair, built round my passion for the countryside, very much the kind of book parodied so devastatingly in *Cold Comfort Farm*. Distressed at the time by the lack of reviews, I now have reason to be grateful for their absence and its total disappearance. There were other outlets. Charles Fenby had moved to Oxford as literary editor of the *Oxford Mail*, of which he would become editor in a few years' time; his paper sent me tickets for London theatres in return for my reviews. I had also managed to get one or two stories into the *New Statesman*, and was elated when I won a competition with a £5 prize for a piece of literary criticism. My contribution was described as having 'a pleasant youthful impertinence ... free from the rather heavy solemnity which overcame most of the essayists who sat down to write about Literature'. Eagerly I went to see the editor, Kingsley Martin, who had not long been in the chair, hoping I should at least get a few books to review from time to time. He explained to me that they were not looking for writers, of whom they had quite enough already; what they *were* looking for was new readers, which the competition I had entered for was intended to attract.

My brother Stephan, having won an open scholarship, had by now gone to Oxford where he was enjoying a career which, if shorter than expected, was sensational while it lasted. Among other achievements he had become editor of the *Isis*, and commissioned me to write a weekly 'London Letter' for a fee of half a guinea. No expenses could be paid, so the letter had to be spun out of my head, but I was allowed to write on anything I pleased. Looking back on what I sent him it is evident that three years in advertising had not freed my writing from undergraduate facetiousness.

Today the airship R100 passed over London. 'Like a gigantic jam-roll,' observed an important City man at my elbow. A small figure was to be seen walking along the top: we supposed for a time he was trying to locate their position. On cries of 'Whip behind!' the figure disappeared, and we later learned he had been looking for Lord Thomson's hat. The great difficulty of airship travel at the present time is that of recovering such small objects dropped by passengers while the aircraft is in motion.

Stephan proved to be a highly successful editor of the *Isis*. He had adopted one of the discoveries of popular journalism, that there is no need to wait for events to happen; they can be manufactured, and manufactured events are both easier to exploit and richer in reader interest than those which turn up of their own accord. One of those he manufactured was a visit to Oxford by Tallulah Bankhead in order to make an ascent in a balloon – a news event from which London newspapers were glad to cut themselves a slice. No wonder that on one of our rare meetings he was able to fish out of his pocket a letter for which I felt I would gladly give one ear. This came from the managing editor of the *Daily Mail*, saying he had followed Stephan's Oxford career with interest and that if he had not yet decided on his future he would be glad to see him in his office with a view to his joining the *Daily Mail*. However, both Stephan's editorship of the *Isis* and his time at the university were fast coming to an end. As Lifeboat Day came round, the magazine's proprietor, a printer, told him to put in the customary full-page appeal. Stephan objected that this had little interest for under-graduate readers, and when ordered to print the appeal 'or else', inserted into the announcement that '£50 will secure a guaran-teed seat in any lifeboat, and £100 gives preference over women and children.' He was sacked, and his successor printed a photograph of him in a sou'wester at the wheel of a fishing boat, captioned, 'The pilot who weathered the storm.'

Bored now with university life, Stephan left a year earlier than expected to join an oil company in Mexico where he would spend the next few years. Meanwhile Jack had got married and settled to legal work in Kendal. Esther, after a year or two in Switzerland, had gone home to work as her father's secretary before taking a teacher-training course, and Paul had launched out into a new career. During his five years spent in engineering, he had joined the Territorials. Finding military life congenial, he decided to take advantage of a transfer scheme to join the regular army; before long he had been commissioned into the Indian Army and was out on the northern frontier where he took part in a succession of campaigns. I seemed to be the only one who had got stuck.

Studying the newspapers eagerly for jobs, I came one day on a small advertisement for a copywriter to do publicity for 'an important newspaper publishing firm'. A newspaper publishing firm sounded a whole stage nearer to journalism than an advertising agency, and I applied. The firm proved to be Odhams Press, where I was interviewed by the head of the publicity department, a large man with sandy hair named Surrey Dane. After negotiation I was given the job at £14 a week, £2 more than my final salary at Crawford's which I left with no regrets.

The extra money was important, since by now I had a wife and two children to support.

10
Marriage

I first saw Antonia White after I had been working in Crawford's for a couple of years. I was walking past the lift shaft on one of the upper floors when I heard the sharp tapping of high heels on a lower level, and looked down. A neat plump figure in a green knitted suit walked past. From her chin thrust forward, and the way she set each foot down as though wanting to knock a hole in the tiles with her heel, the impression I took in was of smouldering indignation. The sharpness of that instant impression remains, as though in it I had seen an essential aspect of her personality, but at the time no doubt I put it on one side since there were plenty of day-to-day reasons for anyone working in Crawford's to be angry.

I knew already who this figure must be. Tony White – for it was only much later that she began to use the name Antonia in private life – had worked in the firm for some four years before I got there. She was not one of the inner directing group, but her skill in writing on what were then considered to be women's subjects – fashion, beauty and the rest – had given her a position of her own, so that she would be called in for consultation when there was work for such clients to be done. But skill alone was not enough in Crawford's; we were all involved in a continual struggle for position, and Tony maintained hers by a combination of obligingness and quick temper. She was not afraid of Sir William, his partner and financial director Florence Sangster, Mrs Havinden, Mills or any of the others, so that she was able to exercise her charm on them as freely as convenient; but if she felt she was being imposed on or her work unduly criticized, she would flare up instantly. With anger her whole appearance was transformed. Her body seemed to thicken and her features set into a stony mask like that of an outraged Roman emperor, so that those who had been making demands or criticisms a moment earlier, were now urgent to pacify and smooth her feathers.

Though she had never broken with the firm, Tony had left Crawford's for a couple of years during 1928–9 to join a new literary magazine, *Life and Letters*. This was a monthly, a good deal more letters than life, edited by Desmond McCarthy; there was virtually no other editorial staff and Tony had joined as assistant editor cum secretary. Now, like most other literary magazines when the initial backing runs out, it was in financial trouble and Tony was returning to advertising. A further reason for her absence, we understood, was that she had been having a baby, which could be allowed for more easily in the less demanding routine of a small office; now, as I got to know her better, I started to learn something of her story.

Her father had been a senior classics master at St Paul's School, whose name, Botting, was familiar to me from Greek textbooks used at school. In middle life he had turned to Catholicism, taking his wife and small daughter with him. He had been a formidable, perhaps something of a tyrannical, father, whose demands on his daughter for mental and moral perfection, deriving from his own difficulties, proved over-whelming. Her mother, whose maiden name had been White,* was sympathetic but vain and ineffectual, so that Tony, an only child, was left with a constant need for comfort and support. She had inherited her father's intellectual capacity and some of her mother's frivolity and wilfulness. Her own inborn passion for literature had been fed by incessant reading and discussion, giving her a wide knowledge of books and an admirably lucid writing style. Eager to get away from home, she had married early – with her father's encouragement but against her mother's good sense – to a young man of a wealthy family which at once cut off the allowance on which they were

*Adopted by Antonia as her pen name.

planning to start life together. The marriage, it seemed, had never been consummated, and was annulled by Catholic headquarters after prolonged legal and ecclesiastical hassle. All that Tony underwent during this period, together with the tension aroused by new emotional relationships, had led in 1922 to a complete mental breakdown lasting for about a year, much of which she spent in the former Bethlehem Hospital. This experience she described poetically and movingly in a story called 'The House of Clouds', which was published in *Life and Letters* while she was still working there.

A year or so after her recovery, Tony had married again, to Eric Earnshaw-Smith, a man of exceptional intelligence and perception with a post in the civil service. Though loving and caring protectively for Tony, because of factors in his own nature Eric did not live with her, and their arrangement, based on a master–pupil relationship, had broken down when Tony fell in love with a young man, recently qualified as an engineer, by whom she had her first child. This had happened shortly after I joined Crawford's, and when I saw her from the lift shaft, the engineer was away on a job in Nigeria, Tony had gone back to live with Eric at his small house in Paultons Square, Chelsea, and baby Susan was in a children's home in Roehampton, at no great distance from the convent school in which Tony herself had been educated.

During 1930, Tony and I spent much time together, causing a good deal of comment in the firm, particularly when we went for a holiday together in the South of France. We did not discuss our relationship with our colleagues, but I had already learned that when a group of people work together, it is hardly possible to keep secret an important factor in the life of any of them. Towards the end of that year the young engineer returned from his Nigerian employment, no more certain of his feelings than he had been when he left, and there ensued a period of much heart-searching for all three of us – as well as for Eric Earnshaw-Smith – which only ended when Tony said it was me she would marry, not the engineer. By the time she reached this decision we were so emotionally exhausted that any end to the argument was a relief to us all; however, the complex story of Tony's previous life made our marriage less than welcome to my parents so that a new series of intense arguments began. Inevitably the question of Tony's mental illness came up and the possibility of a recurrence; it proved difficult to trace the doctor to whom she had been taken on her breakdown eight years earlier, and not easy to secure a statement from him that would be at least partially reassuring.

Much concerned, my father spend some days in London and at the last moment when I saw him off at Euston, walking up and down the platform before his train left, offered, if I did not want to go through with the marriage, to help in disentangling the situation. I assured him that my mind was made up and I should marry Tony with or without my family's agreement. Only later, thinking over his abhorrence for emotional scenes, did I come to appreciate how much this offer must have cost him.

A few days later Tony and I were married in Carlisle Cathedral, where my father was now canon in residence, having left Burneside a couple of years previously. We were married early on a winter morning when there was nobody about and the cathedral not yet warmed up. Afterwards we left for a short honeymoon on the Solway Firth – a long weekend was all I could take off from work – in my father's car. Back in London we rented a flat we could not afford in a block off the Fulham Road called Cecil Court, brought little Susan from Roehampton and settled down, if that is the right expression, to our married life.

Anyone making a book on the way our joint destiny was likely to work out would have found one or two points in our favour to record. We were both young and physically healthy. We both had a passion for writing, liked much the same writers and regarded those we liked with veneration. I had brought what furniture I possessed from Great Smith Street, and Tony some from Paultons Square, but the first we actually bought together were two identical desks made out of plywood for us by a local carpenter at £5 each. These we installed side by side in our main living room, and when my brother Jack, now married and well established in his legal profession, wrote to ask what to give us for a wedding present, we asked not for an eiderdown or reading lamp but for Festing Jones's *Life of Samuel Butler* in two volumes. We had thus one powerful interest in common. On the negative side the list would have to be longer.

Tony loved parties and social life. At parties she brightened up and her face became prettier as she took trouble to attract and charm – whereas I often became gloomy and morose, searching my mind vainly for anything to say, reluctant to speak at all unless I could say something witty or impressive. Sometimes, following the fashion of Bloomsbury, everyone would be asked to make a boast, usually of something extraordinary that had happened to them. Tony's boast was invariably successful: 'I've been married three times and have a certificate of virginity signed by the Pope.' Since we could not afford drink parties, Tony would give tea parties on Sunday afternoons. The people she knew were interesting – Geoffrey Grigson, who worked on the *Morning Post* and was planning to launch a new poetry magazine with his wife Frances; John Summerson, already a writer of authority on architecture; Elliot Seabrook, a heavily built artist who painted landscapes rather too much in the style of Cézanne; Alick Schepeler, a tall elegant woman with a job on *Vogue*, who had been a model and mistress of Augustus John; Frank Freeman, with his talented wife Joan Soutar-Robertson, who painted a mural for us in our hall. These and others were all Tony's friends; the few I might have contributed were now mainly overseas.

Where I felt most at home was not in social life but in the country and though I had already lived several years in London, I still took every opportunity to get out, if only for a few hours and if only into near-suburbia, which was then called Metroland. For Tony the country was endurable as a place to sit in when the sun was shining, though even fine weather brought drawbacks since she felt in constant danger of being stung or bitten. At its best it was somewhere for short visits, since everything of interest took place in London and like many town-dwellers she detested games and exercise.

More seriously, perhaps, we had a different attitude about

money. I could not bear to be in debt and wanted to pay every bill as soon as it came in. Tony preferred always to be not outrageously but moderately in debt, like someone swimming just below the surface. She had accounts with one or two stores which allowed her credit up to £50 or so; this she looked on as a balance in her favour, and if part of it got paid off would rush to rebuild the debt to its full height. Hats, in particular, exercised a powerful fascination for her and more than once when a cheque for, say, £15 was eagerly awaited, what I would find, as keeper of our accounts, would be £10 and a new hat.

Our difficulties over money began immediately. My small capital of about £100 had gone before our honeymoon ended, all except £30 which we were reserving 'for desperate emergencies', but the first of these arrived within three days of moving into our new home.

'There's a man at the door wanting to see you,' Tony said to me at breakfast.

'What kind of man?'

'A rather beagledy man.' This was a word she and Eric used, meaning shabby or down at heel. He proved to be the foreman of the firm which had done the decorating, and he thrust a bill into my hand.

'But it's the agents you want to see,' I told him. 'They undertook to redecorate before we moved in. It's in the lease.'

'These are *additional* decorations, sir. Outlining the panels of the doors and painting the skirting boards in different colours like the lady ordered. The agents aren't liable for that – but the work's been done and I've got to pay my men.'

The bill was for £27, and from that moment we lived on a system of post-dated cheques, carefully spaced out against hoped-for earnings.

Finally, the bookmaking pessimist might have pointed out, neither of us had been particularly successful in establishing any lasting relationship hitherto – so were we likely to achieve this now? Or did Tony know as little about what it meant to be a wife as I about what it meant to be a husband?

*

129

By the time I was in a position to say goodbye to Crawford's, our wedding was long over and we had a new little daughter, Lyndall, named after the chief character in Olive Schreiner's *The Story of an African Farm*, which Tony and I had both recently read. I was so happy over her arrival, which took place around midnight, that I passed the news to the man in the coffee stall where I stopped for something to eat on my way home. His answer was to smile warmly, say he knew just how I felt, and put the change from his closed hand into mine. The way he did this seemed suspicious so I opened my hand and counted it out in front of him. It was five shillings short and I congratulated myself as I walked back to the flat, thinking that with two children to support it would not have done to throw away five shillings.

The publicity department of Odhams Press, to which I now went every day and for a half-day on Saturdays, was a ramshackle building in Long Acre immediately opposite the grandiose entrance to our editorial block in which the *Daily Herald*, *People*, *Sporting Life* and other Odhams papers were produced; scattered here and there, in former shops and up back staircases throughout Covent Garden, were the offices of our numerous magazines.

Surrey Dane, the department's head, was seldom seen. As a director of Odhams, he was either in conference with fellow directors or engaged on matters of policy far above our heads. Meanwhile the department – made up of half a dozen copy-writers, several executives, eight or ten 'artists' or lettering men, and a number of clerks handling the accounts – sweated beneath the lash of Dane's chief assistant, Jerome Chester. Short, grey-faced, over-smartly dressed and with the perky swagger of the stage comedian he had once been, Chester kept watch over us through glass office doors during the day, then, after we had gone home, dictated to his secretary a flood of memos which would be waiting for us, signed charismatically 'J.C.', when we arrived next morning. Chester's sharp tongue and devotion to the firm had so unnerved several of my colleagues that if even a few minutes late for work they would not dare to enter the building but would stop off at a nearby

Lyons teashop, hang up coats and hats to be recovered at lunchtime, and come bustling upstairs with an armful of papers as though just back from visiting an office down the road.

The work I had been hired to do was concerned, oddly enough, more with selling books than advertising newspapers. The early 1930s were the era of the Great Circulation War, in which readers were being wooed by a shower of 'free gifts' to sign an order telling their newsagent to deliver a particular paper for three months or more. Odhams had been the originators of this form of warfare, using it to build the *Daily Herald*'s circulation from around 100,000 to well over two million; though other popular dailies had in varying degrees been drawn into the struggle, Odhams still led the way in variety of offers and success in forcing them onto the public. Some of these gifts were practical – tea sets, cooking vessels, even trousers. But it had been Surrey Dane's achievement to lift the gift business onto a higher plane by offering 'great works of literature', such as the Holy Bible, 'the one book every home in the British Isles needs to possess', or 'the entire collection of masterpieces by the greatest playwright the world has ever known, contained in a single impressive volume'.

Such offers gave cultural tone and educational value to what might otherwise have seemed a sordid struggle to bribe readers away from other newspapers. But they had one drawback – they were one-off affairs. We could not flog the Holy Bible piece by piece, Genesis followed by Exodus, followed by Leviticus and so on. But what about the works of Charles Dickens? Get the reader to sign up for three months to secure *David Copperfield*, and then hammer him to sign on for another three in order to obtain *Great Expectations*. Dickens, happily, had been a prolific writer, and his works were out of copyright. He had also – hadn't he? – been a great reformer, with the first known social conscience, or at any rate *one* of the first known. So what could be more appropriate for possible readers of the *Daily Herald* than to build up for themselves year by year this set of 'immortal volumes containing the greatest galaxy of living portraits ever assembled between covers'? And in the whole-page advertisement with which we launched 'the most stupendous publishing offer of all time', the greatest galaxy could actually be seen pouring out of the half-opened volume – Tiny Tim, Little Nell, Scrooge, Mr Pickwick, David Copperfield, and a host of others whom we came rapidly to loathe. Below we gave weight, measurements, number of illustrations, how many million words ... 'each magnificent volume encased in genuine art leatherette, embossed on the spine with solid gold lettering'. And all this delivered directly to your home at a cost of only three shillings and sixpence, which was described, since the volumes themselves were 'free gifts', as 'to cover packing, postage and insurance'.

In addition to book offers, we also sustained the readership of our journals at their maximum by offering various kinds of 'free' life insurance, and it was in connection with this that Chester, before I joined Odhams, had pulled off a historic coup. Under *John Bull*'s Great Free Insurance Policy, all a fortunate reader had to do in order to 'receive an immediate cheque for £1000' was to get himself killed in a railway accident. If this proved difficult, he could make certain of £500 simply by losing both arms and legs, with pro rata for lesser injuries. To bring this offer before the travelling public, J.C. had hired some dozen or so sandwichmen. Their placards announced the generous terms, while they – like survivors from some horrible catastrophe – hopped along the Strand to meet the commuters coming out of Charing Cross. Not all, however, hopped on crutches. Some had their heads bound with blood-stained bandages and, by a particularly thoughtful touch, the injuries were interchangeable, so that the man who had spent the morning crutch-hopping could relax during the afternoon in the comfort of an injured head.

From us all J.C. demanded a flow of similarly ingenious ideas, plus a high output of forceful advertising copy, plus a devotion to the firm's interests equal to his own. Once when a colleague dropped a box of paperclips and, instead of picking them up one by one, shovelled the lot into the waste basket, Chester spotted him through the glass door. His invective ended with the words (jotted down by me after he stormed out) ' ... an' if I'd been a shareholder in this firm, and seen what you just did, I'd have committed suicide many times over. What's more, I'd have enjoyed it – knowing it was fully justified.'

I had now been with the department for well over a year, and as usual we were under pressure. The Holy Bible had done well but without proving the 100 per cent success we had a right to expect in a God-fearing society. William Shakespeare had been generally approved, but some readers considered his language obscure and others had found it difficult to remember which character was which. Charles Dickens had achieved as massive a success after death as he had in life, but the day came when even those most eager to wallow with Little Nell and Tiny Tim had had as much as they could take. Unless we took a firm grip on our readers, they might soon be sliding off to the *Daily Mail, Daily Express, Daily Mirror*, or even to the *Daily Sketch*.

Before we went home at Saturday midday, Chester summoned us to his office. If we were to keep our jobs, if the department itself were to continue, bright ideas for book publication must be found – and quickly.

'Bring your intellects to the boil, boys!', he advised us sternly, 'and maintain 'em at the boil over this weekend. Then come in here on Monday and spill it all out on paper so that it leaves a big red mark!'

11

The Sum Total of All Human Knowledge

Despite the urgency of his instructions, Chester showed little interest in our ideas when we came in on the Monday morning, and it soon became clear that his intentions had been, first, to keep us concentrated on the firm's business over the weekend in case we might start to enjoy ourselves and be happy with our families, and, second, to build up interest for the announcement he was planning to make. He allowed us to put forward our suggestions, then remarked, 'Having listened to that load of rubbish, boys, all I can say is – it's a good thing for you there's some of us with real ideas in charge of this department . . . ' he then unfolded the project which was to keep us busy from now on. The original idea, like most others, had been Surrey Dane's – an encyclopedia. What we were to offer our readers this time was to be not just entertainment or even spiritual uplift, but knowledge itself. Obviously we could not lash out on sets of the *Encyclopedia Britannica* for our readers, so what we had done instead was to produce our own. Starting from scratch, Chester explained, would have taken too long and cost too much – 'we haven't got half a dozen Doctor Johnsons locked up in the cellar' – so Odhams had bought the rights to an out-of-print Victorian publication upon which 'a posse of high-powered intellects and main-line academicals' had been employed to bring the whole thing up to date. This process was complete and the encyclopedia in print, so that it was now our task to ensure that the public came clamouring for copies. Whole pages had been set aside in all Odhams newspapers and magazines and we were told to 'get your heads down into your blotting paper – even if it makes you cross-eyed', and surpass all previous efforts in putting the encyclopedia over.

We did as we were told, and millions were soon being informed that:

These stupendous volumes – available for the first time in this or any country – contain in their many thousand pages nothing less than the Sum Total of All Human Knowledge, from the first dawn of history down to the latest achievements of the ever-restless scientific mind.... Sumptuously bound and heavily embossed in gold, your treasury of knowledge come to you in handy manageable form such as the great sages of the past were unable to possess....

From this very morning, this priceless heirloom – which you will one day hand proudly on to your children and grandchildren, *and which is available solely to registered readers of this newspaper* – can be yours for no more than the trifling sum required to cover packing, postage and insurance.... Hurry! Hurry! *Hurry!*

Within days the firm's letterboxes were jammed and extra sorting staff had to be called in. The encyclopedia was a winner, and Chester, whose lash had curled so often round our loins, showed himself generous in the hour of triumph.

'When I am reading this ad over my eggs and bacon, boys, I visualize these volumes come steppin' down off the shelf, one by one, in clankin' armour.... It is just like all the pages has been interleaved with five-pound notes. I read every word – right down to the address. An' if I hadn't stopped myself in time, I'd have filled the coupon in and sent my postal order off.... '

But we, or at any rate I, were not to be left basking long in idle satisfaction, and within two or three days Chester sent for me. 'I'm not denying,' he observed, 'that a start's been made – you can even call it a *good* start. But what this encyclopedia needs – if we're to set the country ablaze from end to end – is support from the great minds of the day.'

I sat silent, a horrible suspicion of my own role in regard to the great minds already forming in my mind.

'Begin,' he instructed, 'at the top ... vice-chancellors of Oxford and Cambridge universities, headmasters of Eton,

Harrow an' such, archbishops of Canterbury and York, president of the Royal Society, Lord Chief Justice, Astonomer Royal. . . . And when you've signed that lot up – just a couple of sentences from each saying what it would have meant to have had such a book as this in their own childhood – then you can slip down the ladder. Bring in your successful novelists, your scientific whosits and your non-committal dignitaries.'

'Non-committal dignitaries?' I asked with careful innocence, but he was down on me in a flash.

'Make your list of great minds the way you see it,' he commanded. 'So long as they all say what's expected of them, you won't get hanged from any lamp posts.'

So over the next weeks I found myself entering – at first with trepidation but later with assurance – the studies of a number of eminent men, where the same curiously unreal conversation would take place. I would hand the book over and explain the purpose of my visit; the great mind would then turn to his own speciality, molecular physics or Etruscan art, and read the entry with evident disgust.

'Well of course on my subject it's totally out of date. . . . Might have been written fifty years ago. But in general, I suppose, it's probably all right. What d'you want me to say?'

Far be it from me, I would demur, to put words into such a mouth, but on the way down in the train I had just jotted down a few thoughts, and I would fumble in my pocket for a slip of paper. I had taken care to avoid extravagance, had chosen expressions reasonably suited to the signatory, and once there were a few fish in the bag their presence seemed to decoy the others, but it astounded me that most of those I approached – not quite the full list Chester had drawn up – were willing to sign anything at all. Apart from a useless book of reference, they got nothing out of it.

Only once was I given the bullet I deserved. Unable to see the Astronomer Royal I had left his copy with a covering note, and rang up a few days later to take down his testimonial. He was a long time coming to the phone, and the brusqueness of his manner – 'Well? What is it you want?' – suggested he had been deep in observation of the heavenly bodies.

When he learned who I was and why he had been summoned, there was a moment's silence. Then: 'Are *you* the person who left this load of outrageous rubbish? And are *you* now expecting me to say how valuable it is?'

I admitted this was so.

'Then let me tell you that you, your newspaper, and your whole firm ought to be prosecuted for fraud – and if I had my way ... '

It would be wise, I thought, to end this conversation before it got out of hand.

'Thank God!' I said.

'What the devil d'you mean?'

'I've been hawking this ruddy encyclopedia around for weeks to people who should know better – and all they say is how wonderful it is. You're the first one who's given a straight answer,' and I rapidly rang off.

While I hawked the encyclopedia around for a salary of £14 and, after a while, £15 a week, Tony continued to do freelance advertising work. In the evenings and at weekends we sat for as many hours as we could allow or keep awake at our two desks. What I was writing was a novel – unpublished and happily never to be published – about a young man who gets involved in advertising when he wants to be a journalist; what Tony was writing was a novel about her childhood in a convent school. Quite soon after we moved into Cecil Court she had read me her notes for some half-written chapters which impressed me deeply, and I began urging her to complete the book; to help in getting this done we arranged that she should read a new chapter to me each Saturday evening, and by the beginning of 1933 *Frost in May* was finished. A friend, Wyn Henderson, was connected with a new publisher, Desmond Harmsworth, and urged Tony to offer him the book. He accepted it at once and in June 1933 the novel appeared, to immediate acclaim. . . . 'Intense, troubling, semi-miraculous – a work of art. In the biting crystal air of the book, the children and the nuns stand out like early morning mountains. . . .' wrote Elizabeth Bowen at a later date, and critics at the time were equally enthusiastic.

Tony had suddenly become known, but unfortunately

Harmsworth was a small firm with no real selling organization, and its proprietor a wealthy young man with other interests besides his business. Consequently sales did not follow the book's critical approval and it would be long before Tony got more than her original £50 advance. Meantime our money troubles had closed in on us, and when I got home one night to find a demand for £70 income tax on our freelance earnings for the past two years, we were both desperate. We had sold the only picture we had that seemed saleable in an earlier crisis, and now owned nothing that looked as if it would bring in £20. On top of this Tony, who had worked long hours in advertising, left her bag and pay packet in a taxi, helplessly watching as it vanished down the road. At this point I remembered that many years earlier when we were all still living at home, Austin had written that he was setting aside £1000 worth of stock in his firm for each of us; surely this should be good enough to secure a loan of £100 from the bank? But when I saw the bank manager, he explained that since Austin's was a private company with no Stock Exchange quotation I would need to get a letter from him setting some definite value on the shares. I therefore wrote to my uncle, unaware that he was himself having financial difficulties with his firm. He had written about these to my father, and presuming that I too had knowledge of the situation replied sharply, saying he could not afford to have the bank come down on him for £1000 through my failure to redeem an overdraft. Instead he asked me to return the share certificate and enclosed £500 in final settlement.

We gazed at this lifeline unbelievingly. Tony had often said, 'Why can't we find someone to invest a thousand pounds in us *now*, while we're wanting it so badly? I'm sure we're good bets – they could have it all back with interest in ten years.' And now here it was, or half of it at least. To have sent the cheque back would have been gratifying, possibly noble; but we could not afford gratification or nobility. After paying off all our debts and having the worst parts of the flat redecorated, we still had nearly half the money left. We decided to take £50 each to spend, putting the rest in the bank to be touched only in 'a *most dire* emergency'.

'I'm spending my fifty on clothes,' Tony declared. '*What* a field day I'll have! What will you spend yours on? Clothes, too? I must say you look as if you need them.'

'No. I'm going to buy myself a boat.'

'A *boat*? You mean – to sail about in? Whatever *for*?'

It seemed indeed a crazy plan, but over the next two or three years it proved for me a life-saver. I had given up playing football when we got married, and badly missed the exercise. After six years in London I was quite unreconciled to living entirely among brick walls and found myself constantly thinking of the countryside, at times imagining there were mountains visible from the Fulham Road. Walking one day along the Embankment at high tide and seeing a few small boats tossing at their moorings, I had resolved that if ever I could scrape enough money together I would buy one. There were not many pleasure craft on the London river in those days. With the constant strings of barges towed by tugs and coal-carrying vessels coming up as far as the Fulham power station, it was more like a watery motorway. Up by Teddington indeed were plenty of small racing craft and some seagoing cruisers for those who could afford them, but the former would be useless for my purpose and the latter beyond reach. What I was looking for was a boat I could keep in Chelsea but solid enough for sailing in the open sea; it must have some kind of engine to get home against the tide, and it must not cost more than £50. At last, in *Scud* I found what I thought might serve. She was old and slow, but the hull was solid; there was a cabin the size of a dog kennel, no comforts or conveniences, a fairly new set of sails and an old Renault taxi engine dating from 1910. I got her for £45, and set to work to learn to sail by taking her to a quiet part of the river, putting the sails up one at a time and seeing what happened.

Being an ignorant seaman with a hard-to-handle boat, I several times got into trouble. Once on a specially strong tide *Scud* was carried under an overhead footbridge which ran down to a landing stage – the mast caught in the ironwork and the boat heeled over, over . . . further than she had ever been before. Then, just as the tide started to pour in, the mast snapped, the rigging fell all over me, and the tide swept us through. All I needed now was a new mast, which Bill, an old seaman I had got to know, shaped up for me using nothing but an axe. Another time, trying to moor *Scud* by chains in a racing tide, I pulled myself out of the tiny dinghy into the water. My seaboots filled and I thought I should never manage to clamber back on board. When at last I fell head first over the engine and felt water from the boots pour up my back, I lay for a minute or two, gasping thankfully but without strength to raise myself off the floorboards.

In the course of a tide, using the engine, I could run down to the sea, then sleep on board in some creek or backwater, and come home on the next tide; in this way I got to know a whole new London of the waterside instead of the too-familiar one accessible by tubes and buses. A missing element had come back into my life; I began to feel interested and confident, and the recurring attacks of so-called flu which I had been getting every two or three months – causing me much anxiety when I was forced to miss time at the office – came less often, until finally they vanished altogether.

But it was not only *Scud* which had started to transform my life, there had been a change for the better in work as well. Though I had encouraged Tony to write her book and been happy with her over its success, I was not happy to be introduced at parties as 'the husband of Tony White who's just written that marvellous book'. I longed to achieve some success of my own, and now several factors combined to push me in a political direction.

I was working for, though not on, a Labour newspaper, the *Daily Herald*, whose views I had started to assimilate. Back in 1926 at the time of the General Strike, I had readily come up from Oxford to act as a strikebreaker; in 1931 when the National Government came in, I had voted for it as a matter of course, but I now began to be appalled at its incompetence and complacency. There were other, more personal reasons. Our money troubles of the last few years had made me realize how differently life is organized for those who have and those who lack, and when in the company of rich people I found their callousness – particularly over the rising number of

140

unemployed – as offensive as though it was some repellent disease.

The 'two worlds' of Britain had been brought home to me also in another way. While at Crawford's, uneasy over the work I was doing and seeking compensation, I had become a prison visitor. One evening a week, as far as I could manage, I would go down to Wormwood Scrubs to visit some of the eight or ten prisoners on my list, becoming familiar with the sounds and sights and smells, the conventions and private means of communication of prison life. Each man had a card outside his door giving details of his name, charge and length of sentence. These were kept back to front so that other prisoners, supposedly, could not read them; but all prisoners were adept at flipping the cards up, reading and dropping them back into place. As a visitor, of course, I was entitled to examine the cards of those I came to see, and in my early days would expect a prisoner convicted of violent crime to be a powerful villain, and would unlock his cell door with trepidation – only to find a small man crouched in a corner on his bed, looking fearfully up at me as though I might be intending to do him grievous bodily harm.

My idea in visiting prisoners was not to give them good advice, still less any intention to reform them, but I supposed some might occasionally be glad to talk to a new face or that I might at times be able to assist a man in some practical way. Where this was possible it frequently involved visiting his family in some decaying part of London. Climbing the stairs of a slum building to a single room where a wife and four children lived with rain running down the inside of the wall, I began to appreciate the inadequacy of a system in which a man, finding life unbearable, robs or batters a neighbour and then once inside prison is at least warm and fed, while his family is neither. Often a wife had no idea what assistance might be available nor of where and how to get it, and if she tried to apply could too easily be frightened off by a casual or hostile clerk. There was then no welfare state, but I started to think that there ought to be one.

One of my activities, as Tony and I sat dutifully at our desks, had been to keep a book of newspaper cuttings into which I would paste whatever caught my eye, usually the more heartless and stupid of official utterances.

'I think you are mad,' the magistrate told the prisoner, 'and this Court considers you are mad. If you are found to be mad, you will be sent to Broadmoor where you will be detained for the remainder of your life.'

Now I increasingly began to concentrate on the statements made by ministers on current political issues; friends to whom I sometimes read these out would find them funny, and I began to consider whether I could put them together into a series of newspaper articles or possibly a book. Then one night when Tony was out at a party on her own and I had gone to bed early, I woke up, went directly to my desk and started to write down the title page for a book which had not yet even been conceived.

A STRONG HAND AT THE HELM

Being a Complete and Final Vindication of
the sincerity, lucidity, penetration and profundity
of our Prime Minister, the

Right Hon. J. RAMSAY MACDONALD

Manifesting in the sight of all
the Transparency of his Natural Eloquence
and Providing an Abundant Answer to
the Malevolence of all Carping Critics.

It was to be an attack disguised as a defence and to consist entirely of extracts from speeches made by ministers and a few of their principal supporters. All I should contribute would be the arrangement of the quotations and the dedication: 'with feelings of unspeakable gratitude and awe to the National Government – The Men Who Pulled us Through'. There were not many cuttings in my paste-up book that could be used, but I knew where to find the rest and over the next weeks, much excited, I spent my spare time in the cuttings library of the *Daily Herald* checking through Hansard and reading the reports of political speeches from all over the country. Elated by my haul, I arranged them under suitable headings and combed the

picture library for the most ludicrous and telling photographs –
my first experience of working in photography.

When the whole thing was complete I took it round to Victor
Gollancz, whose Left Book Club was the publishing success of
the moment, and listened as he sat reading my own extracts
back to me.

'Great words and great phrases like justice and so on very often mean
nothing and have serpents concealed in their folds.' – Prime Minister,
in his speech to the Disarmament Conference at Geneva. Reported in
The Times, 17 March 1933.

'Like so many, it [the Labour Party] thinks it can both eat its cake
and have it and carry on a propaganda on that assumption.' – Prime
Minister, in reply to resolution of Bradford Labour Party, *Daily
Herald*, 10 June 1933.

'We may still have to cut our coats according to the cloth, but the
coats will be much bigger than any reflecting man could have
imagined to be possible eighteen months ago.' – Prime Minister, in a
letter to Mr Drummond Wolff, National Conservative candidate at
Rotherham, *The Times*, 23 February 1933.

'Some are already able to point out the light at the end of the tunnel.
I myself see it somewhat indistinctly ... but I like to think we shall
meet here next year, then I believe we shall see clearer where we are
going and be sensible of the rapid pace at which we have been
proceeding.' – Governor of the Bank of England, Mr Montagu
Norman, at banquet given by the Lord Mayor, *Daily Telegraph*, 21
October 1932.

Gollancz brought it out very quickly. Since my name meant
nothing and the book was put forward as a defence of the
National Government, I signed it 'Vindicator'. On the day it
came out, the *Evening Standard* made a half-page from the
pictures, and reviews were soon pouring in ... a whole page
in the *New Statesman*, a leader in the *Manchester Guardian*. The
Daily Herald praised this 'biting exposure of the "National"
Government's incompetence, inconsequence and incon-
sistency'.

At last, I thought, after six years in the barren wilderness, I
am going to be a journalist! My ambition had always been to
join the *Manchester Guardian* and become one of its leader

writers, so might this not now be possible? I rang their Fleet Street office and arranged to see the London editor. He agreed that his paper had rated my book highly, but when I asked whether in view of this it might possibly employ me, he looked blank and inquired what experience I had as a reporter? I recounted all that had happened since the *Westminster Gazette* went down, and he advised me to spend some years on less important papers before coming back to talk to him again. His advice seemed to land me straight back at square one, and at this point I abandoned for good my *Guardian* ambition and made an appointment to see John Dunbar, the grey-haired Scot who managed Odhams Newspapers. He was deaf, inaudible, and seemed at first doubtful of my claim, but when I explained that all the work had been done in the *Herald* library and all the pictures borrowed from its files, he chuckled.

'And you say you're in our publicity department? Just across the road with Surrey Dane?'

I nodded.

'And you want to get into editorial – on to one of our newspapers or magazines?'

'Yes.'

'And so, of course, you should! I shall have a word with Dane about it.'

In this way, without fuss or bother, the wall I had been hammering against for the past six years fell down, and I walked through. When all arrangements had been made and I went into the publicity department to collect my few belongings, the colleagues I was leaving looked at me with envy – all except Chester, who gave me the distrustful stare of a commissar forced to shake hands with a worker he had always suspected of secretly harbouring independent thoughts.

12

A Fresh Start or Two

When Dunbar said he would take me over to the editorial side, he had something definite in mind. A few years earlier when Odhams conceived the idea of making a popular Labour newspaper, their eyes had turned naturally to the *Daily Herald*, founded back in 1912 and edited for years by one of the grandfathers of the Labour Party, George Lansbury. As a newspaper it was a failure, constantly requiring fresh cash transfusions from the party and trade unions, but it had made an honourable name for itself which was worth preserving; also, from a financial point of view, it is often more economical to revive an ailing publication than to start entirely from scratch. In order to get possession of the *Herald* – and to secure the unions' support in building up the new paper's sale – Odhams had been obliged to take over a printing works owned by the TUC, the Victoria Press. This was not so much a white elephant as a moribund mammoth – a collection of elderly machinery and bad debts. Among the latter was a small newspaper called *The Clarion* with an unusual history and, like the *Daily Herald*, an honourable name, though by this time one little known outside Labour party circles.

In the 1890s, before cars came to dominate roads built for the brief heyday of the stage coach, there had been a short alliance between two oddly assorted partners – socialism and the bicycle. Robert Blatchford, a journalist who had spent some years as a private soldier, founded *The Clarion* in 1891 as a weekly paper on a capital of £400. Its blend of biblical socialism with love of the countryside caught the mood of the time and the magazine prospered. Earnest young tradesmen and craftsmen took to their cycles at weekends to explore the 'merrie England' of which Blatchford wrote in a book that would ultimately sell two million copies, and discussed plans for a socialist Britain in evening classes and at Workers' Educational Societies during the week. *The Clarion* was their bible, and a network of Clarion cycling clubs carried its message round the country and pushed its circulation up to 60,000.

By 1934, however, most of the clubs had gone the way of the stage coach, and *The Clarion*'s trumpet call had sunk to a feeble quaver. With circulation at 15,000 and next to no advertising, it appeared doomed to rapid extinction. But then Dunbar had an idea. If encyclopedias and sets of Dickens had induced two million homes to buy the *Daily Herald* six times a week, surely similar offers could entice a quarter of that number, the politically conscious, to pay twopence a week for a 'poor man's *New Statesman*'. He managed to convince his colleagues and the project went ahead.

The chosen editor was a young Australian, Bob Fraser, then a *Herald* leader writer, who would afterwards become better known as Sir Robert, director general of the Central Office of Information, and later first director general of the Independent Television Authority. Our political bloodhound, chief unearther of scandals, parliamentary commentator and diplomatic correspondent was a lean, sardonic young man with a forceful sense of humour and a laugh that could shatter window panes, Claud Cockburn. His privately produced roneoed sheet, *The Week*, after only a few issues had become as much required reading among pre-war journalists as *Private Eye* – in which he would also have a hand – thirty or forty years later.

When I joined the staff as assistant editor in January 1934, we had only a few weeks left before our first issue appeared in March, and by the time it did, advertising and special introductory offers had boosted initial circulation to a ludicrous 400,000. Three months later when the period for which our readers had 'registered' with their newsagents ran out, we came face to face with the harsh facts of life. Each issue had sold less well than the one before and now not even the offer of tea sets and pairs of trousers – for 'merely the cost of packing, postage, and insurance' – would induce them to sign on for another thirteen weeks; the paper provided them, they said, with far too much to read, and far too little to enjoy.

As the extent of our failure became known, depression settled on us like an icy fog. Bob was continually in conference with management. Claud, who had had the good sense not to give up *The Week*, applied himself to its production. I, after reflecting that my second entry into journalism had proved as fatal to *Clarion* (for we had dropped 'The' from the title) as my first had to the *Westminster Gazette*, wrote to Bob offering to jump overboard if it would help to lighten the ship. My letter joined the pile of correspondence the editor had no time to look at, and was in fact only opened weeks later after all our fates had been decided.

At this crisis, Odhams, for perhaps the first and only time in its existence, was prepared to consider something altogether new; and at this precise moment that something arrived in the form of Stefan Lorant, a Hungarian journalist who had been editor of the German picture magazine *Münchner Illustrierte Presse*. Imprisoned by the Nazis in March 1933, he had been released later that year through the intervention of the Hungarian government, and after a spell working in Budapest had recently arrived in London. Something or other brought him to Odhams Press, to whom he now put forward the idea of a picture magazine on the lines of those which had proved so successful in Germany.

Reputations far beyond those of its staff were at stake in *Clarion*'s failure and Dunbar convinced his colleagues in management that rather than close the magazine down, it would be wiser to give this new idea a trial and hope to save part of their investment. And so, with almost no publicity and under the feeble title *Weekly Illustrated*, the first popular picture magazine in Britain came into existence in the summer of 1934, carrying for a very few issues only the message in small type 'incorporating *Clarion*'.

The magazine's formula was by no means new or striking,

but it was at least built around pictures, and for the first months while Lorant was there, it had a touch of originality both in the selection of photographs and in layout. Also it imposed no great strain on its readers' minds, for which they were evidently grateful since the circulation rose as rapidly as *Clarion*'s had fallen, and was soon established at the satisfactory level of over a quarter of a million.

Meantime Bob, eager to join Lorant in the new venture, had been posted back to leader writing, and I, whose chief ambition it was to become a leader writer, was instructed to remain on *WI* and write captions for the photographs. The magazine's first, and indeed its only editor, was Maurice Cowan, who had become well established in Odhams while editing *Picturegoer*, a magazine for film fans. Unfortunately Cowan and Lorant did not get on together, and the fact that Lorant chose to keep his own hours rather than those observed by the rest of the staff did not make things easier, so that after only a few months I learned that he was leaving. In the short time I had been working with him I had come to realize, first, that Lorant understood photographs as no one else I had ever met understood them. He had been both a still and movie cameraman – he claimed to have been cameraman on Marlene Dietrich's first film – and he thought in pictures not words, appearing to possess a mental record of any photograph he had ever seen and where he saw it. Second, I had come to recognize photography as a journalistic weapon in its own right, so that if – like myself at that time – you are determined to promote causes and affect conditions, photographs can be a potent means for doing so.

Towards the end of the year, when Lorant told me he was going, I tried to reason with him. 'Look Stefan, you imagine that somewhere in the world there exists a perfect proprietor. He'll say to you, "Stefan! You're a genius. Just do whatever you want and I'll support you!" But there *is* no perfect proprietor – nowhere in the world. He hasn't been invented.'

'Tom,' he told me. 'I cannot work where I am not appreciated, and no one here understands what I am doing. *No one!* Not even you.'

In a last effort I went to see Dunbar and told him that if

Lorant was sacked or allowed to go, the paper was being sacked as well. Dunbar heard me out and then inquired, 'D'you want to keep your job?'

With a wife and two children, plus a number of unrealized ambitions, I answered, 'Yes.'

'In that case,' said Dunbar not unkindly, 'I advise you to shut up.' And that, so far as journalism was concerned, was what I did. I got on with my work during office hours and outside them applied myself increasingly to my own writing.

During the four years I was on *Weekly Illustrated*, having no Jerome Chester driving me, I started to write stories. I had not the concentration, nor indeed the theme, on which to write a book, which would also have taken too long to be of help in the money troubles which soon gathered round Tony and myself as the last of our £500 melted away. In a single weekend, however, telling myself that as a writer I must surely be able to earn something, I wrote three stories. One went straight into the wastepaper basket. The second, a story about climbing based on memories of the Lake District and called 'Mountain Madness', was at once accepted by *Blackwood's*. The third, which I called 'I Have Been Drowned', would take months, even years, before I could consider it complete. So all the arduous weekend had produced in the present was seven guineas, though the last two stories would be reprinted again and again, earning enough to have solved our money troubles several times over had I been able to draw cheques on the future. On my story of sailing and drowning I worked with special intensity, and at one point during the writing thought, This isn't bad ... but it's a pity I've never actually drowned so as to know what it feels like. It was not long after this that I had the experience already described of pulling myself into the water in a strong tide, struggling to reach my boat, and then feeling I lacked the strength – or in the end could only just find the strength – to clamber out.

Of this story Tony, reading it later on, remarked, 'This isn't really about sailing. It's the record of your marriage to me, which you've welded onto your excitement over the sea and sailing. *I'm* that awful boat – which is sometimes magical but can never be relied on. It's also the discovery of your own powers of endurance.'

After the story had been printed in John Lehmann's magazine *New Writing*, I sent it to the BBC and was asked to read it a couple of times over the air. It was difficult to read, being over-carefully written, but there was a producer at the BBC who took great trouble in helping me turn it from a story to be read into a story to be heard, explaining the sort of changes needed to make a sentence sound natural, and showing me tricks of the trade, such as the difficulty in saying several words in succession which begin or end with *s*. He had fair hair, a roving blue eye and a heated look. Several times over the next few years I would come across him at the BBC when I had stories or pieces to read, and found him always willing to take trouble in getting the best out of them. Some years later I read that he had disappeared, and remembered that his name had been Guy Burgess.

A new job and a boat were not all the year 1934 would bring. As the pressures of our life increased, there were signs that the attack of madness which Tony had suffered twelve years earlier, the memory of which continually haunted her, was about to be repeated. One night she had a dream, and since we both kept notebooks in which we put down whatever seemed to us important, I noted this.

For the past ten days Tony has been upset in her mind. Last night she dreamed that she and I were walking through the streets of a little old town. Down one cobbled street we came to a cinema and went inside. There was a film showing, and the heroine's face came up on the screen. She had fair hair sticking out on each side of her head with a small blue cap on top. 'She looked rather like me when I was sixteen,' Tony explained. Her name, which was also the title of the film, was Sanity Crise.

Following this, her dreams became more frightening. Mushrooms and toadstools were growing out of her forehead. She was consuming her own brains served to her on a plate.... During the day she would be quiet, and managed to continue doing journalistic work and even some writing of her own, but at night she would fall heavily asleep, only to wake in the early hours from a hideous nightmare with the urgent need to talk it over before, by slow degrees, she could be induced to settle down again. A consequence, as I noted in my book, was:

I have developed an odd technique for answering without waking up. The answers satisfy Tony, but are not always to the point. The other night she dreamed there was a man following her round the flat. She woke up in horror – he must be a keeper, and she must already have gone mad.

'Is there a man in the flat?'
'Yes,' I answered, still asleep.
'What is he, Tom?'
'Oh, just a caretaker or animal taker.'

This improbable explanation reassured her; a caretaker would have the right to be around, and by 'animal taker' she understood someone who takes care of animals, whom Tony, with her passion for cats, would look upon as a friend. She turned over and went to sleep.

But such calming incidents were few. I soon began to find on her desk and mine pages in 'looking-glass writing', with everything reversed, and remembered her having told me that she had written like this in the asylum. Before long she had tried to fling herself out of the window, and at other times got up in the night and, half dressed, set off running for the Embankment and the river. At this time I knew very little about psychoanalysis but after discussions with Eric, who knew more than I did, I wrote to the analyst William Brown, much renowned for his successful treatment of shell-shocked men in the First World War, who kindly made time for us both to see him. After the interview Tony visited him a number of times for treatment, and he then recommended her to undertake a full analysis with a much younger analyst, Dennis Carrol.

For her sufferings over these months I had my own responsibility to carry because, though physically present, emotionally I was somewhere else – a fact which Tony would have perceived even if I had been much better at concealment than I was. In the spring of 1934 I had fallen in love; there were factors on both sides which finally drove us apart, but at this

OF THIS OUR TIME

crucial time I was not inwardly present in the same world as Tony and so could not provide the wholehearted support she was looking for and needed.

In the effort to understand and contain an emotional state which carried me far beyond anything I had experienced and shook the pattern of life I had been carefully constructing for myself, I wrote over the next six years two stories. 'Over the Bridge', completed in 1936, is concerned solely with the inner impact of an experience which is never described, since I found myself unequal to writing about my feelings or to conveying an adequate impression of the woman who was their object. 'She isn't pretty,' Tony remarked in one of those flashes of detachment of which she was capable even in the course of a violent argument. 'Really I suppose what she has is a special kind of plainness. But I can see that if you are drawn to such a plainness, then you'll never look at a pretty face again.'

In 'The Third Secretary's Story,' which I wrote during 1940 despite all the demands and pressures of the war, I contrived, by transposing the setting to the Balkans and the period to before the First World War, to approach some degree or two nearer to reality. In this attempt I must have been at least partially successful since a well-known diplomat, who was also a writer, rang Cyril Connolly, the editor of *Horizon*, to inquire who this Hopkinson might be. He had, he said, known all members of Foreign Office staff who were serving in the Balkans in this period, and there had been no Hopkinson among them.

For a number of years it was in my mind to write a third version based directly upon the actual experience, but I was never able to carry out this intention.

Over succeeding years there have been two strange sequels to the appearance of the stories. Cyril Connolly, who first published 'The Third Secretary's Story' in *Horizon* for April 1941, reprinted it two years later in *Horizon Stories*, a selection from those which had appeared hitherto in his magazine. In the same collection he also included 'A Moment of Truth' by Antonia White. Based on a holiday we spent in Brittany in the summer of 1934, this gives her impression of our emotional

152

crisis, and in his introduction to the book Connolly shrewdly observed, 'Antonia White is the author of *Frost in May* and Tom Hopkinson is editor of *Lilliput* and *Picture Post*. Between their two long stories, one so male and the other so female in point of view, there is a link which it may amuse psychologists to try to fathom.'

Evidently catching this hint, James Stern, himself a talented story writer, in reviewing the American edition of the *Horizon* collection for the magazine *New Republic* (28 April 1946) observed:

Of the dozen authors chosen by Mr Connolly, few are known in this country; but there are several who deserve to be. Of these, two – Antonia White and Tom Hopkinson – stand out.... 'A Moment of Truth' is a strange and remarkable achievement for a woman. It is the study of a married couple – a rather dull, long-suffering man and a madly neurotic wife – who "find for the first time in their life together ... complete accord" only after she realizes that he has desired her death and he has acknowledged this truth to himself. Tom Hopkinson's work, oddly enough, has something of the same quality. Both writers are preoccupied with aberrations of the mind. Hopkinson, however, gains his effects by a less strained, less impressionistic prose. Effortless and classic in style, it flows like a river over a smooth bed of sand. And, despite his insistence on realism, he manages to insert into everything he undertakes an element of fantasy, of the supernatural, describing both states in a manner so natural that what is manifestly abnormal human behaviour you accept not only as normal, but inevitable.

The praise, whether justified or not, helped me for a time to overcome my self-doubts as a writer.

These were contemporary reactions to work which had recently appeared. Far more extraordinary to me was the fact that, forty years later, two distinguished actors working with the National Theatre should happen to come across a collection of my early work. This was *The Transitory Venus*, a collection of nine stories published by *Horizon* in 1946 in the course of a brief incursion into book publishing. Two stories in particular appealed to them, and I was contacted to ask if I would be willing to prepare shortened versions of 'Over the Bridge' and

153

'The Third Secretary's Story' for Simon Callow and Paul
Scofield to read for the BBC on Radio 3, which I was indeed
happy to do.

Some time in 1935, becoming more deeply involved in her
analysis, Tony decided to live on her own and took a room not
far away in Chelsea. She continued to come round and see the
children, but inevitably I was now much more in their company
and fortunately it was company I enjoyed, finding it at the same
time stimulating and restful, stimulating because of their
natural intelligence and liveliness, restful because their emotional demands seemed not difficult to satisfy.

Susan, who was at this time about six, and Lyndall, who was
four, were very different in character. Susan was introverted,
self-absorbed, imaginative and poetic. Almost from the first she
attempted to speak in sentences, not broken words; she used
language to be expected from a child twice her age; and would
go white with concentration in trying to find the exact
expression she wanted.

Once I took her down to the Embankment on a day of racing
tide, water pouring past almost level with the pavement,
carrying down planks and tree trunks which rolled and turned
over in the flood. There was a driving mist and I could see she
wanted to go closer still, so carried her along the pier till we
were right out over the river. She gazed silently for a while and
then said: 'I'm the sort of person that likes coldness and wetness
and loneliness and lostness.'*

As both Tony and I worked, from the first we had needed a
nurse for the children and had been fortunate indeed in finding
one who was young, warm-hearted and capable, but not so
strong-minded as to make their life a burden – indeed they
sometimes made life a burden for her. Once a month Mary took
a much-needed weekend off, and then the children and I would
come face to face with reality and one another. On a Saturday in
one such weekend I was woken early by an uproar. Angrily I

---

*Susan today is Susan Chitty, wife of Sir Thomas Chitty, better known as
the novelist Thomas Hinde. Her two most recent books have been lives of
Charles Kingsley and Gwen John.

padded down the corridor to find Susan standing on her bed and Lyndall sitting up in her cot, both roaring and squealing.

'Stop it! What on earth's all this?'

'This is a palace,' Susan explained, 'in the middle of a jungle – the biggest jungle in the world. But the palace hasn't any walls, only statues where the walls are.'

'But statues don't shout.'

'*We're* not the statues,' Susan said disdainfully. 'We're very old stone wireless sets. But the only noise we can get in the jungle is the animals roaring.'

Lyndall's nature was warmer and more gregarious. She was more concerned with colour and form than with use of words. She made friends easily and when I took them both to school she would disappear arm in arm into the throng, while Susan hovered in the doorway. In the evening when I got home and had settled down to read, I would hear Lyndall's step outside the door, call to her to come in and she would appear dangling her favourite toy, Nibby, a rabbit, by one arm.

'Have you got everything you want?' she would inquire. 'Have you got a drink?'

'Yes, thank you.'

'What's that in your wastepaper basket?'

I looked. 'It's *The Times* local government centenary special supplement.'

'*Ooh*! May I have it?'

'Certainly!'

'Can I *keep* it – or shall you want it back?'

'You can keep it for yourself.' She went off happily with her treasure.

After a year or so, Tony's living on her own eased tension for her, and the recovery of her natural wit showed that she was slowly coming back to normal. We would meet for dinner every week or two, and after getting home I would occasionally jot down something she had said, just as I did with the children's talk.

Of a rich friend who was always complaining of his love troubles: 'To listen to the way K. goes on, you'd think he'd never been divorced before.'

155

'When a woman's in love with you, she doesn't want much – only to have you constantly under her eye. That's all.'

'When I'm in love I prefer not to have lunch with the man. There's just enough time to quarrel, but not enough to get over it.'

We had our quarrels too. During one of them at the flat she flung a cup of tea at me, which – having many times watched Tony throwing things at wastepaper baskets – I avoided by remaining perfectly still. Mopping up the mess, we recovered our tempers and she remarked, 'I *do* think you might be nicer to me. After all, I've given you the five third-best years of my life.'

After a year or so, as her recovery continued, Tony decided to return to Cecil Court and take charge of the children, and I accordingly moved out to a room of my own a few hundred yards away. By 1937, both of us having formed new ties, we agreed to end the marriage.

13
Success

After his sudden departure from *Weekly Illustrated* I had not lost touch with Stefan Lorant. I knew he had had some success with his book *I was Hitler's Prisoner*, and that he wrote articles for the *Daily Mirror* and other papers; I would also hear of him from girls I knew, but whom he had evidently got to know a great deal better than I had. Then in the summer of 1937 I came across him again as we were both walking through Covent Garden, picking our way among the squashed fruit and cabbage stalks. He looked despondent.

'How're you doing, Stefan?'

He frowned. 'The editors in this country, they do not like my work. Or if they like it, they do not pay enough. There is only one thing for me to do.'

'What's that?'

'I become an editor myself.'

A few weeks later, on £1200 lent him by a girl-friend, he launched his delightful pocket magazine *Lilliput*, now a collector's item. It was an immediate success, but carried no advertising and at sixpence was costing more to produce than it brought back in sales; in addition it was being publicized, not expensively in the press but with small humorous posters on selected stations in the London tube. Experts at Odhams assured me it could not last three months, but I knew that Lorant was not the man to start a new publication without a clear idea of how it could be made to pay, and *Lilliput* did not fold after three months, nor after six. When the first £1200 was almost gone, Lorant met a shrewd and talented young journalist named Sydney Jacobson,* lately back from India with a gratuity earned by working on the *Statesman*. Jacobson put in the gratuity and took out the post of assistant editor, which is where he was in about April 1938 when, having learned that *Lilliput* actually paid its contributors, I went round to the small office in Fetter Lane and asked if there was anything I could supply.

'Write me a piece about the summer term at Oxford,' Stefan said benignly. 'Make it very poetic and romantic.'

This I evidently failed to do because my article was returned not once, but twice. The second time it was handed back by the editor in person, and he summoned Jacobson from a back room to add weight to the rejection. Nettled, I mounted what was intended to be a high horse.

'Look, Stefan, you have people who write the kind of thing you want, and I know magazines which print the kind of things I write. Why waste time trying to bring the two together?'

'Now Tom, you are very angry,' he said reprovingly.

'I'm not angry,' I lied, 'and to prove it I'm asking you to lunch'.

We arranged a date, but when on a morning in June 1938 I rang to fix a place, the secretary told me the editor had gone over to Shoe Lane to see some new firm called Hulton Press. I was to go round and wait by the front door till he came out. This sounded conspiratorial, but I duly went round and waited. Around 1.30 it seemed there would be no one left inside and I was about to leave when Lorant ran down the stairs. I had just time to notice his new suit and silk shirt when he seized my arm and hurried us down the street. Not until we were well clear of the building did he speak.

'Tom – I am a very rich man! Very rich men lunch only at the Savoy – we go to the Savoy!'

Over lunch he told me that he had lately sold *Lilliput* to the Hulton firm (at a price generally assumed to be £20,000) and was now planning to start a new magazine.

*Now Lord Jacobson.

'They have told me to make a Conservative weekly on the lines of the *Spectator*. But what I shall give them is a picture magazine.'

'In that case,' I said, 'I'm joining you. I insist on being taken on.'

Lorant seemed less than enthusiastic, but before lunch was over had agreed that I should call in and see Hulton's general manager, Maxwell Raison. Raison offered me the post of assistant editor on the new magazine at a salary of twenty guineas – two more than I was getting at Odhams – and when I went to see Dunbar he treated it as an application for more money.

'Go and have a talk with Maurice Cowan. I'm sure he can fix you up with something.'

'But that isn't it,' I said. 'I don't want more money. I'm leaving to start a new paper with Lorant.'

'Lorant? You always did support that fellow – why can't you have more sense? Even if your new magazine got started, we couldn't afford to let it become established. It might affect our own properties, *Weekly Illustrated, Passing Show, John Bull*. ...'

That, I said, would not be my problem. I was now giving in my notice and joining the new paper; and so, after the necessary four weeks, I did.

Unlike most firms which set out to produce new magazines, Hulton Press rested on a secure financial basis, as I had taken pains to find out. Its proprietor Edward Hulton, a year or two younger than myself, was the son and grandson of newspaper owners. His grandfather, a compositor on the *Manchester Guardian*, had launched the *Sporting Chronicle* in 1871, and from this modest beginning his father Sir Edward Hulton had built up a newspaper empire to include the *Daily Dispatch, Daily Sketch* and *Evening Standard*. For this, on his retirement in 1923, he was said to have received £6 million. Young Edward (Teddy), it was understood, had not been able to gain full control of his inheritance until attaining the age of thirty, but this happy day had dawned in November 1936, and the newly established Hulton Press was already owner of the *Farmer's*

Weekly, Nursing Mirror and one or two other journals, to which *Lilliput* had now been added.

Besides Hulton himself, the business side included Maxwell Raison, a man of easy manners, but shrewd under the geniality.* He had only lately ceased to play cricket for Essex, loved the countryside and horses and devoted as much time as he could to such interests and to his young family. W. J. Dickenson, the financial controller, had served Hulton's father as confidential clerk in charge of his horse-racing interests. Bluff, kindly when not thwarted but fond of laying down the law, Dickenson had an acute financial brain. When we journalists read our papers we would be thinking, What will Hitler's next move be? And when will our government wake up?, but the message Dickenson's eyes took in was different. Indeed I don't think he actually *read* newspapers at all. He just looked at them like a medium gazing into a pool of ink; then coloured lights flashed, cranks whirred and a ticket came out saying, 'Sell Consolidated Goldfields and get into cement and bricks.' Or vice versa. Yet he was an emotional man and far from being solely interested in money.

On the editorial side of the new magazine there was nothing but Stefan Lorant, myself and a secretary. We had two German photographers working as freelances, Hans Baumann (later known as Felix H. Man) and Kurt Hubschmann (afterwards Kurt Hutton). They had left Germany in 1934 following Hitler's rise to power, and had contrived with difficulty to subsist in Britain ever since. With the passage of time both today have become internationally renowned as cameramen to an extent the gentle, conscientious Hutton at least would never have expected. Very different in talents and outlook, they made an excellent basis for a photographic team, but we could hardly launch a new magazine on two cameramen and no writers but myself. The arrangement made with Lorant was that he would handle the picture side and I should be

*Later, as an independent publisher he would launch *New Scientist* and *New Society*. One of his sons, Timothy Raison, would become a Conservative MP and a junior minister in Mrs Thatcher's government.

responsible for text and captions. In theory this sounded fine, but I soon found it to be less so in practice, since I could do nothing until he decided what stories to make up and how much space to give them, and Lorant could only work in a creative fervour which would not descend to order, and often not for days on end.

By now we were well into July, and our first issue was expected in September. But we had no dummy and no title, *nothing* indeed except piles of photographs in folders on Lorant's enormous desk. Why, I kept asking, could we not get some of these laid out, so that I could commission articles and write the captions? Why couldn't we make up a dummy so that we all knew what our paper looked like, and the advertising department could go out and sell space?

'Yes, yes ... I do it ... I see to everything! Only not yet. Today I must talk with Mr Hulton. ...' or 'Today I shall argue with the printers,' or 'Today I am having to make up *Lilliput*.' Lorant was a master of delaying tactics, and if pressurized too much would simply vanish. He had kept on his old *Lilliput* offices in Fetter Lane into which he would retreat, a lair to which he only had the key. When at last, however, he could be induced to get down to a problem, he could cut straight to its root. For three weeks now we had been wrangling over just one point – our size of page. Dummies of different shapes and sizes were passed round, and we each had our favourite; management, naturally, wanted the most economical cutting size, but Lorant would not make up his mind. Then one day he handed me a piece of paper. 'This is the size. You must order layout pages.'

'What's so special about this one?' I asked.

The size he had chosen, he explained, was based on the natural enlargement of a 35 mm negative such as all our cameramen would use, plus suitable margins. It was not the cheapest arrangement because some paper would be wasted from each reel, but it meant that we could employ a range of varied layout patterns, using pictures in combinations of upright and across within a single page or double spread. I appreciated the beauty of this at the time, but I appreciated it far more when I came to make the layouts myself; and I appreciate it today every time I look through the Sunday supplements with their boxy, oversquare pages and realize the difficulties the staff are up against in trying to introduce variety into their much too similar displays.

Our next problem was the title. When I demanded to know what the paper was to be called, Lorant had an easy answer. 'You tell *me*, Tom – I am listening!' Our advertising agent, Donald Gillies – my friend from Oxford days, now partner in the firm of Graham and Gillies – had prepared some dramatic material for the launching, but it was all built round the idea that the magazine would be called *Lo!* 'Buy *Lo!* See and know!' was to appear on buses and hoardings, in tubes and mainline stations, backed by a big newspaper campaign.

Most of us were so relieved to have any acceptable suggestion that we were ready to welcome *Lo!*, but again Lorant would not agree. Next day he showed me a page of scribbled suggestions in two columns from which he, or someone, or several of us together, extracted 'Picture' from one column and 'Post' from the opposite one, and this was finally agreed. But there was little enthusiasm for our new magazine under any title. W. H. Smith, on whom so much depended, would order only 30,000 copies for the whole country, which profoundly depressed our circulation department. The advertising people were no happier, having managed to sell fewer than ten pages in an eighty-page magazine out of which they had been expecting to sell thirty.

Top management was just as dubious. Edward Hulton, who had stood twice for Parliament as a Conservative, thought the magazine had a distinctly leftish look. 'Kindly remember,' he instructed us, 'that I am not only a Conservative, I am a loyal supporter of Mr Neville Chamberlain.' To emphasize this, he insisted that the first number must have a battleship on the cover, and to my astonishment Lorant agreed, saying he thought this 'a very good idea'. When at the close of a despondent meeting he and I were asked to give our assurance that the magazine would sell 250,000 copies, I readily gave my guarantee; owning little but a spare suit and a small overdraft,

I considered this a risk I might safely take. But I looked sideways at Lorant who might well – with a presumed £20,000 in the bank from the sale of *Lilliput* – hesitate or blink twice, but his acceptance was immediate. When the meeting broke up I could hardly wait until we were out of earshot.

'Look, Stefan – we've guaranteed quarter of a million. Honestly, now, what d'you think we can sell?'

Lorant shrugged his shoulders and looked down his nose, as he did when he was thinking. 'Maybe hundred thousand. Maybe hundred and fifty. And I tell you, Tom, they are very *happy* if they are getting one hundred and fifty. *Very* happy!'

'But what about the bloody battleship? You know there can only be one thing on the first cover – a girl! A battleship would sink us without trace.'

'I promise you, Tom, there will be *two* girls.'

'Then why did you agree to have a battleship?'

Stefan looked at me pityingly, and vanished shortly – as he did often now that he had become prosperous – to the opera.

At the last moment, with everything ready for the printer, came the scare of war. Chamberlain had gone to meet Hitler for the second time at Godesberg. Could any new project be launched successfully in an atmosphere of crisis? We argued fiercely, however, that if war came everyone would want war pictures so that the magazine would quickly find a public; on the other hand if there was peace, *Picture Post* would be off to a flying start on the general feeling of relief. In the end our argument was accepted and, as we drove down to the printing works at Watford to put the first issue to bed, searchlights and anti-aircraft guns were being sited on rising ground; convoys of troops and guns held up our journey.

Arguing, cajoling, badgering, Lorant had got the initial print order forced up to 750,000 – twice what we expected to sell even with the extra interest every first issue arouses. Vernon Holding, the circulation manager, had performed prodigious feats to get it distributed throughout the trade, while fearing that half at least was likely to come back unsold. On the morning of publication I looked in at his office and saw that he was as exhausted and bad-tempered as myself.

'How's it going?' I asked, when for a moment his phones were silent.

'Don't know. Come back lunchtime.'

'How's it going?' I asked him at midday.

Holding leaned back in his office chair and almost smiled. 'It's gone!' he said thankfully. 'Over the whole east and south of England you can't buy a bloody copy!'

Now, with success, came realization that the effort had to be repeated every week. Because we had had so little time for preparation and not known till a few weeks before the first issue whether we should have a magazine at all, there was virtually no staff, particularly on the writing side. Whenever I complained of this to Lorant his answer had been, 'Find someone to help you out now. Later we look around.' However there had been no time to advertise our wants and none at all for interviewing applicants. I did the best I could, but of the first three to whom I gave a trial, one needed an hour to write half a page; another was tired out by evening, which was when we often started serious work; and the real discovery, Lionel Birch, was carried off to hospital for an appendicitis operation while out on a story late at night. Faced with the task of writing a large part of the magazine myself, I urged Lorant to organize a steady flow of work throughout the week instead of handing me the whole issue in a bundle at the last moment.

'But how do I know which stories I am using till I have planned what is going in the whole paper?' he would snort and glare. 'Anyway I don't know how many pages we are having.'

'But we settled that yesterday – eighty-four.'

'Now I see I was wrong! Eighty-four is not enough. I must have *at least* eight more pages. I see Raison today – or maybe tomorrow.'

Finally the spirit would descend on him. He would gather all the folders of photographs together, order them to be carried to his *Lilliput* office, and from there between seven and midnight a rain of rough layouts would come pouring out, covered with scribbled instructions. 'Get H. G. Wells to write this article. Explain to him yourself exactly what he is to write.' 'This one must be *very funny*.' 'Hore-Belisha [Minister of War] has to see these pictures. He is helping you write the captions,' and so on. Sometimes I would sit looking in despair and rage at the pile of rough layouts covered with impossible instructions before I could summon up the energy to get started. Sometimes we were a day late going to press. Sometimes we were two days late. Once when I remonstrated bitterly that it was hardly worth working that afternoon since we were already so far behind, he replied: 'You are quite right, Tom! We take our children to the circus,' and we did. The printers, astonished and delighted to find a print order for a million copies a week two months after the launching, made prodigious efforts. Once, rather than let us leave their works for dinner, which would have involved an absence of two hours, they ordered in a complete dinner from somewhere which was served to us among the proofs and paste-ups.

When there was snow and heavy frost in the north, Holding and his circulation department organized teams of unemployed men to pass bundles of copies over a snowbound pass to lorries waiting on the further side, having provided supplies of food and hot coffee to keep them working through the night. Success carried everything along. Two months after the first issue our print order was a million. After four months it was 1,350,000.

Though I cursed and complained over difficulties which I felt could be avoided, it was Lorant's sense of timing which made the magazine. He had to feel inside himself just what was wanted. In this way a magazine is something quite different from a newspaper. The newspaper comes in over the tape machines (or 'wire machines' as the Americans call them), also from the dispatches of its correspondents overseas and the material brought in by reporters, so that editing news is largely a matter of selecting, rewriting and arranging material already in existence. But for a magazine like ours, which went on sale more than a week after it had gone to press, the one thing fatal was to follow news. Far better to be capricious – make a number out of life on Mars or the high price of footballers – than base next week's issue on today's events. Anything *can* be right, provided it sells enough copies and contributes to building up the paper's special image.

One morning in November I found Lorant walking up and down his office, black with thought. When angry or concentrated he put on what Raison called his 'rabbit face'; his brow sloped steeply back into his hair, his mouth was compressed to a short line, his eyes glared with suspicion.

'What's the matter, Stefan?'

'This *bloody* Hitler! These *bloody* pogroms! You see the papers?'

'Yes, I know. But ... '

'What do they expect of me? What are the readers wanting me to do? How do I hit back at those *bastards*?'

The result of his hours of walking up and down was a picture story 'Back to the Middle Ages',* in which the most ferocious portraits of the Nazi leaders – Hitler, Goering, Goebbels, Julius Streicher the chief Jew-baiter – were contrasted with the faces of those scientists, writers and actors they were persecuting. Out of all the thousands of picture magazines I have since read and studied, this remains for me the most powerful example of photographs used for political effect. The photographs become cartoons, hammering home their point more effectively than pages of argument and rhetoric, and for me a picture story such as this, or that on 'The Life of an Unemployed Man'† produced by Sydney Jacobson and Kurt Hutton, made up for days of frustration and nights when I walked back to Fulham from Fleet Street because the last tubes and buses had all gone.

Picture Post, 26 November 1938.
†*Picture Post*, 21 January 1939.

14
In Charge

In August 1939 I was in Portugal, having by this time married again. My wife, whose name had been Gerti Deutsch, was Viennese of a Jewish family. She had come into the *Weekly Illustrated* office one day in the early summer of 1937 bringing a portfolio of photographs from an exhibition of her work held at the Austrian embassy in London. Later in that year, together with my brother Paul on leave from the Indian Army, I had travelled to Austria to meet her parents, and in October 1938 we were married. *Picture Post* had only just started and there had been no time for more than an afternoon off, but here we were now on holiday, sitting in the sunshine on a beach at the little fishing town of Nazarré where we had landed up after a slow progress up the coast. It was a truly astonishing place and though we had been here for over a week this was almost the first morning spent in idleness.

In Nazarré there was no port or harbour since the water only just offshore was 100 metres deep; Atlantic rollers pounding in across hundreds of miles of ocean came suddenly up against a shore as steep as a house roof, exploding with a roar which continued day and night, and producing a salty mist which only intensified the sun's heat and glare. The fishermen, barefooted and dressed like biblical seamen in Italian paintings, launched their scimitar-prowed boats into the boiling surf in the interval between two rollers, scrambled aboard and instantly struck out with their oars. On their return, driving high on the crest of a roller, they would crash their boats down onto the shore where teams of dun-coloured oxen waited to haul them into safety. This ceaseless battle with the sea, which went on through all the hours of daylight, so excited us both that from the morning we arrived we had spent almost our whole time working. While Gerti took pictures, dodging around among the fishermen, oxen, drawn-up boats and women spreading sardines on the sand to dry, I wandered about filling a whole notebook with the description of what went on.

But the drama of the beach was not the only one in which we were involved. Living in Nazarré was a little group of expatriates from several nations, centring round two young Germans, a poet, Wolf Berthold, and a doctor, Joe Freyn. Wolf was away, and did not come back until we were actually in the bus on our way to Lisbon, but the others lived in his shadow and talked about him continually. Wolf, Joe said, had left Germany because 'he will not learn to kill other persons. He will rather be killed himself than to kill another person.' Hauled up before a military tribunal and ordered to join the army, he had fled abroad. Joe, with whom Wolf lived, had been imprisoned for refusing to say where he had gone. Since leaving Germany both had been perpetually on the move, unable to get permits to stay anywhere for long, and here they could only remain until November after which they thought they might attempt to find refuge in West Africa.

But now, on this morning of 22 August as we sat at ease in deck chairs among holiday-makers on a part of the beach not used by the fishermen, I glanced idly over a visitor's shoulder at the newspaper he was reading; I knew no Portuguese, but it was not hard to make out what the headline was saying.

'We must go back at once,' I said to Gerti.

'Why?'

'The Nazis have signed a pact with the Russians.'

'So what?'

'So it'll be war tomorrow or next day. I'll phone the embassy in Lisbon.'

The official advised us to take the first boat we could, and after two or three days' hanging around in Lisbon, we found berths on a British ship, the *Delmo*, sailing to Southampton.

There were, I noted, only six passengers abroad, two travelling first-class, two second, and ourselves in the third class. Despite the imminence of war, there was little contact between us, and I spent most of my time writing down all I could remember about Wolf, Joe and their circle, out of which six years later would come a short novel, *Mist in the Tagus*, in effect a memorial to the two wanderers whose wanderings were to end altogether within a year of our meeting.

On 30 August, nearing the coast, it seemed war had actually begun. As we leaned over the rail, a destroyer, her bow wave curling over her foredeck, came racing towards us and, when only about half a mile away, we saw flashes from her guns, heard a shattering report, and a cloud of smoke drifted past. For a moment we thought she must be attacking a submarine, and then far away in the distance saw a tug pulling what seemed like an unusually high barge or a piece of harbour equipment – the target at which the guns were firing. Three or four days later, standing round a radio on a common in Buckinghamshire, we heard Neville Chamberlain declaring war against Germany – the chief reason being, it seemed, that Hitler had lied to him and let him down.

At the outbreak of war many business firms moved out of London since it was generally expected that bombing would begin immediately, there would be wholesale destruction, immense numbers of casualties and disruption of all normal activities. Hulton Press moved to the Watford area, to be near the Sun Engraving Company, which was our printers, and we all found what accommodation we could nearby. Earlier in the summer, convinced that war could not be long delayed I had rented a small cottage in a village called Turville Heath up on the Chilterns between Henley and High Wycombe. Gerti moved out there at once and my daughter Lyndall joined her before long. Then in the spring of 1940, just before the phoney war ended, a lot of firms, our own among them, moved back into London because of the difficulties of operating from outside. I took a room in a small hotel in Lancaster Gate, worked in London all week and went out to our cottage at weekends.

At Christmas 1939 Lorant visited the United States. He had decided to produce a special number of the magazine entirely devoted to the US, much bigger than our normal issues, to be sold as an extra at a higher price. This, he said, would be useful propaganda in winning sympathy for Britain and the purpose of his visit was to collect the necessary material. Before leaving, he talked to me seriously about the running of the paper in his absence; the success of *Picture Post* had been due, he said, to its left-wing policies, determined opposition to nazism and fascism and continued criticism of the Chamberlain soft line on Germany, which the Prime Minister had evidently not abandoned although the countries were officially at war. It was essential, Lorant said, to maintain this strong attitude in the paper and not relax in any way during his absence overseas – with all of which I heartily agreed.

But a few days later, when I was having a drink with the general manager, Maxwell Raison, he remarked, 'What's all this I hear about you being a dangerous Red?'

'What *do* you hear?'

'Stefan has warned us to keep a sharp eye on you while he's in the States because of your left-wing tendencies. He says you're always trying to work things into the paper which could cause us trouble.'

I told him my side of the story, and Raison laughed and asked what I made of it. 'Just keeping us all up to the mark. I'm to be as active as possible. You're to keep careful watch to see I don't get too active.'

Lorant got back to England at the end of January, after which the phoney war did not long continue. The invasion of Norway and the failure of the British expedition sent to help the Norwegians was followed in late spring by the seizure of Belgium and Holland. When, in a few more weeks, France too collapsed, Lorant became convinced that Hitler would be arriving in Britain before long. The British did not mean to fight, and even if they did, their military situation was impossible. The new Churchill government might make defiant noises, but before long it would be forced to accept terms or face invasion; in either case Hitler would soon be in control of Britain, as he was of virtually all the rest of Europe. 'You British citizens will be all right – all you'll lose is the freedom to say what you think. But we bloody foreigners will be handed over.... I've been Hitler's prisoner once in Munich, I'm not waiting for him to catch up with me a second time.' I argued with passionate conviction that somehow this country would survive. America would be forced to come into the war. Financially we should be ruined, but at the end of it we should still be there. He would agree to stay, he said, if he were given British citizenship, which would at least be some protection when the German army landed.

I went to see the Home Secretary, Herbert Morrison, whom I knew from having worked with him in election campaigns, and he told me to go and talk to his assistant, Ellen Wilkinson. She seemed confident that the matter could be arranged, and – following a second interview – I had gone round to her flat for what I hoped might be the final talk, when she surprised me by asking whether I knew that my editor was in negotiation with the American ambassador, Joseph Kennedy, for admission into the United States. I said that I certainly did not know this, and she replied that under these circumstances she could not continue pressing for a special grant of British citizenship.

Only a day or two later Lorant told me he had made up his mind to leave since the British Government had done nothing for him, and he kindly offered to take Tony's and my children, Susan and Lyndall, with him, since a number of people at this time were sending their children to America for safety. I asked Tony her opinion, which was the same as mine. We therefore thanked him for the offer but said the children would remain in Britain. Before he left on the *Britannic*,* the last ship on which it would be possible for private citizens to book a passage, I wrote to him expressing my own debt to him, and thanking him for all I had learned from him. He replied:

I don't want to go. I was never in doubt about this. I want to stay in

*'The *Britannic* held 778 passengers, including 272 children. Among the passengers were Mr Noël Coward, Mr Stefan Lorant, Mme Tabouis and Viscount Stonehaven.' *Daily Telegraph*, 20 July 1940.

this country. I have chosen England as my home – as my fatherland, when I was over thirty – so I knew what I wanted. I love this country with all its faults – with all its weaknesses – because I somehow feel it is my country.

But what can I do – but go?

I have done everything – what I asked was nothing else but a piece of paper which says, 'You are one of us, you belong to us, and if we are attacked you have the right to defend *your* country.' Is it so much to ask for this – for all I have done? Film directors, slick businessmen, German doctors get their naturalizations lately – why should the government keep mine back?

If I would stay and wait – would it be worthwhile to go to a camp – would it influence people's opinion if I did? I came to the conclusion that it would not. Because they wouldn't even know it. I am certain that even my own paper *Picture Post* wouldn't publish *one single line* if I would be arrested. . . .

I am not going for good.

I am hoping that this strange naturalization business gets through when I am away. As soon as I have word that they grant it – I will fly back and go on with our work as though nothing had happened. . . .

In view of his experiences under Hitler, I could well understand Lorant's wishing to have two strings to his bow by applying for naturalization and at the same time arranging for a visa to enter the United States, but it seemed unrealistic to imagine that, once he had gone, there would be any possibility of securing naturalization to allow him to return. In the course of the two years we had been working together, I had come to feel not only great admiration for Lorant but also a real affection for him – or at least for one side of him. For he was, of all the people I had ever known, the one in whom the most contradictory qualities coexisted unresolved. His courage at times astonished me; at others he became preoccupied with self-protection. He could be loyal to his colleagues; or else – overcome with suspicion that they meant to do him harm – would ensure getting his own blow in first. He could be completely realistic or he could expect, and demand, the impossible of life and other people. He could be both generous and its opposite. Thinking over his character after he had left and realizing all he had achieved during only six years in Britain, I felt it was a disaster for the country as well as for the paper that he should now be leaving; but I also, on a personal level, felt relief. This was due partly to ambition and the wish to see if I could cope with the situation left me; but also to the removal of a weight, the problem of working in close cooperation with someone so unpredictable. Yet from his very changeableness, I had learned a valuable lesson. Up until the last two years I had always, I saw, expected men and women to be of one piece; mixtures indeed of a goody and a baddy, but consistent mixtures, or at least more or less consistent mixtures. I knew now that they were not.

I had learned this from looking closely at someone else. It would be some years before I realized that I might have reached the same conclusion much earlier if only I had formed the habit of looking closely at myself.

Lorant had hardly left the country before our two German photographers, Baumann and Hubschmann, were carried off for internment to the Isle of Man. We at once set negotiations in train for their release – which in course of time would prove effective – but meantime we had no cameramen. Sydney Jacobson, with Lionel Birch and Richard Bennett – two of the only writers I had managed to recruit – had all joined the army, so that from a weekly conference of thirteen we were suddenly down to one of five. I was asked by the general manager, Maxwell Raison, whether I thought the paper could be carried on.

The problem weighing on me was that of making the layouts – the choosing, organizing and arranging of the photographs, on which the success of a picture magazine depends just as much as on the work of the photographers. It was this aspect of which Lorant was master, having trained himself in it for the past twelve years, but from the moment he talked of leaving, even though I did not expect him actually to go, I had set myself to learn everything from him that I could. It would always be possible to find someone to take charge of the text, but if the picture side of the magazine were not handled properly our whole enterprise would fail. Accordingly I arranged to see every picture story before it went over to Lorant, and would look carefully through it and try to imagine how I would arrange it into pages; then when it came back later, I would study his layouts and see with how much greater originality he had done the work. But I had been doing this for only a few weeks and was already faced with having to put into practice what, if anything, I had learned.

I asked Raison for a few months' trial, saying that in the meantime I did not want to be appointed editor nor to have my name printed on the title page; we should manage as best we could and discuss my position later when we saw what happened to the paper. With difficulty I managed to persuade my old friend Charles Fenby to leave the *Oxford Mail*, of which he was now editor, and take my place as assistant editor in charge of the writing side. It was a fortunate choice, since with him Charles brought a more thorough journalistic background than I had ever managed to acquire, plus a wide range of acquaintances in various fields of life whom we could call on for articles or advice.

But our first joint task was to gather an effective staff. Honor Balfour, who later stood for Parliament as a Liberal, had been recruited already. Macdonald Hastings – full of knowledge on everything connected with country life and sport – had written several articles for us and now joined the staff. Before long we added Maurice Edelman, a young writer who would become a Labour MP in the 1945 election, and A. L. Lloyd, the expert on folk music, whom the BBC regarded as too left-wing to be allowed to handle programmes during a war for democracy. Our first woman editor was Anne Scott-James, who came to us from *Vogue* and would later become equally renowned for her work in newspapers, magazines and television.

In addition, to my great excitement, we found a remarkable new photographer. Bert Hardy was a young Cockney, the eldest of seven children, who had left school at fourteen. He left on a Friday afternoon and started work on Saturday morning in a printing and developing works at ten shillings a week with sixpence an hour overtime. 'An astonishing number of people sent in filthy pictures. I was fifteen by this time, and when my mother found them in my pocket I told her they were evidence in a court case. My moral sense, I suppose, wasn't highly developed. . . . At ten years old I had been before a juvenile court for stealing "tarry blocks" for the fire.'*

When Bert Hardy came in to see me he was in his twenties and already an experienced cameraman. To try him out I offered him a difficult assignment. The Blitz had started and I asked him to take pictures inside street shelters. No flash must be used and the pictures must make the reader feel he was inside with the shelterers in semi-darkness while bombs were falling. Bert passed the test triumphantly; I at once took him on the staff and he was soon a mainstay of the magazine.

By the end of September I was again sent for by the general manager. He said it was evident that all was going well and they had no anxiety about the paper's future. They asked me to become editor officially and proposed to double my salary, making it up also for the past three months. In this way, just as suddenly as I had found the way into journalism opening out after six years' struggle, I now found my money troubles ended; and in place of a car which had cost £27.10s.0d. and could scarcely ever be coaxed out of the garage, I now had a brand-new one, the first new car I had ever owned, costing no less than £167, and starting whenever I switched the engine on.

*From *Bert Hardy, Photojournalist*, Gordon Fraser, London, 1975. Though the introduction is written by myself, much of the material had been taken down in talks with Bert previously by Brian Dowling, one of his colleagues.

15
Everybody's War

It is hard in the climate of today to form an impression of those times in which men and women having worked a long day in factory or office took on every kind of voluntary work, often for nothing and without waiting for any instruction – and sometimes made free use of buildings or materials without bothering to obtain permission.

All that had happened in the first nine months of war had convinced ordinary people that the country's fate depended on themselves. There was no help in experts; military rank was looked on as a joke and the assurances of politicians had become almost totally discredited. In a statement of sublime fatuity to the House of Commons on 15 April 1940, made the very moment before the storm broke over Europe, Chamberlain declared that Hitler had 'missed the bus'. As country after country fell to the Nazi leaders, his words were quoted again and again as evidence that those in power knew nothing and that we all had only our own determination and commonsense to fall back on. Churchill's accession to power after the fall of France gave confidence that the essentials would now be taken care of, but the old man could not be expected to cope with everything so that we all had still to deal personally with whatever problems came our way.

By midsummer, as the country waited for the promised invasion, one of the most widespread sources of frustration lay with the Home Guard. This body – called originally Local Defence Volunteers and issued with canvas armbands lettered

'LDV' as its sole form of equipment – had come into existence by popular insistence. The War Office, faced with the problem of re-equipping a large part of the British army following the evacuation of Dunkirk, did not want to be bothered with a lot of amateurs and it was only as the result of agitation, particularly in the newspapers, that they had got as far as constituting the LDV an official force at all. The men who immediately joined it in large numbers were not the genial old buffers of 'Dad's Army', but were mainly young men waiting to get into the army or working in reserved occupations, plus a leavening of ex-soldiers from the First World War longing to get back into action. All had only two wishes – to obtain weapons and to secure realistic training. The authorities had their hands full with the armed forces, or thought they had; meantime the LDV were told to wait patiently until someone or other could pay them some attention.

At *Picture Post* we had come to know Tom Wintringham, who had gained experience of German methods of warfare while fighting for the International Brigade in Spain. He was also an excellent writer with a clear style and a vigorous outlook, and in a series of articles during May and June had established himself as the mouthpiece of new ideas and methods of guerrilla warfare. Since these depended little on square-bashing or highly organized staff work – and much on adaptability, local knowledge and ability to live off the country – they made a strong appeal to the freebooting spirit of the day and to the general determination to 'get stuck into things' without waiting for someone in Whitehall to issue permits in triplicate.

One evening in the summer of 1940 Wintringham and I were having dinner with Edward Hulton at his house in Hill Street, and we talked of the frustration in the LDV – recently renamed the Home Guard – over the fact that all they were getting was practice in forming fours when they wanted to learn how to fight, and the question came up, 'Why don't we ourselves provide the training?'

Between dinner and midnight everything was organized. Hulton had a friend, the Earl of Jersey, who owned Osterley

Park, a mansion with lavish grounds just outside London. Hulton phoned him, and he came round at once. Yes, of course, we could have have his ground for a training course; he hoped we wouldn't blow the house up as it was one of the country's showplaces and had been in the family for some time. 'Could we dig weapon pits? Loose off mines? Throw hand grenades? Set fire to old lorries in the grounds?' Wintringham asked. 'Of course! Anything you think useful,' Jersey told him. I asked Wintringham about staff – whom could we get as instructors for such a Home Guard training centre? He at once started noting down the names. Hugh Slater, artist and author, had fought in Spain and planned one of the few success-ful actions on the government side, the crossing of the Ebro; he was also an expert on destroying tanks. Two Spaniards who had been all through the war were now in Britain as refugees and could also be brought in. An expert on camouflage and concealment? Roland Penrose, the surrealist painter. Someone to teach stalking and use of cover? Stanley White, a chief instructor to the boy scouts. Explosives? Wilfred Vernon* – a former senior technical officer at the Royal Aircraft Establish-ment – just the man to improvise mines, grenades and all forms of destruction. For my part I noted down that we should need to rent a couple of small houses near Osterley Park to accommo-date the trainees, but that was no problem since in every London street there were now numbers of houses showing 'to let' signs. We must also get fifty sleeping bags or palliasses to be filled with straw; blankets, cutlery, catering facilities, printed leaflets to send to all units of the LDV offering weekend training. . . .

No time was lost, and the response was instant and fantastic; our 'school' could have been filled three times over. What it taught was simply 'do-it-yourself' war. One afternoon at our headquarters at a small house in Osterley I went through the kitchen to get to the lavatory, passing Vernon who was stir-ring some thick greyish substance in a saucepan. 'What's that

---

*Vernon was later a Labour MP from 1945 to 1951. He died in 1975 at the age of ninety-three.

you've got there?' I asked.

'Dynamite.'

'God Almighty – just let me finish and get out before I lose everything.'

'Don't worry,' Vernon said, 'dynamite doesn't go off from being heated. It goes off from being compressed.'

'Yes – but are you sure it understands that?'

Meantime there was the question of weapons. In our Turville Heath section of the Home Guard, made up mainly of young agricultural workers not yet called up, we had been warned that German paratroops were to be expected and we were encouraged to maintain patrols on the hilltops during the summer evenings. To destroy these formidable invaders, we had in the whole unit a single shotgun with one cartridge intended for deer-shooting. When I managed to buy privately another shotgun and a .22 rifle, we became the most heavily armed unit in the neighbourhood and reckoned the Germans would do much better to land at Lane End or Christmas Common rather than risk a descent at Turville Heath. The solution proposed in Parliament was to issue the Home Guard with pikes. Not satisfied with this proposal, we contacted sympathizers in America, who took steps to collect quantities of privately owned weapons from all parts of a country in which the possession of some sort of firearm is almost a matter of course.

As a result one day in the autumn I received a phone call from Liverpool to say that our shipload of weapons had arrived.*
They were a motley collection, varying from long rifles used in the Louisiana Civil War of 1873, plus Teddy Roosevelt's favourite hunting rifle and a number of ancient buffalo guns, to modern pistols, revolvers and gangsters' Tommy guns. All that could be made serviceable got through to the Home Guard, but the older weapons – which might well today be worth a fortune – must have become one of the casualties of the time. Later on when the regular army had been equipped, rifles from the First

*Picture Post, 30 November 1940. An 'American Committee for the Defence of British Homes' had been specially set up to collect these arms.

World War became available for the Home Guard, but the cry then was for heavier weapons and to answer this *Picture Post** designed its own mortar which could be produced by any garage for thirty-eight shillings and sixpence, and published instructions for its use and manufacture. 'Powder taken from fireworks is not reliable,' we wrote, and advised readers to do as we had done and manufacture their own.

In the autumn of 1940, after our school had been running some months, Hulton and I were summoned to the War Office. We sat for a while in a waiting room, and were then led down a long corridor and ushered in before a certain Brigadier Whitehead, who demanded that we show him our licence to run a military school and – no licence appearing – instructed us that it must be closed 'forthwith'. In the taxi on the way back Hulton asked me what I thought we should do.

'Absolutely nothing.'

'Nothing?'

'The general has carried out his orders by giving us *our* orders, so now he can dismiss us from his mind. It's ten to one he'll be replaced in the next fortnight – they usually are. But if he isn't, let him have the odium of sending troops to close the school, and we'll send photographers to take pictures of them closing it.'

This proved to be unnecessary, for within a month or two the army set up its own centres for Home Guard training and agreed to take over Tom Wintringham and some of his staff, so that our amateur war school could honourably be closed, though not 'forthwith'.

With the autumn came the Blitz, and the reality of war now pervaded every aspect of life. At the office our windows had all been bricked up, leaving only about a foot at the top where a small pane could be opened to let in air, so that we worked always by artificial light. There was much to do and our hours were long; the only time the office became quiet was after everyone else had gone home so that it was then that I would often start working on the layouts, and it would be late at night

Picture Post, 26 July 1941.

before I set off back for the hotel in Bayswater where I had a room.

At Lancaster Gate station I would step out on to a platform which seemed at first sight to be piled up with corpses from some terrible catastrophe. Sleepers of all ages and both sexes lay half-clothed, with arms flung out in every attitude of abandon, leaving a path only a yard wide along the platform's edge. Here and there among the sleepers were a few still sitting up, two women with a thermos flask of tea, a young man trying to read by the light of an electric torch. A child stretched its leg over the path and had to be stepped over carefully. The heat was terrific and the smell appalling, but since it was a daily occurrence one came by degrees to expect it and brace oneself automatically as one stepped onto the platform. No lifts ran at night so there was a long climb up the winding steps, at the top of which was the welcome coldness of the night. There was no light in the streets – once when there was fog I became totally lost on a quarter-mile journey which I made twice every day – but tonight the sky was full of light, an enormous tent of wavering searchlight beams all focused on one spot in the tent roof where two or three silver flies were turning and twisting in the effort to escape. Anti-aircraft guns sounded continuously, but the shell-bursts all fell far short of their targets.

The popular move into the tubes had at first been spontaneous and unorganized, and there was much discussion by authority as to whether they would allow it to go on or not.* Wisely, since it would have gone on in any case, they decided to provide a modicum of comfort and some primitive sanitation. Bunks with wire mattresses were fitted one above the other; regular occupants would leave possessions, such as a rug or coat, to mark their ownership and these would remain all day untouched. Some old people carried their treasured possessions down with them to their bunks for safety night after night, and I would occasionally give a hand to an old lady with a bursting suitcase in one hand and a bundle which appeared to

---

*This nightly occupation of the underground is described fully in *Living through the Blitz*, by Tom Harrisson, Collins, 1976, pages 110–17.

contain all her cooking pots, china ornaments, and her tea service in the other.

At times after working late I would stop for a meal at a little Italian restaurant in High Holborn called Manzoni's, slotted into a chink between larger buildings. One needed to know just where to find the door since no glimmer of light was allowed, but once past the heavy blackout curtain there was warmth, light, food and drink. It did not do to be squeamish, since the distinguishing feature of Manzoni's was the immense age of its waiters. Dressed in ancient tailcoats, heavily splashed and stained, they would come tottering out of the kitchen at the back, negotiate one or two steps, steer round protruding chairs and, with both thumbs in the *minestrone*, plant the soup shakily down before setting off on the risky quest for a glass of wine or pat of butter.

One morning after a heavy night of bombing I left for work at the usual time, but there were no tubes running since a station had been bombed, nor were there any buses because Oxford Street had not yet been cleared of debris. Though the whole network of sidestreets was familiar to me, it took an hour and a half to find my way into High Holborn and as I passed Manzoni's I saw that it and the floors above were a landslide of rubble. In the middle of the road, set among fallen masonry in a couple of inches of water from the hoses, was a desk from which an ARP officer was directing operations. The bomb had fallen, he told me, just as the restaurant was closing; Heavy Rescue men were still at work, but it seemed unlikely anyone would come out of it alive. It had not, I thought, really needed anything so destructive as a bomb – just a sharp push would surely have been enough to finish off those hard-working old grandfathers.

During this winter I met again someone I had come across a few years earlier at Chelsea parties. This was J. D. Bernal, a professor at Birkbeck College known to his friends as Sage, partly because of his vast fund of knowledge and partly on account of his enormous head with its shock of wavy hair. Sage had now teamed up with another still more celebrated young professor, Solly Zuckerman, best known at that time for his studies of apes. During the course of the war they would together undertake a whole series of important assignments, but at this moment they were looking into the precise effects of bombing both on people and on buildings, into which it seemed very little research had previously been carried out. Their immediate concern was a casualty survey* for which they would travel up and down the country to wherever some incident appeared to demand investigation, and I listened fascinated while they told me what they were doing.

'Well,' I said, 'now you've found all this out, suppose you give me some simple precautions for getting around safely over the next few years?'

'We could, of course,' Sage answered. 'But it's a waste of time since you certainly won't act on them.'

I objected that his attitude was unscientific; how could he know without putting the matter to the test?

'Very well,' he said, 'we'll see. If bombs are falling, lie face downwards in the gutter. Gutters give good protection – blast and splinters will almost certainly fly over you. But in case you *do* get injured, always wear a notice round your neck. Something conspicuous – about the size of a school exercise book.'

'Why do I need that?'

'The effect of blast is to pressurize the lungs – equivalent to suddenly giving you pneumonia,' he explained. 'So if a Heavy Rescue man or a sixteen-stone air raid warden kneels on your chest to administer artificial respiration, you've had it! Your notice will say "Weak Chest. Don't touch," or words to that effect. You're a journalist – you can think up your own form of words.'

'Thanks,' I said. 'But if I'm lying in the gutter with my notice, I can't be moving around.'

'Oh, if you want to move around – that's easy! All you need to do is wrap an eiderdown tightly round you. It absorbs the blast and protects your lungs. . . . But of course it won't be much help against splinters.'

*Fully described in Lord Zuckerman's book, *From Apes to Warlords*, Hamish Hamilton, 1978, chapter 7.

That was in 1940. Oddly enough, while putting down these notes forty years later, Sage's advice was confirmed when I came across a short paragraph in a newspaper* headed 'SKIER KILLED BY HER RESCUERS'. It recorded:

A West German skier survived an avalanche but died from rescuers' attempts to revive her according to Austrian coroners. Rosemarie Klimmer, thirty-five, skied into an isolated area in the resort of Zuers when a massive snow drift came loose and enveloped her.

Ski patrolmen dug Mrs Klimmer out of the snow after forty-five minutes and administered first aid. But their resuscitation attempts crushed her ribs, lungs and heart and she died of these injuries.

Inevitably the winter of 1940–41 proved arduous and depressing, so for the first issue of January 1941 I felt *Picture Post* should give its readers something hopeful to think about. I talked this over with the staff at our weekly conference and we agreed to produce a special issue devoted to the kind of country we all wanted to see after the war. It was to be called 'A Plan for Britain', and I asked Julian Huxley – who knew far more than I did about national planning and was acquainted with experts in the various fields – to help me edit it. In that issue we outlined policies most of which later became generally accepted, though not all have survived the economic blizzard of the 1970s and 1980s. Our policies included minimum wages throughout industry, full employment, child allowances, a national health service, the planned use of land, a complete overhaul of education – proposals which would later become the basis of the welfare state.

Though determined that this issue should be published, I was uncertain how it would be received, and so following publication telephoned in to hear what response there had been from our readers.

'I can't tell you how many letters there are,' my secretary, Mrs Brosnan, told me. 'They're still in sacks! We can't get round to unpacking them till more staff can be brought in.' In all, the response was overwhelming; weeks later we were still publishing some of the hundreds of readers' letters. As a

Morning Star, 8 January 1979.

follow-up, we organized a conference – not easy in wartime London – to which we invited a number of readers for a weekend of discussion with the experts who had written the articles.

In publishing our 'Plan for Britain' so early in the war, *Picture Post* was taking the lead in what was to become one of the most controversial issues over the next years – that of war aims. Churchill himself was strongly against any discussion of war aims: Britain, he declared, had only *one* war aim, to defeat Hitler – and his position was understandable. He led a motley coalition; most of his ministers came from the Conservative ranks – in which at this time he himself had no secure roots – but there were also Labour and Liberal members of his cabinet. Winning the war appeared to him the only issue on which all could remain united; over discussion as to what Britain should be like when the war ended they would quite certainly fall apart. But though this might be a good reason for the government to keep silent about the future, it did not stop ordinary men and women – particularly those in the forces with time on their hands – from thinking and talking about it a great deal.

The result of our special issue, therefore, was twofold. It intensified support among readers, who looked upon the magazine as their mouthpiece, almost indeed as their own property, and it increased the antagonism felt in certain government departments, above all in the Ministry of Information. Ministry officials had been incensed early in the war when *Picture Post* had published blank pages with thanks to the MoI for all the photographs they were at that time failing to supply.* We had now doubled the resentment by launching a public discussion on what life was to be like after the war ended.

Picture Post, 4 November 1939.

16
The 1941 Committee

On a pleasant spring evening, 16 April 1941, I was having dinner with my brother Paul at the Café Royal in Regent Street; I was a couple of days short of my thirty-sixth birthday and he would be thirty-five in June. It was some while since we had met and we eagerly exchanged news of the family. Paul, who had been in the Indian army for the past ten years, was already a veteran, having served through three campaigns on the North West Frontier, followed by two more arduous years in the Khyber. Then, after a spell at the Indian Staff College in Quetta, he had been chosen with only five others to attend a course for senior staff officers in the UK. By the time he got here, however, the Dunkirk evacuation was on, and he had been posted to a Scottish division to help organize the coastal defence of Essex. Now that it seemed the Germans had postponed their invasion, he was taking courses in parachuting and gliding before going back to India to raise an Indian parachute and airborne forces battalion, and later a brigade.

Jack, having been a Territorial officer for some years before war started, had gone out to France in December 1939 in command of a company* in the Border Regiment. When the Germans launched their assault in May 1940, his company had been ordered to hold a bridge in the little town of Incheville, a crossing on the river Bresle twenty miles inland from the coastal resort of Le Tréport. Their task was, together with

*D Company of the Fourth Battalion.

a company of the Sherwood Foresters, to cover the withdrawal of the Highland Division by delaying the advance of what turned out to be part of Rommel's Armoured Division. They did this so effectively that they remained in position throughout the whole period of the evacuation from Dunkirk, which began on 26 May and continued until 4 June. In the words of the official history of the Second World War:

Orders for the withdrawal failed to reach these two companies and in default of orders to move they stood fast. For six days they held on, denying for that week the passage of the river they had been ordered to guard. Not only did they beat off all the enemy's attacks and withstand his efforts to dislodge them, but they made prisoner some of their attackers. Only on June 13 when the Germans had brought up artillery and mortars to reduce their position, and when they learned that all other fighting north of the Seine had ceased, did they at last yield. It was a soldierly performance in the best tradition.*

By this time the two companies were completely surrounded and almost out of food and ammunition. Jack, who had lost his right eye on 8 June, had been carried by lorry to Le Havre, from where he was brought back to Britain with other remnants of his battalion. Two years after the war ended, when the German prison camps opened and the full story of the action became known, he was awarded the DSO, but in the meantime after a spell in hospital, he was in one of a number of different training posts, constantly trying to get back into the fighting.

Stephan's life too had undergone a dramatic change. Having cut short a spectacular university career which left little time for the niceties of classical scholarship, he had gone out to Mexico in 1930 to spend four years in the oil industry. Unimpressed perhaps by what he saw, he decided to come home, where he married, attended theological college and became ordained. After a couple of years as a curate in Putney he was now vicar at Barrow-in-Furness on the coast of Lancashire. While he was still at Putney, I had given him my small boat *Scud*, thinking it might provide some diversion from his clerical duties. Too

*Major L. F. Ellis, *The War in France and Flanders 1939–1940*, HMSO, London, 1953, page 283.

busy to make use of *Scud* himself, he had passed her on to his sea scouts, who had just benefited by £80 compensation when she was sunk at her moorings during the Blitz in the tidal wave created by a German bomb.

Esther, after training as a nursery-school teacher, had spent a year teaching in India but was now working among African children in Orlando, then a lively community with a character of its own not far from Johannesburg, but which has today become merged into the enormous African location of Soweto.

All this Paul and I were discussing as we sat over dinner, being joined from time to time by various friends in the agreeable way this used to happen in the Café Royal. Among them was Walter Greenwood, author of *Love on the Dole*, whom I had known since *Clarion* days and who had recently been writing articles for *Picture Post*. Time passed pleasantly and though we could hear much noise outside we had no idea that one of the heaviest raids of the war was in progress until there came a shattering crash, the walls shook and dust from the ceiling came sifting down into our glasses. There could be no more drinking so we paid our bill, said goodnight to Walter, and left. Outside was a feeling of tension and excitement; people were hurrying along in the darkness, bumping into one another, laughing and apologizing good-humouredly as though we were all going to a firework display. As our eyes became accustomed to the dark night, we noticed that there was a lot more light coming from Piccadilly than there ought to be, in the form of a red and flickering glow. Walking quickly down Regent Street, we turned the corner past Swan and Edgar and could see at once where the light was coming from. A heavy bomb had fallen in the very middle of the road almost opposite St James's Church – which was still in ruins from an earlier raid – making a crater which looked capable of holding two buses side by side. The explosion had burst the water mains besides blowing out all shop windows, so that we approached through running water amid the crunch and crackle of broken glass under our feet. The flow of the temporary river was towards Piccadilly Circus and I wondered if it would pour down into the tube. But in addition to the water mains, the bomb had also penetrated gas mains, so that from the surface of the crater a red flame, twelve to twenty feet high, came shooting up at random like a huge will-o'-the-wisp. Everyone in the little crowd realized the flare must bring back the bombers, and that the sensible thing to do was to get as far away as possible at once, but we all simply stood and stared as though at some magnificent stage effect.

Over on the far side of the crater were two air-raid wardens in tin hats, who at first just stood on guard, as though to demonstrate that everything was under control and the incident would be reported to the proper authority in due course. Before long they were joined by a sailor, visibly drunk and with his trousers rolled up to his knees. The problem, he at once understood, was to put out the flame and, looking around, he caught sight of the jagged pieces of concrete hurled up by the bomb. Seizing one of these, he staggered to the crater and flung it in. The flame ignored his effort and continued to shoot up, but he evidently thought that if only he flung enough pieces of concrete, one of them would surely seal off the flow of gas. An ARP man joined in his efforts and as we watched, the two – staggering to the rim of the crater with heavy lumps of concrete – missed their footing and flung themselves into the water with their burdens so that they were, if only briefly, swimming for their lives along Piccadilly.

'I don't think we shall see anything better tonight,' I said to Paul, and we moved on home.

Later on I learned that in the course of that night some 700 German bombers had attacked central and south London for about eight hours. More than 1000 civilians were killed, twice as many seriously injured, and there were many macabre incidents. Antonia, my former wife, was now employed at the BBC, but also did work for the J. Walter Thompson advertising agency which at this time had offices in Bush House. She told me that on the night of 16 April a colleague, after working late, came down to the street door and saw a taxi over on the stand. He was in luck, he thought, and would go the whole way home by cab. He shouted to the man at the wheel, but in the noise and confusion got no reply, so he walked across and took hold of the man's arm to give him his instructions. But the driver's head rolled over and he realized the man had been killed by blast.

Bombing for that year ended with the extremely heavy raid of May 10–11 in which it seemed the Germans were trying to burn down the whole of London at the same time. Coming into the Hulton Press offices after it was over, I found W. J. Dickenson, our financial director, jubilant. He had been in charge of the office fire-fighting arrangements while incendiaries were falling all over the area around St Paul's and Ludgate Circus. Our own team, he said, had been up on the roof half the night, kicking incendiaries off into the street or, as sometimes happened, onto neighbouring buildings. As an additional precaution three or four of the staff, seeing a hose left unmanned by the firemen, had commandeered it and played the water on our building to prevent fire spreading from our blazing neighbours, for whom I rashly expressed sympathy.

'Well,' he said, 'it's their own bloody look out! Half of them had been at the Cup Final or whatever, and the other half couldn't be bothered. They thought the bombing was all over for the winter.'

'And now they know it wasn't?'

'Too bloody right, they do! I feel really proud of our boys!'

Edward Hulton put it more formally in his *World Review*.*
'The offices of *World Review*, *Picture Post* and the *Evening Standard* stand like an island of culture in a sea of desolation. This is largely due to the efficiency of our own fire fighters. Many owners and employers have only themselves to blame. Fire-watching was futile. In many cases buildings were left unwatched and locked up.'

In our immediate neighbourhood that night of fire produced an eerie spectacle. Opposite us in Shoe Lane and tucked in at the back of Fleet Street was a warren of tiny courts and alleyways, most of them built just after the Great Fire, but including a couple of cottages with gardens from a much earlier date. Many of these buildings were occupied by small printing firms which

World Review, June 1941.

kept their machinery on the ground floor, using the upper floors as stores, where in addition to all their paper they kept glass jars of coloured inks. In some of these stores the inner walls had been surfaced with white tiles, and when the incendiaries rained down the paper rapidly began to burn so that before long the bottles and jars exploded, staining the walls with splotches of brilliant colour. I spoke about this to the artist Graham Sutherland, of whom I was seeing something at this time, and he made good use of it in a number of his paintings and sketches.

Earlier this same winter Macdonald Hastings and I had been having dinner with Edward Hulton at his house in Hill Street, Mayfair, to discuss the London conference organized as a follow-up to our 'Plan for Britain'. A noble meal had been provided – oysters followed by partridges, with a fine claret – but there were constant interruptions from the enemy, during which we sometimes ate boldly on and sometimes took refuge under the table. After a specially heavy crash which sounded as though a bomb had actually fallen in the street, the butler came in. 'I'm sorry to report, sir, that the front door has been blown in.'

'Oh – how very inconvenient!'

'Not your front door, sir,' said the butler, as though unwilling to exaggerate the enormity of the enemy's offence, 'not yours, sir. *Our* front door – in the basement.'

Everything must have been repaired, however, because soon after this the Hill Street house became the unofficial head-quarters of the 1941 Committee. This was an organization typical of the time, in that it sprang up spontaneously from the desire of a number of people – mostly in this case middle-aged or elderly and to some extent public figures – to do more towards furthering the war effort. It was a loosely organized group with no rules and no particular commitment, but met regularly for an evening of serious discussion on some aspect of the war. Its motive force was the belief that the country had survived so far by the grace of God and the public's resolution, but that if we were to survive the next four or five years a much more coordinated effort would be needed, with stricter planning of the economy and greater use of scientific know-how, particularly in the field of war production. Though the committee might occasionally publish a manifesto or report, it was felt that its most valuable work would be unofficial, through the influence members could exert on individuals in key positions.

The chairman was J. B. Priestley, whose standing as a public figure had been much enhanced by a series of 'Postscripts' delivered on radio at that key moment of the week following the nine o' clock news on Sunday evenings. 'Priestley,' wrote Graham Greene in the *Spectator* (13 December 1940), 'became in the months after Dunkirk a leader second only in importance to Mr Churchill. And he gave us what our other leaders have always failed to give us – an ideology.'*

The committee over which Priestley presided was a highly individualistic bunch; there was a nucleus of regular attenders, but many more looked in from time to time when a subject interested them or a fellow member urged them to attend. Among the best attenders were the journalists and editors, some because they found good copy, others because they had something valuable to contribute. Among the editors were Gerald Barry (*News Chronicle*), Kingsley Martin (*New Statesman*), Michael Foot (soon to become editor of the *Evening Standard*), David Astor (part-owner and future editor of the *Observer*), with Edward Hulton and myself. Journalists with special knowledge included Thomas Balogh (economics), Ritchie Calder (science), Elizabeth Denby (architecture and planning), Douglas Jay (finance and industrial organization), Tom Wintringham (military affairs), plus the literary agent A. D. Peters. David Owen was a social scientist and the secretary of an influential body known as PEP (Political and Economic Planning). Before long he would become aide to Sir Stafford Cripps who, on his return from the Moscow embassy in January 1942, occupied for a time a position at the very heart

*Quoted in Paul Addison's *The Road to 1945*, Jonathan Cape, 1975. I am indebted to the author for other information about the 1941 Committee, also to the notes made at the time by Sir Richard Acland, a fellow committee member, which I have used to supplement my own records of the period.

of political life, seeing himself and being regarded by some others as a possible prime minister to take over from Winston Churchill when opportunity offered, which – unfortunately for Cripps and for several other Labour politicians nourishing the same ambition – it never did.

Also on the committee were politicians, not all of left-wing views. They included Peter Thorneycroft, MP, later a co-founder of the Tory Reform Committee;* Lady Hinching-brooke, wife of the other founder of the TRC; Richard Acland, then a Liberal MP; Vernon Bartlett, distinguished *News Chronicle* correspondent, who had won a sensational by-election in 1938 opposing the Munich Agreement; Christopher Mayhew, at this time employed at the Ministry of Economic Warfare; Lady Violet Bonham-Carter, whose sharp comments on the proceedings would be circulated afterwards to those too far away to overhear them; and, at the farthest left, Konni Zilliacus, politician and journalist of Finnish origin, who would win a seat for Labour in the 1945 election. There were industrialists and businessmen as well, among them F. W. Miles, an aircraft manufacturer, and Lancelot Spicer of the paper-making firm, who had founded the Liberal Action group in 1940. Occasional attenders were the socialist bishop of Bradford, A. W. Blunt; publishers Stanley Unwin and Victor Gollancz; authors Storm Jameson and Phyllis Bottome; David Low the cartoonist; with academics A. D. Lindsay, C. E. M. Joad and Eva Hubback, principal of Morley College.

The theory on which the committee had been founded was that at this period of the war ministers were all rushed off their feet by the day-to-day demands of their offices, and that a body such as ours, which had time to plan and look ahead, could formulate policy on a longer view. In inviting people to join the committee, the emphasis had been on journalists, who would be in touch with popular opinion, and people in influential positions who could plant the committee's proposals where

---

*Established in March 1943. Besides Thorneycroft and Hinchingbrooke, its thirty-six Conservative MPs included Lady Astor, Quintin Hogg (Lord Hailsham) and Hugh Molson. Thorneycroft, some decades later, would become, as Lord Thorneycroft, the chairman of the Conservative Party.

they would be most effective. It was not to be an agitating body seeking to attract public notice but the opposite, one which kept out of the limelight to concentrate on practical results. In his *World Review* column 'Thinking Aloud' for March 1941, Edward Hulton wrote optimistically,

The 1941 Committee, under the chairmanship of J. B. Priestley, is forging ahead. It is at present the only group uniting a large body of progressive leaders, and uniting them not for general mateyness, but for action. A statement of aims headed by the words 'We Must Win!' has been published. The drawing up of such an agreed statement from about thirty intellectuals and others is itself a genuine epoch-making event.

By Christmas 1941 the committee had drawn up a 'Memorandum on Production'. Bottlenecks in production and the continuing failure to bring Britain's full industrial potential into the war effort were at this time major causes of concern, and the committee urged as 'steps which can be taken *now*':

1   Public control of railways, mines, docks, partly as a valuable token of the Post-War New Deal.
2   Pooling of essential (civilian and war) industries within wartime state-financed holding-and-operating companies, with fair compensation for owners.
3   A national wages policy....

There were seven more steps listed.

By May 1942 the committee had got so far as to issue a 'Nine-Point Declaration' calling for a programme to include not only a wide degree of common ownership and establishment of works councils, but 'Maximum freedom of expression', 'Elimination of Red-Tape in the Civil Service', 'British initiative in planning an offensive Grand Strategy' and 'Preliminary Post-war plans for the provision of full and free education, employment and a civilized standard of living for everyone'. Something or other had evidently gone to our collective heads, since no unofficial body making such sweeping demands could expect to be taken seriously.

The only way a group with a membership so mixed as ours could remain united would have been by concentrating all our

194

efforts upon limited objectives. Nor indeed did we remain united. Only a couple of months after this manifesto, in July 1942, the 1941 Committee merged with a band of Richard Acland's supporters known as Forward March to form a new political party under the name Common Wealth, and almost the only members of the committee who stayed on were Vernon Bartlett, Tom Wintringham and J. B. Priestley, who became chairman. Before autumn, both Priestley and Bartlett had resigned. Common Wealth never succeeded in its aim of becoming a mass movement, probably because under Acland's direction its drive was more towards encouraging moral revival than to attracting public support; but in the curious circumstances of the time – in which the main political parties, being in coalition, could not oppose each other at by-elections – it did succeed in winning three by-elections against Conservative candidates, giving it, including Acland himself, a total of four Common Wealth MPs.

Did the 1941 Committee achieve anything worthwhile in its short life? Among its members one heard claims to have influenced this or that piece of legislation, notably the introduction of clothes rationing in June 1941. But the justification for this must be very doubtful, and at best it could have been no more than the speeding-up of an inevitable decision. Paul Addison's conclusion* is, I think, a fair one. Having described the committee on its formation as 'a ginger group designed to collect informed criticism and communicate it to the government', he records that in July 1941, 'In the House of Commons, Clement Davies† was the unofficial organizer of the ginger opposition: outside it was expressed by the 1941 Committee.' A less kindly view came from H. G. Wells, who described the committee as a 'well-meaning (but otherwise meaningless) miscellany of people', and spoke of them 'earnestly and obstinately going in every direction under their vehement professions of unity'.‡ He also spoke dismissingly of 'the

*Addison, op.cit., pages 188 and 197.
†A Liberal MP who later became leader of his party from 1945 to 1956.
‡H. G. Wells. '42 to '44, Secker and Warburg, 1944.

flights and plunges of the Acland kite'. Wells's own contributions to the discussions at the few early meetings he
attended seemed to me designed rather to confound and confuse
than to achieve results. After one of his interventions, Lady
Violet Bonham-Carter remarked that his baiting of the chairman, Priestley, was like 'watching an aged but still skilful
matador handling a vigorous but inexperienced bull'.

Priestley's own point of view was contained in a letter he
wrote me in January 1941.

I do not agree that this is simply a Win The War Quickly group. It is
much more to organize the country on certain lines both to win the
war and establish a proper peace movement.... While this war can
obviously be lost by a shortage of ships, planes, guns, I do not believe –
unless Germany is weaker than I imagine – that it can be soon won
simply by having plenty of these things.... I believe it can be won
only by these things plus what amounts to a revolutionary outlook
here, which will inspire Western Europe to give us every possible
piece of assistance.... The last vestige of any suggestion that this is an
'imperialist' and 'plutocratic' war must be removed....

Seen in this light, the 1941 Committee should perhaps be
reckoned among those bodies making a useful contribution to
the controversy over war aims, a controversy which would
grow in importance as the war progressed, eventually providing the issues on which the post-war election would be fought.
And Churchill, by his refusal to accept plans for the future of
Britain as part of his wartime policy, was making certain the
Conservative Party entered the 1945 election without any
agreed policy for reconstruction, and so paving the way for his
own defeat and ensuring the return of a Labour government.

Meantime with the ending, at least temporarily, of the Blitz,
followed by the attack on Russia which appeared to have
removed any immediate danger of invasion, some degree of
social life was starting up in London. Such contact as I had with
it was mainly through Cyril Connolly and his dinner parties at
the flat in Bedford Square where he lived with Lys Lubbock,
one of the two attractive and talented secretaries on the
magazine *Horizon*, the other being Sonia Brownell who would

later marry George Orwell. I had met Cyril before the war at Chelsea parties, and at the end of 1939, when the magazine *Horizon* was launched with himself and Stephen Spender as joint editors, I at once took out a subscription. I admired the magazine, and before long sent in 'The Third Secretary's Story' which I had lately written.* Connolly was pleased with the story, that of a young diplomat stationed in some Balkan country before the First World War who involves himself, almost as a matter of routine, in a casual love affair only to discover that he is entrapped in a memory which haunts him for the remainder of his days.

Following this we met fairly regularly, Cyril from time to time inviting me to a dinner party and I, having no home in London, asking him to restaurants in return. On one evening at his flat, following my journalistic habit of arriving everywhere on time, I got there before anybody else and Cyril, an excellent host, led me down to a coal cellar where he kept his wine, while he selected the bottles for the evening; afterwards, since no one else had yet appeared, he started showing me volumes from his library. Gradually as he talked and I listened, his other guests arrived and when there were enough of us assembled, he announced, 'I must tell you all that I have discovered something terribly important!'

'What's that, Cyril?' we all asked.

'Nothing less than the true religion.'

'Good heavens! Tell us – what is it? Does it accept converts?'

'It's Taoism,' Cyril declared solemnly.

'*Taoism?*'

'Yes,' he replied. 'It has *everything* one needs. . . .' He was unfolding the merits of his discovery when he checked himself. 'Sage Bernal is coming here this evening,' he remarked. 'You must all promise not to say *one word* of this to him. I know Sage. If he hears about it, he won't be happy till he's undermined my belief.'

We all swore that nothing would induce us to betray his secret and allow the cold breath of scepticism to blast the tender

*See pages 152–3.

197

sapling of his faith. But Cyril found it impossible to keep his own secret, and halfway through dinner said, 'Sage – I *must* tell you – I have found the true religion! It has already given me great happiness and peace of mind. But knowing your scorn as a scientist for everything beyond the material world, I've no intention of telling you what the religion is that I've discovered.'

'Oh, but Cyril,' Sage remarked, 'I'm afraid you've gone too far already.'

'What d'you mean?'

'If one knows a man really well, that must be enough to tell one what religion he is going to take up.'

'Tell me, then – what is it in my case? Go on – tell us!'

Accepting the challenge, Sage laid down his knife and fork and took a drink. 'In the first place, Cyril, it has to be something unusual, something nobody else has thought of yet – I don't imagine you've suddenly discovered the underlying truths of Protestantism. Nor do I suppose you've decided to follow your friend Evelyn Waugh into the Catholic Church . . . seeing that he's got there first. Nor do I fancy you'll have been attracted into a warlike religion such as Shintoism. And I don't even think you've become a Moslem – despite the attraction of four wives. Buddhism – that could be tempting. . . . Except, of course, for one difficulty.'

'What's that, Sage?'

'You'd have to look on the whole material world as an illusion – *maya*. I can't imagine you doing that. Food, drink, even claret like this – an illusion? Not the religion for you, I fancy, Cyril.'

By now, as the possibilities narrowed, Connolly had begun to look uneasy, but Bernal went on remorselessly. 'The really important thing for you, Cyril, in choosing a religion, must be that it makes absolutely no demands on you. You won't want to attend temples or churches, give up a lot of your income to the poor, be obliged to say prayers at all odd hours . . . that's not *your* religious cup of tea, I fancy. And certainly you won't want a spiritual programme that tries to turn you into an ascetic. . . . So if you've *really* discovered the religion that suits you, Cyril – plenty of quiet contemplation, vague in character, with no demands for a change of any kind in your way of life – I can only suppose you've become a Taoist.'

17

'Undermining Morale'

Already from as early as November 1940 *Picture Post* had been following a policy of criticizing, sometimes strongly, what we believed to be avoidable failures or defects in the conduct of the war. During that month, in an article called 'A Question for Mr Morrison', who was then Home Secretary, we attacked the conditions in air-raid shelters, particularly the big shelters into which thousands of people crowded every night.

One small Salvation Army canteen hands out penny cups of tea (the queue may be a hundred long). One water-tap serves all these thousands. And the sanitation? A handful of lavatory buckets in the dark, behind a canvas screen.... And all this while good shelters are shut to the people ... big business buildings, vast pyramids of steel and concrete, deep below which is a labyrinth of rooms and passages which could shelter thousands, are locked to the public at night, and great notices are posted outside, saying, 'This is not a Public Shelter'.

Six months later, with the Blitz for the time being over, criticism was directed to the disaster in Crete, where towards the end of May nearly 30,000 British, Australian and New Zealand troops together with two divisions of the Greek army had been overwhelmed by a German airborne attack – which had been confidently, almost boastfully, anticipated. From the resulting defeat little more than half our forces finally escaped in a naval rescue operation which cost the loss of three cruisers and six destroyers, with thirteen other ships badly damaged, including two battleships and the only aircraft carrier then in the Mediterranean. Public confidence was badly shaken, not merely by the scale of the disaster but because of the optimistic statements put out by Middle East Headquarters early in the attack, and handed on by Churchill in the House of Commons, to the effect that the invaders were being 'wiped out' and 'mopped up'.* Moreover the Cretan defeat followed closely on the chasing out from Greece within three weeks of the small army sent to help that ally, plus a further setback in the war against Rommel in North Africa.

The state of public feeling was summed up in an article in *Picture Post*, 21 June 1941, which was signed by Edward Hulton:

Here is the heart of the criticism. Not that we suffer disasters – but that we suffer disasters through failing to appreciate the power of our enemy and the new technique of war he has invented. We do it time after time, and each time it happens we find excuses for it, but we do not learn from it.

Three months laters, in September 1941, we published an article by Sir John Wardlaw-Milne, a Conservative backbencher who had begun to make speeches critical of the conduct of the war, particularly in the matter of supply. Entitled 'Are We Working All Out?', this called for a speed-up in arms production and an end to the prevailing muddle and confusion, which he ascribed to conflicts between departments and the consequent delay in making decisions. 'The US has one head of production: we have four!' and he quoted from a report by the Amalgamated Engineering Union stating that out of thirty-one aircraft factories visited, there was actually a shortage of work in twenty-two, with shortages in certain departments of a further three.

Nor were American supplies the answer to the country's needs – in either quantity or quality. In November 1941 we quoted articles from the American magazines *Life* and *Look* which showed that so far from the flood of tanks, aircraft, ammunition which was generally assumed to be pouring across the Atlantic week by week, a mere trickle was in fact arriving.

*B. H. Liddell Hart, *History of the Second World War*, Pan Books, 1970, pages 141–3.

Britain's main theatre of war at this time was popularly known as 'the Middle East', but essentially it was North Africa plus the army's supply bases in Egypt, and the issue of *Picture Post* which carried these American reports, that for 22 November, was banned from being sent out to the whole Middle Eastern Area. Such action was farcical, since – though our magazine could be banned – the American magazines from which we quoted could not be. However, the banning of this single issue was only a foretaste of official reactions soon to come.

The following month, on 20 December 1941, we returned to the attack with an article by Tom Wintringham, 'What Has Happened in Libya?' He had prepared the article after much careful consultation, both with war correspondents and army officers back from the North African campaigns. In it he wrote:

We have an army that is very good. As Churchill has told us, it began this job with equality on the ground and superiority in the air. Can Mr Churchill find leaders for it who will understand what Rommel was being taught from 1935? Can we find a staff worthy of the fighting men and commanders? That is the key question raised by the fighting in Libya, and what we know as yet of how that important battle has gone.

He went on to criticize war material being issued to the North African armies whose tanks, throwing 2-pound shells, were often up against German tanks throwing shells of 5 and 15 pounds.

Wintringham's article proved to be the last straw, and I was summoned to the Ministry of Information where Brendan Bracken had taken over as minister only a few months previously, in July. I was seen not by Bracken himself but by one of his chief henchmen, a lawyer in civil life, who told me that the magazine's criticism was causing much anger in high places. There was particular concern over what we were saying about the quality of war material, much of which we had described as second-rate. Even if this were true, which he was not admitting, it was all that could at present be provided, and to weaken the troops' confidence in it was 'doing the enemy's job for him'. We were, he declared, 'undermining the morale' of the armies in North Africa.

To this I answered that the man on the spot – in this case the man in the tank – knows very well whether his equipment is as good as that of the enemy, which he is up against every day, and has no need to buy a magazine in order to find out. We knew very well from the hundreds of letters we were getting from the North African army – as well as from the reports of correspondents and others who had recently returned – exactly what the men felt, particularly about the quality of our tanks and guns. What the man in the tank wanted, I suggested, was not a barrage of government publicity to the effect that his equipment was 'the finest in the world', but evidence that people in this country were aware of the true situation. They wanted to know that their families and friends realized the difficulties they were up against, and that the government realized them too and were taking urgent steps to put matters right. If this were being done and known to be being done, it would not undermine morale, but reinforce it. What made the troops sick – as the letters they wrote so plainly showed – was the sense that people at home were blaming them for the continual reverses our armies were suffering. Boastful statements about the quality of material being sent out only served to give fighting men the impression that authority was quite happy with the existing level of equipment. Over-optimistic official statements, I said, were doing far more to 'undermine morale' than factual criticism.

Since we were both convinced of the rightness of our arguments the discussion was a warm one, and I left the building without giving the official any of the assurances demanded. The MoI's next step therefore was not to engage in more discussion but to act; and they now banned, not just a single number, but the sending out of any issues of *Picture Post* in future to the Middle East. This was not difficult for them to arrange since magazines and papers were sent to overseas forces under a subsidy scheme, paid not to the publishers but to the wholesale export firms, thus enabling them to put publications on sale at roughly the prices which obtained at home. So that all the ministry needed to do to stop the 10,000 copies of our magazine sent overseas each week was to notify wholesalers that the subsidy which applied to *Vogue*, the *Tatler*, *Punch*, the *Illustrated London News* and so on would no longer apply to *Picture Post*. At the same time the British Council was ordered to stop sending the 332 copies going weekly to Iran, the 162 copies for Turkey and the single copy sent out to Transjordan. In telling our readers of these events, we printed the words Brendan Bracken had used to the Foreign Press Association shortly after taking office: 'A free press is the most watchful sentry of the state, a "Yes" press is fatal to good government.' We asked, 'Do these words apply to British and Dominion troops? Or are these men of ours the exception – do *we* need a free press, and must they be protected from hearing the voice of criticism raised?'

Happily the issue was not complicated for us by any question of advantage. Under the paper-rationing scheme in force, we were not able to print anything like the number of copies we could sell, so that the spare 10,000 were simply reallocated to outlets in this country.* But the incident was an example of the way in which, though there was no regular wartime censorship in Britain, a ministry could sometimes achieve a similar effect by other means. In *World Review* for April 1942, in his column 'Thinking Aloud', Edward Hulton wrote, 'If suppression is to be applied to a free press, why cannot it be done openly and above board, and with all reasons clearly stated?'

We were now at the end of 1941 and if the war had hitherto gone badly in almost all respects, there was worse to follow. Such scant successes as Britain had achieved hitherto had been either in the air or else at sea, elements in which it was generally believed that we still retained some of our traditional superiority. But early in 1942 came a blow to British confidence in both these elements at the same time. Three German battle cruisers, the *Scharnhorst*, the *Gneisenau* and the *Prinz Eugen* – of great potential as commerce raiders, in which capacity the first two

---

*Paper rationing, which applied to all publications (except those put out by the various government departments) was based on a percentage of the quantity used in the last year before the war. At this time it was around 25 per cent of 1939 consumption, but would later go as low as 21 per cent. For a full examination see J. Edward Gerald, *The British Press under Government Economic Controls*, University of Minnesota Press, 1956.

had already caused us heavy losses in the Atlantic – had been safely bottled up, it was thought, in the port of Brest for almost a year, continually under watch from the navy and the RAF. On 12 February 1942, however, they succeeded in slipping out of harbour at dawn, and were not detected until well on in the morning by two Spitfires. The battleships were supported by strong air cover, and in a series of attacks Britain lost over forty aircraft, despite which all three enemy warships got safely through to Norway or the Baltic. Coming shortly after the fall of Singapore, with the accompanying loss of two British battleships sent to oppose Japanese landings, this was a shattering blow, and the 'Home Intelligence Weekly Report' spoke of this as 'the blackest week since Dunkirk'.

A consequence of this seemingly unending series of disasters was that now for the first time there began to be criticism of Churchill as Prime Minister. This took two different slants. Popular criticism, such as was to be heard in pubs, air-raid shelters and in general talk, took the line that the 'old man' himself was still the only possible war leader, but that he was failing to share the burden sufficiently with others, and also being 'let down' by commanders in the field. Simultaneously a body of 'insider' criticism began to be heard which followed an opposite line, that it was Churchill who was the cause of our continuing setbacks through his taking far too much upon himself. Confidential meetings took place, at one or two of which I was asked to be present, attended by MPs of all parties, two or three editors and influential journalists, and some renowned admirals and generals no longer in active posts but carefully briefed, it seemed to me, by top brass who were unable – or thought it unwise – to attend in person.

The argument there put forward was that the effective conduct of the war was being hampered by Churchill's constant interference in military matters about which he was not competent to judge, and that in view of the continued setbacks being experienced he should now be replaced by Attlee. Attlee, it was accepted, was a far from dominating personality, but at this moment it was not a dominating personality who was required but someone who was 'a good chairman of committee', that is, who would listen to the arguments on both sides, sum up carefully, and be guided by the consensus of opinion. I listened in silence to the prolonged discussion, and when eventually asked my view said that I knew nothing about the main point at issue, Churchill's supposed interference with the chiefs of staff, but that I did have some contact with public opinion, and that to the ordinary man and woman Churchill, despite all reverses, remained the embodiment of British determination to defeat Nazi Germany, so that his replacement by Attlee or anybody else would be regarded with intense suspicion. I also asked how it was proposed to effect such a change, and received the extraordinary reply that the King, as head of state, could assume power for the time being before handing it back to Churchill's successor.

Echoes of these meetings can be traced, I think, in Edward Hulton's *World Review* for April 1942 (page 7), in which he argues that, 'We cannot go further without a Minister of Defence – or rather of Attack – separate from the over-burdened Prime Minister.' And in the following July (page 5), he wrote, 'Mr Churchill is playing far too big a role in the field of strategy.'

The culmination and the final dispersal of these behind-the-scenes efforts came with the vote of censure on the central conduct of the war moved in the House of Commons on 1 and 2 July 1942, following yet another major disaster and further shock to public confidence, the fall of Tobruk on 20 June. Sir John Wardlaw-Milne, who, as chairman of the Select Committee on National Expenditure was in a position of considerable influence, had put down a motion censuring the central conduct of the war, a motion clearly aimed at Churchill himself. As a result of his influential position and his articles in *Picture Post* and elsewhere, Wardlaw-Milne now had a number of adherents among Conservatives, and there were dissidents in the Labour Party, loosely grouped around Stafford Cripps, who might be expected to lend support. Two days had been allotted to the debate which had aroused much speculation in the press. But though some important points were made, the main attack fizzled out because two of its leaders called for opposite solutions. Wardlaw-Milne wanted Churchill to remain as Prime Minister, but delegate military decisions to a Minister of Defence, and Admiral Sir Roger Keyes wanted Churchill to take all such decisions personally. Finally the debate from which so much had been expected ended on a note of complete farce with Wardlaw-Milne's proposal that the Duke of Gloucester, the King's brother, should be made commander-in-chief – a proposal which echoed the suggestion about the King's taking over power put forward at the private meeting I had attended. No wonder, after this, that the vote was lost by 476 to 25, and from this point onwards serious opposition to Churchill as wartime Prime Minister was confined to those who felt they could do the job better themselves if the opportunity were to be given them.

Later in the year, in any case, the military situation was looking very different. It began to be accepted that popular opinion had been right all along in believing that Hitler, in attacking Soviet Russia a year earlier, had 'gone the wrong way and made a big mistake'. In particular the defence of Stalingrad – whose resistance continued long after the city's fall had been reported and where it appeared that the all-conquering German armies were now actually grinding to a standstill – had caught popular imagination. Then in November came the successful Allied landings in North Africa, to be followed in early 1943 by the Eighth Army's victories over Rommel.

As a minor consequence of the North African landings, I found myself faced with an unexpected problem. On coming into work one morning I was told by my secretary that an air force officer had arrived some time before and was demanding to see me urgently. He proved to be a young squadron leader, pale and visibly distracted, who almost before giving me his name burst into a demand that I should promise to print the story he was about to tell. He was, he said, ready to risk arrest and the finish of his career by signing his name to it. Seeking to calm him down, I said I was sure what he had to tell me was important and that I would listen to it sympathetically; however an editor has responsibilities which he can no more abdicate to another than a squadron leader can abdicate his, and

I asked him why he had come to me with his story rather than taking it somewhere else.

'Because *Picture Post* has published a lot of criticism which other papers wouldn't use.'

'All right – so you had enough confidence to come here in the first place. But now you've either got to take a risk and tell me your story – or take it somewhere else. There can't be any question of a guarantee.'

In the end, of course, he came out with his story. It concerned a new type of plane which was, in fact, not so much new as a modification of an older one, designed to keep the production line of a famous firm running a while longer. According to him, the plane was described as a 'fighter-bomber' but was not truly effective in either capacity. It had not the speed or armament for a fighter, while as a bomber its load was too small, its take-off and landing speeds too high, and it lacked the necessary range. His squadron, operating in North Africa soon after the allied landings, had been one of the first to be equipped with the modified plane, a number of which, he said, had simply fallen into the sea before ever reaching Lisbon on the way out. He came close to breaking down when he described how some of his squadron never got as far as the target on their first raid, and others destroyed themselves on reaching base owing to the plane's excessive landing speed. He said he intended writing all this out in detail, that he would sign it, and was willing to be shot for doing so. He added that I owed it to him and to his dead comrades to publish his account straightaway in the form in which he wrote it. Was I willing, he demanded, to give this undertaking?

I said that I accepted his story as true, though obviously it would be necessary to obtain confirmation, but that there were several things I had to consider before deciding whether to put it in the paper. The public had endured a long diet of failures and disasters; the landings in North Africa and Montgomery's recent desert victories had been their first taste of success. It would be bitter for them now to be told that the same muddle and confusion which had haunted us from the beginning was still going on.

Some *Picture Post* people

When photographers went out on assignments for the magazine they would often take shots of the journalists who went with them. These would be pinned up on a board in the editor's office — and he, or someone else, would write captions under the pictures. On the following pages are a few of these pictures, with others taken at parties when the staff celebrated the past and looked forward to what we all imagined would be a golden future

Above Edward Hulton, founder and proprietor, on holiday at Gstaad, with editor Tom Hopkinson

Right Stefan Lorant, the magazine's first editor, plans an early issue

Below Ted Castle, assistant editor, John Ormond, who wrote the TV programme 'The Life and Death of *Picture Post*', and H.J. Deverson, picture editor

Left Kurt Hutton, one of the magazine's first two photographers. *Above* Fyfe Robertson, staff writer, doubtful about his health. 'My God! It's stopped!' was the caption written under this picture

A.L. Lloyd, whose left-wing views disturbed the proprietor

Lionel Birch, first writer to be recruited to the staff

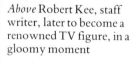

Above Robert Kee, staff writer, later to become a renowned TV figure, in a gloomy moment

'Slim' Hewitt, photographer, descends into the depths in the course of duty. Later he faced the same perils as a TV cameraman

Above Assistant editor Castle, right, interviews Tory leader, Anthony Eden. But they are not in full agreement

Above Sports writer Denzil Bachelor shows how it should be done
Above left Cameraman Haywood Magee operates sitting down

Science writer Wragge-Morley is given an injection of electrical horsepower for an arduous assignment

The end of the road: North Korean prisoners roped together before being shot by their South Korean captors. It was the end of the road for them. The end of the road also for the editor when he insisted on publishing the pictures

Above Photographer Bert Hardy in full battle equipment for the Korean war
Left His pictures of the Inchon landing receive the highest award for 1950. From left to right, Lionel Birch, H.F. Deverson, Tom Hopkinson and Bert Hardy

'You mean you'll do nothing?' he broke in.

'I mean that if the result you want can be obtained without making the matter public, I should think it wiser. And there's something else.'

'What's that?'

'It's possible that we might print your story in the magazine, but that it might never reach the public.'

'How?'

'Because of our criticism in the past, we're under official suspicion. I don't know how these departments operate, but it would seem to me natural for them to have a man of their own inside the printing works. If they found a way to stop our magazine going overseas, they might well find a way to stop it appearing in this country. Then your story won't be published, and we shall have lost a whole issue.'

'So what do you propose?'

I asked the officer if he would give me one week. I suggested that he go away and write his account in detail, giving dates, times and the names of men who had been lost. Meantime, I told him, I would see whether the matter could be dealt with in another way. I had kept notes of what he had told me which would be sufficient for my purpose, but if my efforts failed he would have his own written account to take elsewhere. We made a date for him to come back to the office in seven days' time.

Sir Stafford Cripps was at this period Minister of Aircraft Production; I had met and knew him, but only slightly. It would be better if he could be approached by someone he knew well and who had both political and scientific status. Professor A.V. Hill was currently the MP for Cambridge University, he was the secretary of the Royal Society and a member of the War Cabinet Scientific Advisory Committee. He was also a Nobel prizewinner, had written several excellent articles for our magazine and I had been impressed by his authority and directness. I arranged at once to see him, showed him my notes, and explained that I was reluctant to publish a story so damaging to public confidence, now just beginning to revive, but was prepared in the last resort to do so if no better way could be found. I remarked that the minister himself would surely be eager to take action providing the matter was brought to his notice in the right way by somebody he trusted.

Professor Hill wasted no time. A week later when the officer returned I could tell him that all planes of that type had been grounded, and before he went back to North Africa that they had been taken out of service altogether.

18

The People's Beveridge

From the end of 1942, the feeling began to spread throughout the country that the tide of war had finally turned. Following the victories of Alexander and Montgomery in North Africa, it was evident that the right commanders were at last coming to the top; the problems of supply also seemed on their way to being solved so that there were fewer complaints about the quality of equipment. But after three and a half years of war, with at best another one or two more to be expected, there was a general sense of war-weariness. It was thus not only possible to believe in the future but it was also a relief to think about it in contrast to the present; so, on both accounts, the question 'what will life be like when the war ends?' began to loom larger and larger in people's minds.

Hitherto the War Cabinet had managed to keep official discussion of what was called 'post-war reconstruction' safely under the desk. They did this by the usual government expedient of handing the awkward subject over to a committee with no powers, under a chairman who was not likely to make trouble. Back in January 1941, Arthur Greenwood, a Labour stalwart long past the peak of his energy and application, occupying the undemanding post of Minister without Portfolio, had been made chairman of a Reconstruction Committee. A survey of their task as its members saw it was put out – dividing problems into 'economic' and 'social' – which – had they all been seriously tackled – would have left no economic stone unturned and no social avenue unexplored. But after this imposing start the committee met only four times during the next twelve months before Greenwood was sacked and Sir William Jowitt, the Solicitor General, put in his place. Jowitt was even less of a political heavyweight than his predecessor. As a politician his efforts had been devoted chiefly to his own survival, at which he had shown himself adept, slipping dexterously across party boundaries no fewer than four times in ten years. He was thus not a man likely to create difficulties for himself and others by working out and putting forward policies which would be unwelcome to Churchill and his colleagues in the War Cabinet. Before he had been in his position for a year, however, an extremely hot potato landed on his desk in the form of the Beveridge Report.

At the crucial moment, December 1942, Sir William Beveridge was the master of University College, Oxford. After a successful career in the civil service, he had been made director of the London School of Economics, remaining there from 1919 to 1937, when he moved to Oxford. His concern with social problems had been lifelong, from his early days as a Toynbee Hall social worker and a protégé of Sidney and Beatrice Webb around 1905, to his appointment in 1934 as chairman of a government committee on unemployment insurance. During the first weeks of the war, in an article published in *The Times** he had called for a full-scale planning of the wartime economy, and his convictions had been strengthened by what he had seen since 1940 – in his role as temporary civil servant in the Ministry of Labour – of the failure to organize manpower as he felt it should be organized.

The opportunity which would lead Beveridge to much more than instant fame had been presented to him inconspicuously enough, back in May 1941, with his appointment as chairman of an interdepartmental committee, its brief being to prepare 'a survey of the existing schemes of social insurance and allied services, including workmen's compensation, and to make recommendations'. An innocent enough way of keeping a body of senior officials occupied, it would appear; yet from

The Times, 3 October 1939.

this modest cocoon would emerge a plan to establish full security for all British citizens 'from the cradle to the grave', and lay practical foundations for the post-war welfare state. This was the renowned Beveridge Report.

Its author's assets for drafting the report were an immense capacity for hard work, strong convictions and a thorough knowledge of his immensely complex subject. He was also, within the limits set by his character, a skilful political manipulator whose experience of Whitehall from the inside, understanding of politicians, and shrewd evaluation of the effect of popular opinion and of press support in putting his work across, would stand him in good stead. A serious obstacle in his way, however, lay in a certain aspect of his character. He had now been in positions of authority for over twenty years and his urbane assurance of his own superiority, turning rapidly to irritation were he in any way challenged, alienated many of those whose backing he most needed. Indeed the hostility which his manner provoked might well have destroyed the effect of all his valuable work, but for extreme good fortune in the matter of timing.

Published as a White Paper on 1 December 1942, his report saw the light of day just when the minds of people at home and in the fighting forces were hopefully turning towards peacetime life, in a widespread determination that the future should be very different from the past. Coming at this moment, the Beveridge Report put into practical form the hopes and dreams of millions, who could provide the determined backing Beveridge was bound to need if his project was not to be half-welcomed by the men of power, and then gradually shuffled on to one side before being finally elbowed into the wastepaper basket as an impracticable dream.

Those of us who knew of the report beforehand and had some idea of what it contained were well aware that it would arouse opposition at the highest level, and throughout most – but not all – of the Conservative Party. We were convinced that the only way such far-reaching proposals could be realized was to secure at least a degree of government commitment to them while the war was still on. Once the war ended financial arguments would predominate, as they had always done, and *Beveridge* would be filed away and postponed till the millennium. In the weeks before publication the government line was to play down the coming report and afford its author no facilities for publication. But by the end of November this attitude had changed, largely because of the great propaganda value which could be got out of the report in broadcasts to occupied Europe. The idea that the British were so confident of victory that they were already planning their own post-war future, coupled with the appeal to war-weary masses in Europe of this vision of a better life for all, offered an irresistible opportunity. Brendan Bracken, who as Minister of Information had been anxious in October to play the report down, now took the opposite line. And though there was a further change of heart in December, resulting in some back-down on official publicity, this came too late. Press welcome in Britain had already been widespread; only the Berry brothers – Lord Camrose in his *Daily Telegraph* and Lord Kemsley in his *Daily Sketch* – seriously opposed Beveridge's recommendations, and a fantastic total of over 600,000 copies of the report was sold.

In February 1943 came the parliamentary debate. The report's popularity with the public, backed by its massive welcome in the press, made it impossible for the government to reject it out of hand. After much discussion within the War Cabinet as well as in the Conservative Party, the line decided on was a tepid acceptance of a number of the separate proposals, while avoiding any general commitment on the ground that it was impossible to foresee what the country's financial position would be when the war ended. This policy, of getting all possible propaganda mileage out of the report in broadcasts overseas – and encouraging our own people to look forward to the better future outlined it, but without undertaking to *do* anything – struck me and others as a low trick even by political standards.

Accordingly, when the debate on the report took place, I sent a cameraman to photograph Beveridge's arrival at the House – looking like a benign bird of prey with his sharp eye, long beak and flapping overcoat for wings – and then after the debate was

214

over I did what I very seldom did at any time, wrote a signed article for *Picture Post*.

The House of Commons has said its say. It has not precisely rejected the Beveridge Report – indeed, so far as words go, it gave it a kind of welcome.* It has not even quite killed the Report. It has done something different. It has filleted it. It has taken out the backbone and the bony structure. It has added up the portions that are left – and assured us that they amount to 70%. Sixteen portions out of twenty-three by the Herbert Morrison reckoning – and the only proviso attached is that none of these portions is quite definitely and finally guaranteed. . . . The opponents of the Report – from Sir John Anderson† all the way down to Sir Herbert Williams – spoke as though the basis of the Report were an attempt to cadge money off the rich on behalf of the not entirely deserving poor.

Yes. They might be willing to give something. They recognised the justice of the claim. But not all that was asked. And certainly not now. And, above all, they could not make promises for the future. Sir Arnold Gridley wondered 'how want is to be defined. Can it necessarily be met by any specific monetary sum? The family of a hard-working and thrifty man can live without want, perhaps on £3 a week, whereas the family of a man who misuses his money or spends it on drink or gambling, may be very hard put to it if his wages are £5 or £6 a week.'

The fear that small children or old age pensioners may take to drink or gambling is a very real one to large sections of the Conservative Party.

Sir Ian Fraser congratulated the Chancellor on having 'done a most difficult thing'. He had called the House back 'from the fancy fairyland in which it loves to indulge, to reality, and thereby rendered a great service to us all. . . .' Further on in his speech Sir Ian carried misrepresentation to the pitch of mania. Objecting to Sir William's plan to make insurance compulsory and national, so as to cut the cost of collection to a fraction, he declared that Sir William's object in doing this was 'to steal a capital asset so as to get some revenue for his scheme'.

Finally, Sir Herbert Williams let out of his own private bag the largest cat released on the floor of the House of Commons since

*The vote in favour had been 335 to 119
†Lord President and chairman of the Reconstruction Priorities Committee. Later on, in 1943, he would become Chancellor of the Exchequer.

Baldwin explained why he had to fight the 1935 election on a lie. He did it with the words 'If the scheme is postponed until six months after the termination of hostilities the then House of Commons will reject it by a very large majority.' Exactly. If we don't get the foundations of a new Britain laid while the war is on, we shall never get them laid at all. Sir Herbert Williams and others of the same kind – or nearly the same kind – will see to that. For so huge an indiscretion the Conservative Party should un-knight Sir Herbert instantly.

These snivelling objections are quoted for one purpose only: to show the low level at which the opponents of the Report chose to conduct the battle. They fought it on the Poor Law level, the three ha'penny, ninepence-for-fourpence, Kingsley Wood and Means Test level. The common people of this country were asking for more than their directors and controllers chose to give them. They could get back where they belonged, and say thank-you the mercies were no smaller. . . .

The article went on to record the astonishing effect the Report had produced in occupied Europe when put out by the BBC.

The very day the Report came out Dr Schmidt of the Nazi Propaganda Service was put up to try to answer it. All the leading Axis paper followed suit. . . . The Axis shook at the thought that Britain would grasp the leadership in social reform which they claimed as the basis of their own New Order. But then, immediately following the Commons debate, had come relief. On February 17, after the first day's debate in the House of Commons, the German News Service was able to declare: 'The Beveridge Plan was given so much publicity for the sole purpose of demonstrating to the world Great Britain's claim to leadership in the social sphere. In Europe . . . there has been nothing but laughter at this attempt. . . . It now transpires that the whole Beveridge humbug has feet of clay. The wine of enthusiasm of the British leftists has been watered down by insurance experts, doctors, pensioned officers and big business-men. . . . Nothing will remain of the comprehensive social scheme but the ensuring of a State grant for the veterinary treatment of cats and dogs.'

So, for the time being, the battle for the report ended. But it would come to the surface again in 1945, when the lukewarm reception offered by a largely Conservative government, and the efforts made by some Labour followers to prevent it from being altogether watered down, would play an important part in Labour's victory. But it deserves also to be recorded that even within the Tory ranks there had been a division. A group of forty-five Conservative MPs, mainly the younger members with experience in the armed forces who had banded themselves together into the Tory Reform Committee under the leadership of Captain Quintin Hogg* and Lord Hinchingbrooke, backed the report, though not to the extent of voting against the government. Instead they put down the amendment calling for the immediate setting up of a Ministry of Social Security. And in the same issue of *Picture Post*† in which my article appeared, Quintin Hogg wrote 'An Open Letter to the Tory Party'. In this, in a visionary moment, he called on his fellow party members to consider '... where exactly are we going? I will tell you. As a nation we are heading for political chaos. As a party we are heading for political suicide.'

It would be dishonest not to add that in my own long – indeed much *too* long – article, I included a passage so wildly utopian as to cause me now, nearly forty years later, some doubts as to the writer's sanity. I was answering Conservative arguments that Britain could not guarantee to provide a comprehensive social service after the war, since if we did we might not be able to compete economically in the post-war world. Their argument, I wrote, is 'not that we definitely cannot afford the proposals – but that we cannot know whether we shall be able to or not. An excellent idea – that of eliminating want, but who can say whether this country can afford to have want eliminated? Maybe it will need to have a certain amount of want in order to keep going.' So far, so reasonable. But not for long, for in the next column I went on:

And what of the export trade? Well, what of it? To me, and to those who think as I do, the idea that after this war we are all going straight back to cutting one another's throats in the effort to export more and import less ... is delirium. There could only be one answer to that – a

*Now Lord Hailsham.
†6 March 1943.

217

general refusal. *A World Strike.* The only account book that ought to matter after the war should be the world account book – by which raw materials are directed to where they can be manufactured, and products of industry sent to where they can be used. We reject altogether the idea that the British people must force down their standard of living for the sake of trying to undersell the Japanese. . . .

Well, well. It was written a long time ago, and we have all learnt a great deal since, perhaps.

On *Picture Post* we had not altogether finished with Sir William Beveridge. Following the debate, Edward Hulton invited him to lunch, with myself and a few others, at his house in Hill Street. When after lunch Hulton asked what he was intending to do next, Beveridge replied that he was planning a further report on the maintenance of full employment, but that he was not certain where the funds were coming from since the inquiry would be his own undertaking, not the government's. Hulton, in a handsome gesture, at once offered to provide some thousands towards the cost.

When we got back to the office late in the afternoon, Hulton walked along the corridor leading to his own room. I followed, as I wanted to have a word with one of his fellow directors, W. J. Dickenson, and thus was witness to a curious little scene. Hulton was a heavily built man, fond of wearing thick tweed suits with waistcoats, which made him bulkier than he need have been. On top of this, he wore a heavy tweed overcoat, half open with the ends of a belt hanging loose. He wore his hair long in those days, fringing out over his collar, with a small black hat perched uneasily on top. He walked jauntily down the corridor, which he almost filled, till he came at the end to his own room with the name 'EDWARD HULTON' on the door. There he stopped, as though surprised by what he read, and caught sight of a second notice, put there to prevent stray visitors from wandering in on him, which read 'TO MR EDWARD HULTON'S OFFICE', followed by a hand pointing to the door behind which his secretary worked. He stood there leaning back on his heels while he read both notices through, visibly hesitating which way to go, turned to follow the pointing hand – and then, as though recollecting that he was after all Edward Hulton, opened his own door and went inside.

People who have never worked in offices, I thought, can have no idea of the ceaseless flow of interest to be found in office life. Apart from the work one does, which might be all-absorbing like my own or utterly boring and mechanical, there is always the varied company and strange behaviour of one's fellows – and for them, no doubt, the strange behaviour of oneself. I should miss all this, I thought, if I were ever to lose my job or one day, conceivably, retire. Meantime I had already opened the door of Dickenson's room and begun my conversation. I had grown to like Dickenson increasingly over the years I had been working with him; he was always direct and to the point, stating his objections but without making a meal of them.

I was looking in on him now because he had lately sent someone to see me, an acquaintance of his who had a project – also it seemed the patent – for a particular type of colour camera. After looking at the idea carefully and talking it out with our cameramen, I had concluded that the idea was not worth following up; there were other better and simpler systems already being developed.

'Very well, then,' said W.J.D., 'tell him to bugger off.'

'I can't say that to a friend of yours. How d'you *really* want me to write?'

'Just tell him to get stuffed.'

'But seriously, W.J.,' I foolishly persisted, 'what d'you want me to say to your friend?'

'Tell him he's barking up the wrong horse's backside.'

Which, in rather different words, was what I did.

19

A Very Strange Lunch
or Two

Our struggle over post-war planning led to one further skirmish before the Second World War ended and the future turned into the present. This involved the awe-inspiring figure of John Reith. Following his long spell at the BBC and the later task of transforming Imperial Airways into a state-run corporation, Reith had been brought into politics by Chamberlain, who made him Minister of Information in January 1940. When Churchill took over in May, he gave Reith the post of Minister of Transport to which he applied himself with his habitual energy. He was also just starting to feel at home in the House of Commons when in October 1940 he was shifted again, this time to the Ministry of Works, with a peerage which carried him out of the Commons and into the Lords.

Churchill disliked Reith,* whom he blamed for having kept him off the air during the crucial years of the thirties, and may have imagined that, shoved into the Lords, in a post that had little to do with the conduct of the war, he would fade into obscurity. Instead Reith set to work, with determination and efficiency, to make the most of this new opportunity and in particular to extend the powers of his office. One aspect of his work was concerned with repairing bomb-damaged buildings, but another involved the planning and rebuilding of cities after

* 'Thank God we have seen the last of that Wuthering Height!' quoted in Collin Brooks, 'Churchill the Conversationalist', in *Churchill, by his Contemporaries*, ed. Charles Eade, Hutchinson, 1953. See also *The Reith Diaries*, ed. Charles Stuart, 1975, page 267.

the war ended, thus opening up the whole field of post-war reconstruction. It did not take Reith long to draw up an imposing list of objectives which included a central planning authority: 'controlled development of all areas and utilization of land to the best advantage; limitation of urban expansion; redevelopment of congested areas; correlation of transport and all services; amenities; improved architectural treatment; preservation of places of historic interest, national parks and coastal areas....'* Followed, inevitably, by his recommendations for immediate action.

'I was looking beyond the war to the problems of planning and reconstruction,'† he wrote, and again: 'All this was a war aim.... I was not frightened about the war, but I was frightened about what would happen when the war was over.'‡

Nor was his list of objectives the whole story. In addition he appointed a panel of experts to advise on post-war planning, put in hand a plan for post-war rebuilding which covered the whole of central London, besides setting up committees to deal with particular aspects – such as the future of the countryside and the problem of compensation. When the mayor of Coventry came to see him with a deputation to ask about rebuilding their battered city, 'I told them that if I were in their position I would plan boldly and comprehensively; and that I would not at this stage worry about finance or local boundaries.'** He gave similar advice when he visited Southampton, Portsmouth, Liverpool, Glasgow and Plymouth. There had seldom been such a wholesale slashing of red tape, and red tape has always many friends in key positions. Reith was on risky ground, since he had as yet no definite authority, but for the time being all went well, and in February 1941 he succeeded in securing a general acceptance of his plans by the War Cabinet.

From February 1941 to February 1942 he was involved in a further struggle, trying to secure the necessary powers for his ministry to take their agreed policies a stage further. But in this

*J. C. W. Reith, *Into the Wind*, Hodder and Stoughton, 1949, page 422.
†Ibid, page 407.
‡Ibid, page 440.
**Ibid, page 424.

he was up against opposition from Arthur Greenwood and his Reconstruction Committee, which regarded Reith's activities as poaching on its preserves, and also against hardening resistance from a number of Tory MPs who opposed planning of any sort. Yet this battle too Reith appeared to have won when on 9 February 1942 the War Cabinet agreed to hand over further powers to his Ministry of Works, symbolizing the change by its new title of the Ministry of Works and Planning. It was to be a short-lived victory, however, for less than a fortnight later, in the reconstruction of his government following the loss of Singapore and other military defeats, Churchill dismissed Reith, who was easy to get rid of since he belonged to no party and therefore lacked solid political support.

To those who looked on the planning of post-war Britain not as a harmless pastime for intellectuals but as an essential part of the whole effort of our time, Reith's abrupt dismissal – coming at the very moment when he had been given the powers needed for his job – implied the relegation of post-war planning to outer darkness, if not directly to the dustbin, and this interpretation was confirmed by the choice as Reith's successor of an obscure millionaire crony of Churchill's named Wyndham Portal. As expected, Viscount Portal soon showed himself just as eager to reduce the importance of his ministry as Reith had been to expand it, and in December 1942 he announced to the House of Lords that a new, separate Ministry of Town and Country Planning had been set up, to which a whole section of his own ministry's work was being handed over.

Following his dismissal I wrote to Reith, and in April he asked me to lunch with him at the Athenaeum. His account of the meeting was as follows:

23 April 1942. Lunched with *Picture Post* editor and was very forthcoming with him. He said it was a great pity I had not done some advertising of myself. He thought I ought to create a nuisance value for myself. I said it wasn't in my line at all.*

These few lines cover what was for me a truly extraordinary meeting. Reith was a man of commanding presence. It was not

*The Reith Diaries, op. cit., page 292.

only his great height, domed head, bushy eyebrows and the impression he gave of being in uniform even when in civilian dress; he wore, at least on the few times I met him, a sombre, scowling look, as though the whole of humanity was a vast defaulters' parade on which he would shortly be pronouncing sentence. But it was apparent before we had been talking long that behind this formidable exterior was a sensitive, perhaps over-sensitive, human being who had been deeply hurt by his dismissal and, even more, by being deprived of the opportunity to carry through a piece of work on which he had set his heart, believing that no one but himself would do it properly.

My interest in coming to the lunch had been to extract from my host a strong article on the need to press ahead with the planning of post-war Britain, and particularly with getting the necessary legislation put in hand. This must take years to carry through and unless it were put in hand now, men and women in the forces would come back to the same pattern of indecision and frustration as their predecessors in 1919. Reith at this moment was directly in the public eye. His work at the ministry had attracted widespread notice; the dramatic manner of his sacking posed him in the limelight as a victim of the old gang of Chamberlain Tories and their financial allies. Other papers besides ours had supported his efforts and were concerned over his dismissal, among them *The Times*, *Observer*, *Daily Mirror* and *News Chronicle*. Anxious that he should not disappear despondently into the background, I felt I could assure him of powerful press backing if despite being out of office he continued drawing up plans for the country's future. What I had vaguely in mind was that he might – if the necessary finance and office staff were provided – produce a 'Reith Report' that would do a similar job for the use and development of land to the one Beveridge had done for health and social services. With two such reports drafted out and accepted, covering such vital areas, we should be well on the way to an agreed plan for post-war Britain.

I said nothing of this for the time being, waiting to see how he reacted to the idea of an article. To this he raised various objections, though not, I thought, with full conviction, and then astonished me by changing the whole course of our conversation and asking my advice about his career. 'What would you yourself do if you were in my position? How would you be acting at this moment?'

I looked at him. The question, however odd, seemed serious enough. I thought for a minute and then asked whether he wanted to continue with a political career, or at least a career in public life. I had in mind what was currently said of him, that the height of his ambition was to become Viceroy of India. He replied that he most certainly *did* want to continue in public life, and that he had enjoyed both his ministerial work and his time in Parliament.

'Your recent painful experience,' I said, 'must have convinced you that in politics one needs allies. A lone figure is everybody's target.'

'What are you suggesting?'

'The need for party backing.' He began to scowl and snort, but he had asked my advice and I meant to give it to him.

'You have a tremendous talent for administration. You've proved that several times over. You know where you want to go, and can get people to work for you. But the Tory Party's full of administrators and ex-administrators, party servants of long standing with claims on its patronage. . . . It would also seem that it contains some characters hostile to yourself.'

He shrugged his shoulders. 'If you do a job properly you're bound to make enemies.'

'Yes. But it's useful to remember just where they're placed. And if I were in your position, I shouldn't expect much in future to come my way from the Conservatives – even supposing they manage to come back to power when the war ends.'

'But I'm not a party man in any case. Never have been.'

'Whereas,' I went on, 'the Labour Party is extremely short of good administrators. You're not a party man in the strict sense, I know. But both at the Ministry of Transport and the Ministry of Works what you were doing was far more in line with Labour than Tory policy. You believe in controls in the national interest – not in a free-for-all in which the richest take all they can grab, and the rest pick up what they can.'

'Hmph,' he said. 'But I don't see myself as being part of *any* political party. My idea is that I should be available for whatever I'm called upon to do in the national interest by either party.'

'But doesn't "being called upon" follow party lines? And won't it do so still more when the war ends? If you ally yourself now with Labour in the House of Lords, you'll be directly in line for "being called upon" for something very important later on.'

He did not answer, and I wasn't sure if he had even heard, but after a minute he remarked: 'Anyway I can't write anything about post-war planning. It would look as if personal feelings were involved.'

I was about to ask what on earth personal feelings and the look of things mattered compared to all that was at stake, but stopped myself in time. What an extraordinary mixture, I thought, of ability and determination hampered by a maidenly concern over what people would think.

It was more than a year before I lunched with Reith again, also in the Athenaeum. Still hoping for an article which might lead to further developments, I had written to him on 4 August 1943.

Can I persuade you to come out in public with a strong article about the trifling and almost frivolous way in which the government is handling the basic problems which underlie post-war planning?

The last time we talked this over, you felt, I know, that such an article coming from you would have the appearance of personal feeling. Surely after this lapse of time, any suggestion of this sort must now have gone?

We met a week later on 11 August at his suggestion. This was a meeting quite unlike the earlier one. In the dining room Reith spoke only briefly about politics and his own plans, before proposing that we have coffee somewhere else, and I imagined the reason why he had invited me along was now going to emerge. He led me not to some quiet room but to a seat at the head of the club's main staircase, where he could see everyone coming up and they must inevitably see him. More than that, since they had to approach up a number of steps while he reclined in an armchair, I had the sense of being present at a reception, almost as though he had already become Viceroy. A number of members stopped for a few words, their manner conveying to me the impression that they were both glad to see him and relieved to get away. After several such interviews, when it was evident that he had nothing he wanted to discuss, I said I should get back to my office, but asked first whether he had given any thought to the question of an article. He replied that he did not want to criticize the government, and that in any case, as a naval officer* it was not possible for him to do so. I had not asked him to criticize the government, nor did I want him to do so except in regard to the one aspect of post-war planning on which he was an authority, but thought it better to let this pass. Why, I wondered, had he gone to the trouble of asking me to lunch if he had nothing to discuss and no possibility of writing anything? Or had he invited me in one frame of mind, but then changed it before we actually met?

As I went down the stairs and out of the club, I had the impression that I had been watching some machine of great potential whose system of controls only allowed it to operate in limited directions so that its full possibilities were never going to be realized. Many years later I was reminded of this when I heard him in an interview on television complain of never having been 'fully stretched'.

It was not until nearly forty years after our last meeting, and more than ten years after his death, that I read the two following entries in Reith's diary.

11 August 1943. I am very busy now and presumably will stay so. Lunched with Hopkinson, editor of *Picture Post*, who wanted me to write a strong article attacking the government. I wouldn't and anyhow as a naval officer can't.

15 August 1943. I wasn't feeling at all happy. I have made such a mess of everything and I wish I had never been born.

On reading these notes and thinking back to our two meetings I felt that, though impressed at the time both by his capacity and

*Since the middle of the previous year he had been a lieutenant commander in the Coastal Forces; later he was put in charge of the material side of the navy's part in combined operations with the rank of captain. *The Reith Diaries*, op. cit., page 308.

his ambivalence, I had quite failed to appreciate the extent of his inner conflict. I had been given a glimpse into a truly terrifying struggle between an ambition – which in his case was harnessed to a genuine wish to serve – and that paralysing inhibition, the need for general approval. How much better for himself, and probably also for his country, if ambition had been allowed to gain the day.

Besides my work on *Picture Post*, I had also since 1941 been responsible for *Lilliput*, the pocket magazine started by Stefan Lorant to which some six years earlier I had vainly tried to contribute in the hope of earning three guineas. *Lilliput* was a delightful little publication, well printed, with an attractive coloured cover always drawn by the same artist, Walter Trier. One of its best-known features was the 'doubles' – two look-alike photographs on facing pages, a pouter pigeon opposite a cadet on parade with his chest thrown out; Hitler giving the Nazi salute to a small dog with its paw raised; a pear opposite a publican with a pear-shaped face.

In wartime particularly, *Lilliput* was an easy magazine to sell. It made no demands. It did not attack or criticize. It simply made one laugh, providing a couple of hours of easy enjoyment. Writers, artists and photographers seemed happy to work for it despite the ridiculously low fees it paid, and the sales soared before long into the hundreds of thousands. One of the theories on which the magazine operated was that all kinds of well-known people who don't normally write articles – archbishops and admirals, sportsmen and scientists, film stars and prime ministers – have some personal interest they will be happy to write about if asked. It may be the only article you will ever get from them, but at least it will make your contributors' page impressive. Those, for example, who wrote in December 1942 on 'The Foulest Christmas I Ever Had' included Arthur Koestler, Rex Harrison and the Dean of Canterbury, for which each probably received something like £5. The magazine had very few 'returns' (unsold copies), but at the end of the year we would bind any there were into a canvas cover and sell them off as the *Lilliput Annual*.

For me the one or two afternoons each month which I spent working on the magazine were made easy and enjoyable because all the real work had already been done by the assistant editor, Kaye Webb, and her helper Mechthild Nawiasky. Kaye, who would later become known as the extremely successful editor of children's books for Penguin, was a lively and attractive girl, so that writers, artists and photographers were constantly coming into the office to talk to her and going away finding they had promised to do a couple of drawings or write a funny article by the day after tomorrow. She could even perform the same magic on the telephone. Recently – in the course of looking through back numbers of the magazine – I noticed that we had had an article by Bernard Shaw and asked how on earth, for the few pounds we offered, she had ever managed to get an article out of him? 'Oh, I just rang him up and we had a chat.' And Max Beerbohm? 'I wrote to him. . . . He wrote back – "Dear Miss W. How can I resist your letter? But you must promise not to alter a single capital or comma."' And James Mason? 'I just asked him.'

Julian Huxley, Feliks Topolski, Stephen Spender, Professor Joad, Geoffrey Grigson, John Betjeman, Compton Mackenzie, Osbert Lancaster, Beatrix Lehmann, Robert Graves, Leslie Henson, Walter de la Mare . . . the list of noted contributors was endless. But she was excellent also at discovering the unknown. One of these was Bill Naughton. 'He was a lorry driver with a bright blue eye who came wandering into the office with a badly typed story – it was the first one he ever got published. I remember I took him to the dogs with my mum.'

More than twenty years later, just back myself from nine years in Africa, I would come across Bill Naughton playing football in Hyde Park against a team of waiters from Grosvenor House.

'You must be doing pretty well nowadays, Bill,' I said. 'A play running. Pieces on television. Stories in magazines. Articles in the dailies. What does it feel like to be famous?'

'It feels fine,' he said. 'And the cheques come pouring in through the letterbox like soap coupons.'

Bill Brandt, today a venerated father-figure in photography, took many picture series for *Lilliput*, photographing young poets, taking pictures on film sets, in pubs, in Soho, in the London parks. One day in the summer of 1942 we suggested to him that these wartime nights offered a unique opportunity to photograph London entirely by moonlight. Because of the blackout there was no street lighting, no car headlamps, no light of any kind; never in history had there been such a chance, and once the war ended it would never come again. He returned to us weeks later with a beautiful set of mysterious photographs out of which we made ten pages. He had been obliged to give exposures of up to half an hour, and had once found himself suddenly surrounded by police. An old lady had seen him standing beside his camera mounted on its tripod, and dialled 999 to say there was a man in the road with a dangerous machine.

But the feature which gave me the greatest pleasure during the whole five years were the shelter drawings of Henry Moore. How I had come to know him I no longer remember, but we used to meet regularly for lunch, sometimes every week, at a restaurant called Gourmets in Lisle Street, just north of Leicester Square. I looked forward to these lunches keenly for I had never met anyone so calm, so certain of himself and of what he was doing, and so generous towards the work of everybody else. One day he produced a book of drawings which he was making around the tubes and underground shelters. I looked through them fascinated and asked if we might reproduce some of them in *Lilliput*. He was happy to let us use them, and Bill Brandt took a series of shelter photographs to appear in the same number. Later Henry Moore's notebook of shelter drawings would be published in facsimile with great success.

Lilliput at this period must have been the most oddly staffed of magazines, at least of any successful magazine. Neither Kaye herself nor Mechthild Nawiasky – who had a keen eye for photographs and would be for many years picture editor of the *Observer* – had received any regular journalistic training. In addition we had on the staff a lean, exceedingly pale young Londoner, John Symonds, who had been recommended to me by Feliks Topolski and also by a friend of my Oxford days, a poet named Tom Good. When I asked the young man what his experience had been on newspapers and magazines, he answered engagingly that he'd had 'almost none'. And when I inquired what he had been doing for the last five years, he said he had spent this time 'reading in the library of the British Museum'. Later I learned that he had spent not five but eight years in this form of study, researching for his father's books on English furniture and clocks, as well as delving into his own much more esoteric interests. This seemed to me such an unusual introduction to working on a popular magazine that I suggested he join us for three months on a minimum salary till we saw how useful such self-training might prove. At the end of three months we were glad to keep him on, though the gaps in his knowledge of everyday matters were as surprising as the depth of his reading in alchemy, magic and the less familiar aspects of religion.

When the article which Kaye had so skilfully extracted from James Mason disappeared from the office, John admitted that he had put it in the 'Rejects' basket, never having heard of the author. On the other hand when he went to Hastings to see Aleister Crowley they spent the whole day in discussion.

The story in the office, perhaps apocryphal, was that following their talk Crowley was deeply impressed by John's knowledge of his own specialized fields of magic and occultism, but not quite so certain of his practical capacity. On the understanding that his visitor intended writing an article for *Lilliput* about himself, Crowley was planning to ask him for something substantial on account. But before he could come out with his demand John had successfully touched him for £1 to pay his own fare back to London.

This must have relieved Crowley of any doubts about John's ability for handling the material world, since before long he appointed him his literary executor. And this was indeed an inspired choice since the revival of Crowley's fame owes much to *The Great Beast* (1951; enlarged and republished 1971) and *The Magick of Aleister Crowley* (1955), both by John Symonds; as well as to *The Confessions of Aleister Crowley*, of which he was co-editor.

20
Changeover

In November 1944 we gave up the cottage at Turville Heath in which Gerti, Lyndall and Nicolette had spent most of the war, I left the one-room flat which had been my London base for the last couple of years, and we moved into a house in Chelsea. At that time it seemed that half London was 'For Sale' or 'To Let'; all you had to do was to choose the street where you would most like to live and walk up and down selecting the house you preferred; the terms would certainly be reasonable. I had no doubt what street I wanted to live in. Ever since I first came to London in 1927, I had thought Chelsea the place to live and Cheyne Row the handsomest street in Chelsea; number 26, next door to Carlyle's old house, was to let, and we took it for £175 a year. Inside, it was exactly as it had been left on the date, presumably in September 1939, when the owners had packed up and gone, even to the teacups and sandwich papers on the floor. Though a fine house, with a beautiful panelled room taking up the whole of the first floor and a staircase you could not walk down without feeling noble, it was chill, especially in those winters of fuel shortage; it was damp from lack of human occupation and, being on five floors, difficult to run. Common-sense would have dictated some less splendid home. Moreover, though the big bombing raids were over, and the buzz bombs, or V1s (which had killed nearly 6000 people and destroyed 25,000 London houses), seemed to have ended too now that their launching sites had been overrun by Allied armies, there were still the rockets, or V2s. These gave no warning and

231

caused damage over a wide area, but there were fewer of them and since you could not see or hear them coming it was easy to forget about them until one fell close by.

Other members of the family were arriving in London too. Stephan had left his vicarage in Barrow to take over one just across the river in Battersea. My father, typically, had given up the peace of a Westmorland village and the dignity of an archdeacon to join him as assistant curate – the level at which he had started nearly thirty years earlier in Colne – so that he and my mother were now installed in a small flat overlooking Battersea Park. Jack was still stuck protestingly in one of his army training posts, and Esther was at a wartime nursery school. A few months later when Paul came home for a short time from Burma, my mother remarked that it was the first time for seven years that all her children had been in England together.

Paul had had a unique experience of war. Appointed in 1943 as commanding officer of an Indian parachute battalion, he had been leading his men in 1944 on what was intended to be a training exercise in the Burmese jungle; most of the brigade was still in transit by train and river steamer when Paul's advance battalion found themselves right among the advancing Japanese. After several days' fierce fighting, he was badly wounded in the leg by fragments of a hand grenade flung from close quarters by a Japanese who had infiltrated their position. Put in the care of two British soldiers who were ordered to 'get him out of this', he heard them during the night debating what to do with their charge. He was too badly injured, they considered, for them to have a chance of making it back to safety with him in tow, and their best hope was to leave him and clear off. 'I could hear them talking,' Paul said afterwards, 'but was so doped up with morphia that I couldn't speak. Otherwise I should have told them to clear out – which they soon did in any case.'

Next morning, abandoned by his two comrades, he was sitting beside the track wondering what to do next when in the remoteness of the jungle he heard English voices. By what, for want of a better expression, is called a stroke of luck, some other wounded men were making their way down the same trail. In this manner Paul became one of a band of men amounting to a dozen or more, varied in colour, nationality, rank and the nature of their injuries, who stumbled, staggered and hopped on a seemingly endless journey through the forests and across range after range of the Burmese mountains. For a whole week they contrived to keep going, holing up in the daytime and travelling at night, finding sufficient water and shooting an occasional animal or bird once they were out of earshot of the Japanese. Throughout the journey Paul leaned on the shoulder of a Gurkha who, when the last food had been eaten and there seemed no prospect of shooting anything, produced out of his clothing a tin of bully beef which he had been saving for this moment.

When finally they reached something like a road and followed it down to the outskirts of Imphal, where defences against the Japanese were being hastily prepared, they were confronted by a young officer with a squadron of tanks. Appalled by their appearance, he ordered his men to hand over their rations, radioed back for ambulances and had them all conveyed to hospital. In the course of a dreadful week they had covered about thirty miles.

Meantime in the quieter world of *Picture Post*, the last year of the war was bringing big changes. I had lost Charles Fenby, the assistant editor, who had gone to take over another Hulton magazine, the *Leader*, recently bought from a character known as 'Cosher' Bates. Cosher, who derived his nickname from his business methods, had been a financial associate and crony of the Labour leader and railway union boss, J. H. Thomas, with whom he had shared some profitable speculations. But by this time Cosher was very near his end and no match for W. J. Dickenson, whose natural kindness of heart did not prevent his driving the hardest possible bargain on behalf of the Hulton family, to whose interests he was devoted.

To replace Charles I managed with difficulty to persuade Ted Castle, husband of the renowned Barbara, to forsake the *Daily Mirror*. Ted was a journalist of wide experience and many contacts, a good organizer, liked by everyone. But now

233

suddenly others as well as Charles were leaving. MacDonald Hastings, who had been invaluable as a war reporter almost throughout the war, left just before it ended for a romantic project – nothing less than to revive the old-time *Strand Magazine** – taking with him the photographer Felix Man. Anne Scott-James, about to marry Mac, left at the same time, going back to fashion magazines and then to a distinguished career in Sunday journalism. Maurice Edelman, who had covered the North African campaign for us, left too but in a different direction. In the early summer of 1945 he had been in Blackpool covering the crucial Labour Party conference which would settle the character of post-war Britain. Summing this up, he wrote:

A new spirit had taken hold of the Labour Party. You felt it in the first hours of the Blackpool Conference. It expressed itself in the faces and voices of the delegates who came to the microphone. It communicated itself to the Executive.

It made itself heard in the speeches of Labour leaders. Labour has recaptured its old evangelical fervour. More than that, Labour has won the will to win.†

Later he described watching Attlee, the party's leader, in his hotel, 'fretful and insecure, tormented by self-doubt, walking alone up and down the corridors, mentally composing the letter accepting or rejecting Churchill's proposal that the Coalition should continue. Now at last the decision was made, and with Ellen Wilkinson in the chair the Conference was dressed for action with the speakers of the New Britain – young soldiers like Denis Healey and John Freeman – coming to the rostrum to give their testimony.'

Maurice's own life, as well as the country's future, was to be changed by this week at Blackpool. Strikingly good-looking, friendly in manner and a fluent speaker, he was having a drink after the official conference ended when a group of young people sat down at his table. They were looking, they said, for

*A project which, sad to say, never materialized, the publishing firm backing down before the first issue appeared.
†'Labour Makes Its Plan for Power', *Picture Post*, 9 June 1945.

a candidate for their division of Coventry.

'What sort of person are you looking for?'

'Someone like you!' one of them exclaimed.

'Well, what *about* me?'

A few weeks later he had become their candidate, and not long after that their MP.

One I was anxious to retain was Edgar Ainsworth, the art editor, whose job it was to work out the layouts for the various pages in detail. Known to us all as 'Grumpy' from the air of truculence surrounding his small figure, he was an excellent draughtsman who had come to the paper by way of advertising. Perhaps as some form of compensation for lack of size, he was boastful and assertive; most of what he said about himself we would discount – only to find out afterwards that it was largely true. His method over work was self-protective. He would complain that the set of photographs given him to make up was incomplete and that the whole story ought to have been done differently, but when I answered 'Leave it to me, Grumpy! I see just how to make this story up,' he would carry it off and come back, often enough with something original and interesting.

I was fond of Grumpy, either because of or despite his abrasive manner, and was sorry when one summer evening during the flying-bomb period it seemed he was about to go up in smoke. I had been working late and around seven in the evening went downstairs to go home. Outside all main entrances in those days was a stout brick wall to act as baffle and prevent bomb blast entering the building. Hearing the hammering noise of a V1 flying bomb, I stopped by the baffle wall and looked up. It was coming in over the river, quite low down, only a short distance away, and appeared to be heading directly up Shoe Lane. As I watched, two things happened simultaneously; the bomb's engine cut out – which meant that it would start to come down leaving just ten seconds before it hit the ground – and Grumpy, who had been drinking in the pub opposite our offices, started to walk out around its baffle wall.

'Poor old Grumpy!' I thought. 'That's the last I'll see of him! Hope he had a few good drinks.'

At the same moment, as he told me later, he was catching sight of me for what he supposed was the last time.

'Poor old Tom! He's gone! Serves him right for staying on working after everyone else had left!'

We were both wrong, however, for the bomb veered away in its descent to explode with a shattering crash and a column of filthy smoke and debris in Clifford's Inn, 100 yards behind Grumpy's pub, and almost directly opposite Manzoni's restaurant where the elderly waiters in their stained evening suits had been interred in the rubble four years previously. Having lost so many good people to other employment, I was not willing to lose Grumpy too, and Grumpy, who had been offered a job in an advertising agency, was persuaded by a pay increase to stay on, being assisted in his layout work by young Rosemary Grimble who would later make a name for herself by her exquisite line drawings, particularly of scenes in the Gilbert Islands where she had lived as a girl and her father had been governor.

For a few months longer we hung on as best we could, and then back from the army came Lionel Birch and our ace photographer Bert Hardy. Sydney Jacobson, whose distinguished war service on several fronts had brought him a decoration, wanted something closer to political life than *Lilliput* could offer and so joined *Picture Post* as a trouble-shooting special correspondent, while Richard Bennett took over the editorship of *Lilliput*. A newcomer was Robert Kee, sent on to me by Sonia Brownell;* Kee, just back from the army, was taken on at sight and quickly started to become one of the best writers on the staff.

In those days journalism as a profession had not yet been structured and an editor enjoyed much freedom as to whom he employed, subject of course to his proprietor's agreement. When a young student just leaving his Welsh university wrote asking for a job as a reporter, I replied asking for samples of his writing. All he sent me were poems, but they were remarkable

---

*She would become George Orwell's wife shortly before his death in January 1950, and later his literary executor.

enough to secure him a three months' trial, after which everyone agreed we should keep him on. We knew him as John Ormond Thomas and were sorry when after only a few years he returned to Wales to work for the BBC and to make his name – now John Ormond without the Thomas – as a poet and a television producer. Some thirty years later in his programme, 'The Life and Death of *Picture Post*', he would pronounce an eloquent requiem for the magazine.

Another of our most successful writers was discovered lurking on the paper's administrative side. Fyfe Robertson, a lean Scot whose ruddy features and rich accent would one day become familiar in all British homes, had come from the northern edition of the *Daily Express* to do the job known as picture editor. This involved looking after negatives and prints and in addition acting as a kind of wet-nurse or nanny to the photographers. It was his responsibility to see that when a cameraman went out on a story – which might involve visiting half a dozen countries spread over two continents – he had everything he needed, passport in order, visas, inoculations, plane and rail tickets, travellers' cheques and money in the necessary currencies.

'You treat these cameramen like bloody royal children!' Denzil Batchelor, our new sports reporter, objected, coming back from his first assignment. 'They seem to think I'm there to hold their hands and wipe their noses.'

'Not royal children,' I said, 'more like racehorses. You don't expect racehorses to make their own travel arrangements – and when they get to the course they need looking after, too. If the cameraman gets his pictures, and you miss your story because you were helping him – that's okay, we'll get the story somehow. But if there are no pictures we've got nothing.'

The making of complicated arrangements, however, was not Fyfe Robertson's strong point. Cameramen complained that something or other they should have had was missing. Occasionally too film or prints I needed had managed to get themselves lost, and one day I asked the picture editor into my room.

'Robbie,' I said, 'you and I have got a problem.'

'What's that?' he asked, concern visible down his considerable length.

'You aren't good in the job we hired you for. However, we all like you, and nobody would want to see you go. Isn't there another job on the paper you could do, supposing someone else took over from you as picture editor?'

'I think I could write,' Robbie answered, much to my surprise. Told to choose his own story and the cameraman he could work with best – something never normally allowed – he went away, coming back before long with clear proof of his claim. Within a few months he had established himself, and an old friend from *Weekly Illustrated* days, Harry Deverson, was persuaded to leave the fast-disintegrating Ministry of Information and take Robbie's place. Deverson's conscientious nature and unfailing good temper made him an ideal 'photographers' nanny'. He had also an excellent eye for the right pictures to print out of the two hundred or more negatives a cameraman might bring back from an assignment.

So now, with old hands and newcomers, we had got a real team together. I summed them up as individualistic and assertive, full of ideas, distrustful of authority and not apt to accept instructions – whether from editor, proprietor, or officialdom – without giving their own views and sometimes arguing the toss. So far as they had any common political alignment, it would be left, but not far left, of centre.

With the staff organized, my next concern was of a different sort. On a magazine there is continual need for reference material, often in the form of drawings or photographs from the past to help build up some story in the present. In a single week one might have to send out for, say, every picture in existence of the island of Diego Garcia; portraits of all Queen Victoria's prime ministers; a photograph of the first Test team to visit Australia; and a reproduction of the Great Seal of England. In the whole of London there were only about half a dozen sources from which such requirements could be met, the so-called picture libraries; hitherto these had served us well, but could we be sure such service would continue?

Often during the war I had been impressed by the scale of

operations of the big American magazines, which would send four or five cameramen and reporters on a story where we sent one of each, and whose editors and executives moved around in state as though they were ambassadors. Evidently they had vast resources, and I began to fear that when peacetime conditions returned and the free-for-all began, they would decide to invade the British market. *Life* and *Look*, to name only two, were far glossier and better-printed than our own magazine would ever be. Lavish presentation might be countered by our greater knowledge of British conditions, but where should we be if they used only a fraction of their profits to buy up the picture libraries? Accordingly I suggested to Raison and Dickenson that we should buy them up first – and they agreed.

The most important of these libraries was known as the Rischgitz Collection. I had spoken the name a thousand times, but had no idea what reality corresponded to the title. It proved to be a comfortable house in Notting Hill, owned by a Mrs and Miss Boutroy, relatives of the original Edouard Rischgitz whose story they now told me. Exiled from Hungary following the Kossuth Rebellion, he had gone first to Geneva to study art, acquired in Paris the craft of painting on porcelain, and then in 1866 had been asked over to this country by the firm of Minton to make designs for an important exhibition. Around 1870 he had settled down in Linden Gardens, which was then on the outskirts of London, and where his family had remained ever since. It was a fair-sized house with a large garden in which several studios had at different times been added on to the main building. In one of them the Victorian artist Mulready had worked, as had also a painter named Creswick; a successful actor, Alfred Wigan, had enlarged one into a private theatre, which Henry Irving had made use of for his wedding reception.

However, Edouard Rischgitz's hopes that his home would become the centre of a small colony of artists were never realized, and after his death his son Augustine had founded the Rischgitz Collection almost incidentally. A teacher by profession, he adored his mother and from his school in Hampshire would cycle home every weekend in order to be with her. Always a great reader, he made a point of finding drawings and photographs of places he read about or which interested him, amassing by degrees a large collection. Eager to find some way of life which would allow him to stay at home, he started to exploit his collection. He would note anniversaries or centenaries and take round appropriate illustrations to magazines such as the *Bookman*, *Everybody's Weekly*, *John O'London* and others, which soon began to depend on him for any illustrations they required. Before long Gus was extending his activities to provide illustrations to publishers for books, encyclopedias and so on. When his nieces Alice and Louys Boutroy started to grow up, he took them on to help him, doing research in the British Museum and elsewhere for a modest ten shillings a week, of which some proportion had always to be saved.

In the early 1920s when Augustine Rischgitz died, he left his collection, by now well established, to his nieces who had added to it considerably, in particular by buying up the stock of the London Stereoscope Company when it gave up business. During the intervening years Alice too had died, leaving the knowledgeable and vivacious Louys, to whom, with her mother, I was chatting on an evening in the gloomy winter of 1943–4. After telling me a little of the collection's history, they invited me to test its resources, which I did, asking them for portraits of Samuel Richardson, engravings showing the Great Fire of London, and photographs of John Ruskin and his home at Brantwood. After a brief whispered discussion as to where these would be found, the ladies dispersed, to return in a minute or two with all I had asked for. It was evident, as I already knew, that the collection was an excellent one, but also that it had little by way of a filing system. If we were to buy it, therefore, we should need to persuade its owner to work with us while the material was being reorganized to form part of a much larger library.

Over a cup of coffee I suggested that if the ladies should ever consider selling their collection, Hulton Press would like to have the opportunity of buying it and of employing Miss Boutroy as one of the librarians, proposing that if the idea interested them, they should talk it over with their advisers and suggest a price. This they did. It was reasonable indeed, and before long Hulton Press had become the owners of the Rischgitz Collection, to which we added the Gooch Collection and one or two others, until I was confident that – with the negatives and prints from our own cameraman, plus all the pictures from the Ministry of Information we had accumulated during the war years – we would have the basis of the finest photographic and reference library in London.

For the present the war was still in progress so that it would be unwise to bring the various collections together where one bomb might destroy the lot. The Rischgitz Collection itself was in fact very nearly destroyed during the last winter of the war when a canister of incendiaries was dropped on the house in Linden Gardens during an air raid. The two ladies at once set to work to put out the blaze and when it seemed to be growing beyond their capacities to cope with, they phoned the fire station in Queensway for help.

'Sorry we can't help, miss,' was the reply. 'All our appliances are out.'

Thinking she might achieve more personally than she could over the phone, Miss Boutroy set off into the night to run the mile or so to the fire station. Some American soldiers in a jeep gave her a lift, and she was soon explaining to the fire officer the importance of the collection which was often called upon to supply pictures to the Ministry of Information.

'Oh, if it's ministry work, that's different,' said the officer, and called out the reserve appliance which was kept for government work or special emergencies. In this way the collection had been saved, and only in May 1945, when there were no more bombs likely to fall, did we take over the top floors of a disused warehouse near our Shoe Lane offices, and start bringing everything together under one roof. Knowing nothing myself about filing systems or the organization of a library, I consulted Charles Gibbs-Smith, then just returning to his post at the Victoria and Albert Museum after working for the Ministry of Information during the war. He soon drew up a plan, of whose execution a delightful and capable librarian, Mrs Mona Parrish, was put in charge. She assembled a team of librarians which included Miss Boutroy, ordered the necessary filing cabinets and equipment, and embarked on her lengthy and exacting task.

I was happy to see the work underway at last, never imagining that – in little more than ten years' time – the library, known today as the Radio Times-Hulton Picture Library, would be almost the only part of our whole enterprise still in existence.

21
Seeds of Conflict

With the war's end and the build-up of our staff, it at last became possible to create a magazine according to a plan instead of printing war pictures and living from hand to mouth. In addition our paper ration had started slowly to increase, so that we could again tackle subjects needing to be treated at some length, the sort of subjects around which today television documentaries would be made but which in the 1940s were not handled by the media at all, being considered too controversial and distressing.

I was convinced that a readership which had just been through the war must be a lot less squeamish and easily upset than most editors and managements believed, and that – if it were to hold existing readers and attract new ones in a period of competition – *Picture Post* would need to be provocative, grappling with the subjects people talked and argued about among themselves. This was not primarily a matter of morals or ethics but of knowing what niche the paper filled. By following its own path it would attract a section of the community whose interests were not catered for elsewhere, and I was never happy to let the paste-up of an issue leave our office for the printers unless I could see something in it which was going to be argued over in the pub or around the breakfast table. Buying a newspaper is a matter of habit, so that it can remain unaffected by a few poor issues, but most magazines – and certainly ours – were bought casually on impulse. When we put out a feeble issue it might sell no worse than the previous two or three, but the following issue would show a drop of twenty or thirty thousand from disappointed readers.

Among the longer picture stories we now printed were one on life in a mental hospital – where Fyfe Robertson and the photographer Kurt Hutton lived for a fortnight while building it up. Sydney Jacobson and the same Kurt Hutton made the first picture story ever inside Holloway prison, and Bert Lloyd with Bert Hardy recorded 'The Life of a Prison Officer' (20 November 1948) at Strangeways prison, Manchester. In his article Lloyd wrote that 'The notion of educating men in gaol and giving them a sense of purpose is winning small success because prisons are overcrowded (so that rooms for leisure are turned into cells), and there just aren't enough prison officers to tend men outside their cells after teatime.' That was nearly thirty-five years ago, and today overcrowding is still the complaint, but with far stronger cause and less justification than in the immediate post-war period.

Even more topical in the 1980s appears the investigation made by Robert Kee, also with photographs by Bert Hardy, into the question, 'Is there a Colour Bar in Britain?' (3 July 1948). Kee wrote:

Although there are no official figures, the coloured population of Great Britain is estimated by both the Colonial Office and the League of Coloured People at about 25,000, including students. This total is distributed over the whole of Britain, but there are two large concentrated communities: one of about 7000 in the dock area of Cardiff round Londoun Square, popularly known as 'Tiger Bay', and the other of about 8000 in the shabby mid-nineteenth century residential South End of Liverpool.... It is most important to remember that all colonial coloured people, of whatsoever origin or class, have been brought up to think of Britain as 'The Mother Country'.... This is particularly true of the West Indians, who no longer have the tribal associations and native language which can still provide some fundamental security for the disillusioned African. The West Indian disillusioned with Britain is deprived of all sense of security. He becomes, quite understandably, the most sensitive and neurotic member of the coloured community....

The British colour bar, one might say, is invisible, but like Wells' invisible man it is hard and real to the touch.... And it is when you get

lower down the social scale that you find it hits the hardest....
For Britain's colour problem there are a few practical and remedial
steps that can be taken.... But it can only be solved by a true
integration of white and coloured people in one society. And for that
to take place there must be some sort of revolution inside every
individual mind – coloured and white – where prejudices based on
bitterness, ignorance or patronage have been established.

Parallel to this inquiry and connected by its theme was another
into that revival of fascism which would in course of time lead
to the founding of the National Front. The article, headed 'Why
Should Anyone Still Follow Mosley?' appeared in May 1948,
and it is indeed strange to realize that Mosley's meetings should
have been attracting big audiences only three years after the war
against fascism had ended in seemingly total victory. But most
surprising of all perhaps, looking back on these old issues, is
that in November 1945 we should have had the prescience to
send a cameraman and a journalist, Hilde Marchant, to
Manchester to cover one of the earliest Pan-African Conferences, an event which attracted almost no attention from the
British press as a whole – and still more extraordinary that
among half a dozen pictures published we should have included
a portrait of Jomo Kenyatta. Then a quite unknown farm-
worker in Sussex, he was destined to become first president of
an independent Kenya where I would one day spend several
peaceful and happy years under his rule. Inaccurately described
by us as 'the Abyssinian delegate', Kenyatta was asking for
an Act of Parliament to make discrimination by race or colour
in Britain a criminal offence. Another to whom Hilde spent
time talking was George Padmore, a West Indian journalist,
with whom I would have talks in Ghana fifteen years later
when he was adviser to Kwame Nkrumah, the first head of the
first of the newly independent African states of the 1950s and
1960s. Nkrumah himself, a student of law and economics at the
London School of Economics, was then as unknown as
Kenyatta. Concerning this same conference Nkrumah would
write that the nature of the delegates was important since 'they
were practical men and men of action and not, as was the case of
the four previous conferences, merely idealists contenting

themselves with writing theses'. Also, since 'the preponderance of members ... were African, its ideology became African Nationalism – a revolt against colonialism, racism and imperialism in Africa – and it adopted Marxist socialism as its philosophy'.*

Another African delegate, Ndabaningi Sithole – destined to play a prominent part in the long struggle to create Zimbabwe out of Rhodesia – has described how the conference came to be held only a few months after war ended, and how the war itself had served to inspire the movement for African liberation.

World War II had a great deal to do with the awakening of the peoples of Africa. During the war the African came in contact with practically all the peoples of the earth. He met them on a life-and-death struggle basis. He saw the so-called civilised and peaceful and orderly white people mercilessly butchering one another just as his so-called savage ancestors had done in tribal wars. He saw no difference between the primitive and the civilised man. In short, he saw through European pretensions that only Africans were savages. This had a revolutionising psychological impact on the African.

But more than this, World War II taught the African most powerful ideas. During the war the Allied Powers taught the subject peoples (and millions of them!) that it was not right for Germany to dominate other nations. They taught the subject peoples to fight and die for freedom rather than live and be subjugated by Hitler. The subject peoples learned the lesson well. . . .†

Presiding over the conference was the truly legendary American Negro leader, Dr W. E. B. DuBois, who had flown over from New York – a somewhat less comfortable journey then than now – at the age of seventy-three. Back at the start of the century when the white races could see no challenge to their superiority anywhere in the world, DuBois had made the astounding prophecy that colour was to be the great problem of the twentieth century.

*The Autobiography of Kwame Nkrumah, Nelson, Edinburgh, 1959, page 44.
†Ndabaningi Sithole, African Nationalism, Oxford University Press, Cape Town, 1959, pages 19–20. Born in a mud hut of illiterate parents, Sithole has written one of the books most influential in the African struggle for independence.

246

One delegate present whose speech would return to haunt him was Joe Appiah, delegate for the West African Students Union and later to become the son-in-law of Sir Stafford Cripps. 'The only language the Englishman understands is force. Others plead for more diplomatic negotiation, but I am for firmer action. Only force will take us out of our disgraceful plight.' In years to come Joe Appiah would himself become the victim of force, and spend long years of suffering in prison; not, however, as a prisoner of the English, but of his fellow delegate and national leader, Kwame Nkrumah.

Yet another question which is more urgent and topical today than it was when we discussed it then, was that of how far a United Europe could be organized, and of what Britain's place in it should be. 'Is Europe Nearer Union?' by Lionel Birch and Kurt Hutton (29 May 1948) and Birch's follow-up story a year later with Felix H. Man, entitled 'Europe: Dare We Face Real Union?' (27 August 1949) are articles which can be read with interest more than thirty years after they were written. But the one which provoked the biggest explosion outside the office – for there were several which caused much greater upheavals in it – was a well-documented exposure of the disastrous Tanganyika Groundnuts Scheme, produced on the spot by Fyfe Robertson with Raymond Kleboe, one of several new photographers we had by now taken on. This appeared in the issue for 19 November 1949, raising a storm in the House of Commons and in the country which went on for weeks.

All these serious articles were only one aspect of the magazine, which depended for its success primarily on being enjoyable to read and look at. Such picture stories as that of Elizabeth Taylor at the age of sixteen (29 January 1949), or the young and beautiful Audrey Hepburn visiting Kew Gardens (13 May 1950) are as enchanting now as they were then. Every magazine deserves an occasional piece of luck and we had one in September 1948, when we made a single page filler from a small set of photographs under the title 'Schoolboy Jockey'. Its almost unknown subject had just won his first big race at the age of twelve, and the short article reported, 'Just now it's only holiday work. But crack jockeys may look out when

Lester Piggott leaves school.'

'What kind of magazine *is* this?' a newcomer to the paper once asked me at the weekly conference where next week's issue was being hammered out in general discussion among the staff. 'Is it a do-gooding paper? Or is it out for popular success?'

I answered, rather arrogantly, that any competent journalist can make a paper that is popular but useless, and anyone with a social conscience can produce a do-gooding paper which no one buys. Our task was to make a worthwhile paper which millions would enjoy looking at and reading.

The years from 1945 to 1950 were years of consolidation, following the drama of the magazine's launching and the period of the war, in which virtually every publication sold all the copies it could print. And the fact that at a time when competition was becoming fiercer – many journals were faltering and some had already collapsed – the sales of *Picture Post* were rising, seemed to indicate that the choice and blend of subjects was right for the audience the magazine was reaching. And rise the sales certainly did, from under 950,000 in December 1943 to just over 1,422,000 in December 1949. The magazine was also getting as much advertising as it could carry on its still restricted paper ration, and the profits remained steady.

But if, with the ending of the war, the excitement and enjoyment of editing had really started, so also had the difficulties, which centred round my relationship with the proprietor, Edward Hulton. Hulton was by nature a kindly man, anxious for people in general to be happy and to have what they needed for a reasonable life. He was hospitable, fond of company and could be generous. Once I had approached him on behalf of a member of my staff who was in trouble, asking him if he would be willing to give X £200 – equal at that time to £1000 or more today.

'Why?' he asked, laying down his pen and leaning back in his revolving chair.

'Because he's desperate. His work's vital to the paper, but he can't work with this matter hanging over him. He's got no savings. We shan't get any good out of him till this is settled.

We'd pay that amount for a camera without thinking twice. X is much more valuable to us than a camera.'

Hulton fished a chequebook out from somewhere and handed me a cheque for the amount.

But if enterprise, gregariousness and a lively – though not always clear – mind were among his virtues, he had other qualities which made him difficult to work with. His manner was brusque and he wanted everything settled in a moment; quickly bored, he was unwilling to explore any issue thoroughly and would often agree to some proposed action without being convinced, because he wanted to get back to his newspaper or to make a telephone call. He was also extremely susceptible to the last opinion he had heard, particularly if it had been violently expressed. A member of some half-dozen clubs, he would go for lunch to one or other and, on coming back, send for me to complain that some article or pictures he had approved a week earlier was 'a disastrous mistake'. When I asked in what way it had been a mistake, he would reply in general terms that it had 'given great offence to influential people', and I must take care that this did not happen again. When I tried to open out our discussion and arrive at the real issue behind his objection, he would place the tips of his fingers together, lean back in his chair, frown and indicate that there was no more to be said. He had expressed his opinion, and that was that.

In the days when *Picture Post* was still only an unnamed project, Hulton had once called Lorant and myself to order with the words, 'Kindly remember that I am not only a Conservative, but I am a loyal supporter of Mr Neville Chamberlain!' Edward Hulton had in fact contested both the Leek division of Staffordshire in 1929 and Harwich in 1931 in the Tory interest. The fall of France, however, which he ascribed to the refusal of the unprivileged many to risk their lives in protecting the possessions of the privileged few, had had a profound effect on him, as it had on other very rich people at that time, so that for a while his whole outlook seemed to change.

Not only had he flung himself energetically into helping to

organize the Home Guard school, and into the work of various committees concerned with the conduct of the war and the planning of post-war Britain, but in 1943 he had written a book, *The New Age*,* of which an anonymous *Times* reviewer wrote (2 October 1943):

Mr Hulton ranges over a wide field of human activities, political, social, economic, sometimes discussing them very briefly. One chapter may be twenty-one pages, another only as many lines. A lurid picture is drawn of the period between the wars. 'It was chaotic and evil, it was obviously and palpably bad.' This was due, not entirely to the incapacity of a ruling class, but to the disintegration of society which began with the break-up of medieval Christendom....

A rather fuller review by Tom Clarke, former editor of the *News Chronicle*, writing in Hulton's own journal *World Review*, described *The New Age* as '... a brave, eager book, a refreshing adventure among ideas. The result is a mental shake-up likely to shock the Blimps who fondly await peace to bring back their "good old world".' It called, Clarke said, for 'a change of heart and a new spiritual and social urge', and he described the Utopia as envisaged by the author:

There will be no Stock Exchange ... no speculations in shares, no genuflexions before an obsolete gold standard, no money 'talking' as if it were a commodity. Business will be more controlled, internationally and internally, in an economic system combining nationalisation and private enterprise.

This mood was still dominant in August 1945, when Hulton wrote a resounding welcome to Mr Attlee's new Labour government.

The great victory of the Labour Party at the General Election was a surprise to everybody, to Labour people almost as much as to anyone else. We now have, for the first time in British history, a Labour Government in power with a large majority. Wise men have long realised that Labour must some day come to power; and it is well that

*Edward Hulton, *The New Age*, Allen and Unwin, 1943.

it should do so unfettered. More will be relieved that the form of Conservatism represented by Lord Beaverbrook, and aided and abetted by Mr Churchill in his latest phase, has been flung indignantly overboard. . . .

I am not personally a Socialist; I do not think that nationalisation will produce a 'universal panacea', still less am I a materialist. Yet I rejoice that latter-day Conservatism has been overthrown; and that we now have in power a party which is pledged to improve the social services – Beveridgeism if you will – and to provide the houses, and the land for the houses, without which there may well be a revolution.

I am more delighted than I can say that Mr Ernest Bevin has gone to the Foreign Office. . . . At the Blackpool Conference he stolidly refused to dub every Pole a Fascist, and it is reasonable to assume that he will be as firm with Russia as with the United States.

In thus rejoicing that Conservatism had been overthrown, Hulton referred to fears that unless houses, land and social services were provided 'there may well be a revolution'. Before long, however, he had evidently become convinced that any danger of revolution by the masses had gone by. And as memories of the war years faded, as the world increasingly split into two halves, West and East, and as the Labour Party ran into the economic difficulties of the post-war years, the views of our proprietor moved one way and the views of editor and staff either did not move or moved another. I began to receive a shower of notes complaining that the paper was too left-wing; that we were 'soft' on our attitude to the 'People's Democracies' of Eastern Europe; that we were guilty of 'appeasement' in our attitude to the arch-enemy Russia, so that responsible people now 'looked askance' at the magazine which was 'going rapidly downhill'.

In August 1945 Hulton had praised Ernest Bevin, the Foreign Secretary, for refusing 'to dub every Pole a Fascist', but eighteen months later, following an article which he felt was unduly sympathetic to the transitional government in Poland, he wrote me a long, explosive memorandum:

I am totally at a loss to know why *Picture Post* should become more Soviet than the Soviets themselves. . . . I must ask you in future to submit all political matters to me. I cannot permit editors of my newspapers to become organs of Communist propaganda. Still less to make the great newspaper which I have built up a laughing-stock.

Not long after this again, in March 1948, his views had hardened further since he ordered me to dismiss Bert Lloyd, who had now been on the staff for nearly eight years, on the ground that he could not have someone on the paper who was an admitted member of the Communist Party, adding that he had no wish himself to be regarded as a 'fifth columnist' or 'sent to the Isle of Man'* in the event of war with Russia. I was determined not to lose Lloyd, who was an excellent writer; nor did I think it would improve the image of Picture Post if we were to sack a capable reporter for his political convictions. I therefore offered to write Hulton a formal letter saying that I was aware Lloyd was a Communist, that he had never made any secret of the fact, and that I accepted full personal responsibility for continuing to employ him and for ensuring that his views did not colour any articles of his we printed, nor influence the paper's attitude in general.

This offer was accepted, and so from month to month and year to year our uneasy collaboration was maintained. Long ago I had told Stefan Lorant that he was unrealistic to imagine he was going to find somewhere in the world a proprietor who would say, 'Stefan, you are a genius! Just go ahead and do exactly as you want.' I had no expectation myself of finding such a paragon, but I used to dream of a proprietor who would say, as Lord Thomson was later reported to have told his editors, 'Make the paper a success. So long as you do that, so long as circulation rises, advertising comes in and profits are maintained, I shan't interfere.'

But that was very far from being my own case.

---

*The Isle of Man had been used for internment of people of German origin, or possible Nazi sympathizers, during part of the First World War.

22

Tension Mounts

While still a very young man, Edward Hulton had married the daughter of a general in the Imperial Russian Army, a marriage which ended in divorce. In 1941 he married again, his second wife being the daughter of a Russian councillor of state and chamberlain to the Tsar. Her name was Princess Nika Yourievitch and she had been brought up in Paris, to which after 1917 so many Russian exiles were attracted, partly no doubt by the city itself but also owing to the long history of contact between the Russian and French courts – before revolutions removed them both – and to the widespread use of the French language among the Russian nobility. Nika herself might well have been taken for a Frenchwoman; she was beautiful and talented, with a passion for clothes and a cultivated interest in art. The stir of social life was a necessity to her, and being purposeful and strongwilled with the fortune of her husband as backing, she was determined to establish whatever may be the present-day equivalent of a *salon*. To this end she gave big dinner parties, wanted important people to be present at them, was anxious that she and Teddy should be asked everywhere in return, and – though normally impatient and quick-tempered – was ready to exercise much diplomacy to realize her social ambitions. Teddy himself was a lavish host. Fond of political discussions and interested in political gossip, he had not yet, it seemed to me, altogether given up his pre-war parliamentary ambitions.

During the latter part of the war the Hultons had established themselves in the Dorchester Hotel, Park Lane, which was not only comfortable and well-provisioned, even under wartime conditions, but also solidly built, an important consideration at that time. A number of other eminent figures in the social and publishing worlds had moved in too. On nights when bombing was severe, the corridors were considered safer than bedrooms since their ceilings were narrow and so less likely to fall in. Consequently there were times when a late-night visitor returning to his room, or making his way from someone else's, would have to step over or round a number of famous bodies laid end to end. For a while after peace was signed and before they bought themselves an imposing house near Guildford, the Hultons continued living in the Dorchester, and it was here that they did much of their entertaining.

Among their guests would often be a number, sometimes a preponderance, of Conservative politicians: Anthony Eden, Oliver Lyttelton (later to become Lord Chandos), Sir John and Lady Anderson, Oliver Stanley and others. Almost the only Labour figure I ever met as guest was Hector McNeil, the still youthful Minister of State. Another politician present from time to time was Leslie Hore-Belisha, who had been War Minister at the outbreak of hostilities but was demoted rapidly by Chamberlain, supposedly at the instigation of the French generals* whose reputation and influence ranked high until the fighting started. After the war Hore-Belisha renounced Liberalism – he had been one of the small group of so-called National Liberals – and joined the Conservatives. Shortly after this I was present at one of the Hultons' dinner parties when he happened to remark of a young Labour MP, Raymond Blackburn, whose maiden speech had been praised by Churchill, 'He's not a convinced Labour supporter. I'm pretty sure that – with a little persuasion – he could be persuaded to come over to our side.'

'I dare say he would,' Oliver Stanley remarked coldly. 'But you know we never really *like* people who join us from another party.'

*See Liddell Hart, op. cit., page 45.

Hore-Belisha became silent.

Less easily put down was C. E. M. Joad, the popular philosopher,* who attended one or two of these dinners. An engaging figure, good-natured and a fluent conversationalist, Joad was at the height of his fame as a member of the 'Brains Trust' – probably the most celebrated of all radio programmes at a time when there was virtually no television – but had found himself in trouble for persistently travelling without a railway ticket. A less ebullient spirit would have been dampened by so conspicuous a humiliation and many public figures would probably have retired altogether into private life. But not so Joad. When a fellow guest at the dinner remarked that he had to go down to Brighton for something or other next weekend, Joad from the far end of the table piped up in his peculiar high-pitched voice: 'If you are travelling to Brighton, let me tell you, you have no need to book any further than Three Bridges. When you get there, you must hop out and nip across the line . . .'

Nika could make her own contribution too, but more often quietly to her neighbour than to the table as a whole. Once when she remarked to Cyril Connolly that she had just bought herself a new grey Rolls-Royce, Cyril – who wouldn't have minded being a rich man himself – remarked sententiously, 'You realize, Nika, that buying a Rolls-Royce is not going to make you happy?'

'Yes, I do realize that, Cyril,' Nika replied. 'But when I'm very *unhappy* it will comfort me to go and look at my Rolls-Royce.'

As the pace of social life increased and dinner parties grew more frequent, I found it difficult always to be present when invited – often, no doubt, having only been asked to make up the numbers when some more influential guest dropped out. I have never cared for social life, would almost always prefer to stay at home rather than go out, on top of which I was finding it impossible to edit the magazine by day and stay out late in

*Joad was head of the Department of Philosophy at Birkbeck College, University of London, and author of *Common Sense Ethics*, *Common Sense Theology* and a number of other works.

255

the evenings. I used to wish I had a twin brother, or could appoint someone as 'social' or 'dinner party' editor who would eat and drink on my behalf and make the kind of entertaining conversation required. As between planning and making up its pages, or having a social life with compulsory attendance at parties, I should not have hesitated for a moment; I positively enjoyed my daily work and would gladly have signed a pledge never to attend another dinner party for life, or at any rate for ten years. Occasionally I would call on Lionel Birch to help me out. Tall and good-looking, he was very soon welcome on his own account, but his taste for the luxury life was also limited, and there came a day when I asked him to stand in for me and he refused, having something more interesting on hand.

'Well,' Nika told me over the telephone, 'if you *won't* make an effort yourself to help me out, and if Birch *can't* come, then the very least you can do is to find someone presentable to take your place. I shall expect him here at eight o'clock!'

Shortly before that we had taken on to the staff a young man called David Mitchell; like Birch, he was tall, good-looking and an Oxbridge graduate, and having joined us so recently could not protest when I told him he must get out his dinner jacket and turn up at the Dorchester that night. He was an unfortunate choice, however, since, when Anthony Eden started expressing his opinion on some political issue after dinner, Mitchell contradicted him and put forward his own very different view. Encouraged by the general silence and fortified by a glass or four, he went on to develop this at some length. Later when the party broke up, Nika told him to stay behind and, after telling him off roundly for his indiscretion, ordered him to ring the bell for a bottle of champagne to be sent up. She added, ' . . . But of course you won't know how to open it. I can see you're not used to champagne.'

'I'm quite used to *drinking* champagne,' Mitchell replied. 'But I must say I usually have it opened for me.'

When I learned of this next day, I congratulated Mitchell on his reply, but told him that if he intended to go on contradicting ministers and giving sharp answers to employers he would do better in some other career than journalism. In fact he soon became a capable journalist, and after a life of varied activities has established himself with success in the arduous career of professional author, being particularly attracted, oddly enough, by the history of the suffragette movement.

From time to time, despite our differences, the Hultons would ask me to accompany them on a short holiday and in April 1948 we all set out for Norway by way of the sea ferry from Newcastle. Besides Mr and Mrs Hulton, there were two children and a nanny, an accompanying Norwegian lady and myself. We were seen off from King's Cross by two secretaries, a maid and two chauffeurs, who disposed of our twenty-three pieces of luggage among which was a large wooden box, the size and shape of a croquet set, which was brought into the compartment. This, I knew, was to be a skiing holiday at a place called Finse high up on the bony spine of Norway where the conditions are like those of the Arctic and blizzards often go on for several days, so I was puzzled as to when we should play croquet. Perhaps, I thought, it was some kind of indoor croquet which could be practised on the carpet.

By midday, however, the box had already been opened up and found to contain a sumptuous lunch with four bottles of Burgundy, which we were all soon enjoying. Everything went smoothly until our eventual arrival in Bergen at 6.45 a.m., with a train leaving at 7.30 and a taxi journey from the quay to the railway station. By 7.10 after a great deal of effort we were all out of the ship and on the quayside with our twenty-three pieces of luggage ranged in front of the customs officer. The officer started by asking for the keys, but then, realizing that the situation was beyond him, hastily chalked the lot. A seaman helped to get us and our belongings into two big cars but by now it was almost 7.30. We arrived as the train was pulling out, but the effect, as we poured onto the platform followed by a posse of luggage-bearing porters, was so impressive that the engine was stopped and we were all soon installed in three compartments.

Our hotel, which looked like a gigantic station buffet plonked down between the railway and a frozen lake, was comfortable and crowded. There was skiing all day and dancing every

257

evening. Teddy on holiday proved to be a relaxed, even jovial, companion, drinking as heartily as I did, singing aloud any songs or tunes he thought he recognized, beating time to the rest with the cutlery, and dancing energetically. On the dance floor he made a formidable figure and the Norwegians soon learned to allow him elbow room.

As an important British publisher, his visit to Norway so soon after the war ended had attracted much attention, and a number of Norwegian journalists had either travelled up on the same train or were already established in the hotel. It was possible on the first evening to keep them at bay, but next morning when Hulton and I started out after breakfast some four or five of them emerged from the entrance hall and followed. Skiing in Norway proved to be quite different from skiing in Switzerland and elsewhere; there were – at least at this time and place – no ski lifts and no *pistes* or headlong descents. One trudged along on short skis over the powdery snow, which was continually taking off and blowing away in clouds as though before long there might be none left. In the blizzard-like conditions, visibility seemed to sink to almost nothing, but the tracks were marked out by birch wands planted in the snow about twenty yards apart, and however thick the air, one could somehow always catch sight of the next wand.

But before we could even set out on our route we had first to manoeuvre awkwardly up a small hill and as we paused, panting and sweating at the top, the press closed in. One or two took out notebooks and it was evident they expected a statement of some kind. As Hulton looked round at them, mopping his brow, I wondered whether between us we ought not to have prepared some kind of speech. However, before reporters could put their questions, Hulton put one of his own. He had a keen sense of history about which he was unusually well-informed, and the matter he raised was evidently one to which he had been giving thought.

'Correct me if I am wrong, gentlemen,' he inquired. 'Correct me if I am wrong – but I *believe* your Norwegian constitution was founded by Gustavus Adolphus?'

The reporters looked at one another, clearly wondering

what sharp questioning might follow such an opening gambit, but finally one of them spoke up and agreed that this was indeed the case; the Norwegian constitution *had* been founded by Gustavus Adolphus.

'As I thought, gentlemen. As I thought,' observed Hulton and planting his sticks firmly into the snow levered himself off onto the trail. I followed, and looking back after we had gone a short distance, saw that the reporters had made tracks for the hotel. As we battled our way along I found myself wondering what kind of interview with the noted English proprietor they would soon be phoning through to their offices in Oslo. Happily, I thought, we were unlikely ever to see the Oslo newspapers and would understand no word of them if we did.

When we got back to the hotel shortly before lunch, Nika was downstairs and dressed, but in no happy mood. She demanded that I come with her at once to interview the manager and force him to see reason. I followed her to his office. It seemed there was to be a special dance that evening and Nika was demanding that a hairdresser be brought from Oslo to do her hair which, she declared 'looks simply terrible'.

Patiently the manager explained for what was evidently not the first time that he would indeed be happy to summon an excellent hairdresser from Oslo, but it was now after twelve and the only train of the day left before nine. It was perfectly impossible for anyone to travel from Oslo to Finse until tomorrow morning, even if it were a matter of life and death.

'But you're just not trying!' Nika objected sharply. 'You *could* arrange it if you wanted to – I know you could!' And towering threateningly over him, she declared, 'You'd better do exactly what I want – otherwise I may come back and stay in your hotel again!'

This holiday, and another in Gstaad in January 1949, were no more than agreeable interludes in a relationship which was growing more difficult month by month. As the situation between East and West grew tenser, my employer's concern over what he felt was imminent war with Russia increased and I received numerous memoranda accusing me of 'appeasement', of 'reiterating Soviet propaganda' and publishing 'weak and foolish' articles which did not make the national peril sufficiently clear to our readers. Moreover I had lately lost the only person on the management side with whom I had been able to talk freely and whom I felt I could count on for support. For in 1948 W. J. Dickenson had relinquished, or had been persuaded to relinquish, his charge of the company's finances, though he continued to hold the title of director.

Despite our hardly having an idea in common and never meeting outside office hours, a relationship of affection had grown up between us. This was based on my side in an appreciation of the strength of character and warmth of feeling which underlay a certain unscrupulousness and readiness to exploit all situations to the full. In a sense, this unscrupulousness was a measure of his devotion to the family he served and not to his own interests. When I wrote to tell him what I felt about his leaving, he ended his reply with the words, 'I have been in the Hulton family thirty-three years now and perhaps I'm a bit possessive, so to relax may be a good thing.' He had named the house in Leatherhead where he and his family lived 'Hulton Way'.

In 1949, Hulton Press had been transformed into a public company. It had at the time been tentatively suggested to me that I might become a director of the new company. But I had during the last few years become disturbingly aware of the conflict between an editor's various loyalties; the first, in my view, was to the readers and the second to the staff, most of whom, as it happened, I had taken on. The third was to my employers – and, though I did not know much about business and finance, I knew enough to realize that their interests and those of the shareholders were by no means always identical. Not wanting to add another to an already oppressive list of loyalties, I showed no enthusiasm for the offer, which was not proceeded with.

By 1950 the Attlee government was running out of steam. It had by and large carried out its mandate and for the moment had nothing except more of the same to offer. Its policies were associated with rationing and controls which five years after war ended had become increasingly unpopular. There was a powerful barrage of newspaper support at the election now coming up, for the return of a Tory government which would 'make a bonfire of controls'. This, we were assured, would 'set free the spirit of national enterprise' so that Britain could once again take her rightful place as a world leader in industry and trade. I was not convinced by this vision of management and workers itching to take on the world in competition, and was in favour of the magazine continuing to support Labour, while giving equal prominence to the plans of all three parties. Finally it was agreed after much argument that the magazine should remain neutral, but that Edward Hulton would write as he pleased in his own column, and in one of the issues for February 1950 he put down the reasons why he would vote Conservative.

Nearly everybody is now persuaded that the Soviet Government constitutes a grave menace, not only to Peace, but to our very lives. The Soviet Government, with the Communist Party, is what Mr Churchill would rightly call 'a relentless foe' – determined on the complete destruction of all peoples who will not obey their dictates one hundred per cent. Although it may very well be true that the Kremlin does not desire war at this particular moment, this is merely because it is waiting, crouching, for a better opportunity to spring upon us. All and every form of appeasement is worse than vain....

At this perilous moment, I am, personally speaking, appalled that the conduct of our foreign policy should be in the hands of Mr Ernest Bevin.

What effect this may have had on Ernest Bevin as Foreign Secretary, I cannot say, for he was one of the Labour ministers with whom I had never exchanged a word, but it spelled out sufficiently plainly the change that had taken place in the opinions of *Picture Post*'s proprietor over the past five years, and the yawning gap which had opened out between his views and mine.

23

Pause for Reflection

Meantime I had anxieties of a different order; it was evident to me that my marriage with Gerti was coming to an end. We had too little in common to become united and were now living side by side in the same house with scant contact and following separate interests. I was concerned – much too concerned indeed – with the magazine and its success. I woke up in the morning thinking about what to put in the next issue, shaved myself and ate breakfast still thinking about nothing else, got out the car and drove to the office continuing to make plans, and was thinking about *Picture Post* and its problems as I drove home again at night. I seldom left the office until everyone else had gone, the rush hour over, and I could drive back along the Embankment to Chelsea in the same state of preoccupation as I had set out in.

Most of the staff would go across to the Two Brewers, the pub opposite our office – in whose doorway I had once seen Grumpy about to step off into eternity – for a couple of drinks before going home, but I would sit at my desk writing letters or looking through picture magazines from other countries to see if there were good ideas to be borrowed or any pictures we might want to buy; the word 'workaholic' had not then been invented, but if it had it would have fitted me all too well. My spare time occupation was another form of work, my own writing. At the weekends or on holiday I had always some task which absorbed me, short stories mostly, but also a couple of novels and a long piece or two of criticism. For relaxation I attempted to cultivate the garden of our Chelsea house where the soil was so sour that little ever grew and that little needed – or seemed to me to need – endless attention.

My main enjoyment was the company of the children. Lyndall was now living with her mother, Antonia White, and going to the Old Vic Theatre School, so that I saw far less of her than I wished and particularly missed the long rides we used to take together over the grassy slopes and commons around Turville Heath. But Nicolette, and Amanda, born late in 1948 and so still hardly more than a baby, were a constant source of happiness. I have always looked on children from the moment they are able to talk, or even earlier, as people, to be treated with as much respect as grown-ups if not more, and have seldom found it difficult to make contact with them. Moreover, in addition to their personal qualities, some children possess for about their first seven years of life extraordinary intuitions and perceptions which amount at times to thought-reading. But the term 'thought-reading' already gives too positive an impression, since the process is not deliberate but automatic, and would be better described as a capacity to pick up the thoughts and feelings of those with whom they are in close or regular contact.

This capacity I found fascinating since for me – as perhaps for most would-be writers or artists – intuition is a higher power than ratiocination, and flashes of perception offer a more valuable guidance in reaching decisions than brain-racking. My notebooks for these years are full of the children's comments and expressions, and a dozen times when I have turned to them to confirm my memory of some important event I have found nothing to the purpose. All I had recorded during some critical month of the war or time of political upheaval have been notes of conversations overheard, glimpses of the children playing, or perhaps a dream in which one or other of them figured. As for their special quality of perception, one example must serve for many.

We had had from early in the war a grey poodle, given to us by a lifelong friend, the painter Sine Mackinnon. Jenny was an enchanting creature. Lively and sportive, she would play with any dog she met, and on the common at Turville Heath where the bracken grew waist-high would go bounding through it on stiff legs like a springbok pronking, looking around for a rabbit at the peak of every bound. When one of the children munched a rusk or biscuit temptingly at nose height, she would never try to snatch it but would hoover up the crumbs, until, if they happened to drop it on the floor, the rusk would be gone in a flash. But now Jenny had grown old, slow in her ways, her coat was dark and greasy, difficult to clean, her eyes were filmed and she had become incontinent. I would begin every morning by mopping and drying up after her, though in the daytime she would go out into the garden to meet her needs. On this occasion, however, at midday and with the garden door open Jenny had made a puddle on the floor upstairs, which I was now duly clearing up.

'Couldn't she be given some medicine?' Gerti asked me.

'I doubt it. She's very old. If she goes on like this we may have to think of something else.'

We spoke quietly, indoors, saying nothing more explicit, but my unspoken thought was that Jenny might have to be put down. I went downstairs and out into the garden where Nicolette was playing with her toys just as she had been when I went inside.

'Who are you going to kill?' she asked me.

'No one. We aren't going to kill anyone.'

'Oh! I thought you were going to kill Jenny for making puddles.'

For some time now Nicolette and Amanda had provided the only real link between Gerti and myself, and their activities were the only subject on which we could converse with mutual enjoyment. Gerti's own chief interests were her piano-playing and listening to music; her photography – for which she had real talent, but less application; her friends, particularly Austrians with whom she could talk about her childhood and life in Vienna in the days before the war; and the holidays she took abroad, particularly visits to her own country. We went together to Austria once or twice, but as Europe grew more settled she began to travel on her own. I could see that she looked forward to visiting places and people connected with her early life, and I too had started to look forward to her absences. And now, late in 1949, we were beginning for the first time to quarrel; having lived for some years in a condition of detachment, a note of hostility was creeping in. Finding it more and more difficult to work peacefully at home, I one day suggested that I should take a room nearby as a study where I could do my own writing for one whole day at weekends. I could see that she did not like the idea, but neither did she try to dismiss it altogether.

Such was the situation between us in October 1949 when I went away for a fortnight's holiday on my own. I took the car and a supply of maps, my riding clothes and boots, and was drawn first, without thinking, to a part of the country I had never visited, Lincolnshire and the Wash, where my mother had lived as a girl and of which I had often heard her speak during my own childhood. Here I visited the tomb of her father, the Rev. Thomas Fountaine, after whom I had been named. I had never met this grandfather, but knew that he had been fond of games and sport and, it would appear, was a lively character until struck down by paralysis in middle life, being obliged to spend his last decades in a bath-chair. Having paid belated respects, I drove up to the borders of Yorkshire and East Lancashire. I wanted to be near enough to Colne to visit the scenes remembered from my own childhood, but far enough out on the moors to be able to take long solitary rides.

Why I was spending my holiday in this way, and why I should be coming to this part of the country when I could go anywhere I pleased, I never asked myself. I had the impulse to come here, and I came. Perhaps because I was acting on impulse and following no conscious plan, everything that happened during this fortnight seemed charged with meaning and significance. It was like the interlude between two lives in which one is seeking to understand the lessons of the life just over and to make plans for the one that lies ahead, hoping to avoid making the same mistakes but aware that mistakes of some kind, indeed of many kinds, will be inevitable.

For some reason – perhaps from a forgotten conversation – I

had it in my head that I would be able to hire horses at Gisburn, and on my way there stopped at Bolton Abbey, wanting to see the abbey itself and to walk across the stepping stones we had run across as boys on a day's outing from the Colne vicarage with my father and our kindly friend Canon Dempsey. I also wanted to see again the famous Strid where the waters of the river Wharfe are forced boiling through a narrow gorge into a pool overhung by ledges of rock beneath which – it is said – anyone who falls in will remain trapped, perhaps for days. The gorge itself is not too wide for a good jumper, but the take-off is treacherous and the risk intimidating. Here, we were told, my grandmother as a girl – it must have been some time in the 1860s – had gathered up her skirts, taken a short run and gone flying over in her bonnet and buttoned boots. Having looked once more at the scenes of long ago and found them much less altered than myself, I went for a cup of tea into the muddy garden of a café where the leaves came floating damply down among the scones and teacups. A man of about my own age came and looked inquiringly round as though expecting to see some friend. I could tell he was not really expecting to see anyone he knew but was shy and uncertain, so beckoned to him to sit down at my table where he immediately began to talk.

He was a German, he said, living in Rochdale, having left his country before the war because of his Jewish origins. He made his living now working for a tannery as an expert in judging different qualities of leather which was something that could not be done mechanically. 'So, you see, there is still a use for human beings,' he added with a smile that was both sad and awkward. He had, he told me, lost his wife, but had a young daughter still at school. In return I told him that I was a journalist living in London, where I had a wife and daughters. 'Yes,' he said, 'when I was married I too used to like to get away for holidays by myself – but now I have too much of it!' After an hour, he said goodbye, but returned with a map of the district which he thought might be useful. I supposed that was the last I should see of him, but later when I was sitting in my car about to drive away, he reappeared with a list of hotels where I might like to stay, adding about one of them the unexpected words, 'If you are wishing for a very lonely place, where you can find yourself by losing yourself as it were, this is the one I recommend to you. . . .'

All worked out as I had hoped: I found stables in Gisburn where I could hire horses for a daily ride, and at a pub high up on the moors a few miles away there was a room in which I could stay and the landlady would give me meals. And then one morning soon after my arrival I went over to Colne to look at some of the old scenes. I intended to park in the yard outside the station – which had seen a good many tears when we all went back to school – but instead drove on to Penrith Road, had a look at our old home, now modernized and turned back again into two houses, and then on an impulse set out to walk across the hills to Trawden by the footpath we had as boys so often taken. It was a pale October day with a low-hanging mist, but already warm and with a brightness which showed that the sun was trying to break through.

Once up on the hillside my eye was caught by a single point of light shining through the mist like a planet in the evening sky. It must be coming, I thought, from across the valley on the outskirts of Colne, and I was expecting it to fade or vanish with every step I took, but it continued to shine steadily, indeed to blaze. What could it be? Car headlights left on – but there was only a single point of light. Could it be coming from some industrial process? I concluded at last that it must be a reflection from the sun shining on to a glass roof or open window at some spot from which the mist had already lifted. As I walked on, the light did not vanish, nor did I move out of its orbit. It stayed with me for a full half-hour, and in the mood I was in, in which the smallest happening seemed significant, I took the light to be a sign – but of what I should have to think out later.

As I neared Trawden a man was gathering mushrooms in the field above me. He called out and I waited till he came up. He was wearing bright brown trousers tucked into topboots, a coloured shirt with an open neck and a soft grey knitted cardigan. His hair was red and he had a red moustache and side-whiskers which sprouted vigorously; I put him down as an art student who had been some time in the army, and asked if

267

there was any café or pub in Trawden where I could get some food.

'Help me find a few more mushrooms and I'll run you up a snack myself.'

We searched around for half an hour while he told me his story – so many years in a minesweeper and so many more in the Red Cross. Invalided out, and married. He was now the gravedigger and cemetery-keeper at the Trawden Forest Cemetery, a steep patch on the hillside given over to dead human beings instead of to live sheep. He didn't mind the work, he said, was quite happy to dig graves all day, didn't mind wandering around among the tombs at night. But once, he said, he had slipped and fallen onto a coffin of which the lid had rotted. His hand had gone through onto a dead man's face, and all the skin had come off on his hand.

'Hundreds of times in the day I've washed that hand! It isn't that I'm frightened. I just don't like to think of it having happened.'

Back in the cemetery house he showed me some of his paintings, as well as photographs, newspaper cuttings, boxes he'd carved and models he had made. His name was Tom Seel and he was an artist, but not one who just painted pictures; his art spread all over his everyday life at which he was wonderfully handy and expert. He reared hundreds of chickens, cultivated flowers to put on the graves, kept a pig and had a collie as alert and competent as its master. He had only to whistle and nod to the dog, and it drove all the cows at a good round trot out of the cemetery or away from the patch where his hens were feeding. The cows were always breaking in, he complained, as he fixed the loose gate with a heavy stone. A few days ago he'd nearly lost his pig when one of the cows struck a horn into its backside and it had taken him six hours to staunch the bleeding.

We had eaten the mushrooms and much else beside before I started back over the hills, wondering if I would still be capable of living in the country and writing only what I wanted to write; whether I had anything important enough to be worth saying; and how I could meet my various obligations if I gave up journalism. I thought of a friend, editor at different times of two Fleet Street newspapers, who had talked of giving it all up and going into politics or, perhaps, writing biographies of politicians.

'How is X nowadays?' I had recently asked a mutual friend.

'X,' he replied, 'has now reached the stage where he not only has to have supper every night at the Savoy – he feels he owes that to his image – but has also to send champagne to the band.'

I had never yet sent champagne to any band and couldn't remember when I had last had a meal at the Savoy, but I knew that in my own way I had become just as entangled in the life I led, though it was in the work rather than the accompanying luxury.

The pub where I was staying was as quiet as a barn during the week, but at weekends exploded into noisy life. Businessmen and shopkeepers came out from Skipton and other nearby towns. Farmers from all round drove in with their wives. The bars were packed and the uproar – out here where no policeman ever came – went on long after closing time. It was Saturday night, and I sat back in a corner, listening. At the table beside me an auctioneer was telling an audience of farmers about the chestnut pony he'd just brought from Ireland ... 'a reet butty-un', bringing his hands together to show he meant short-barrelled, short in the back. 'Fourteen-one. Three pairts bred.'

'But 'ow doos he roon?' a listener inquired.

The auctioneer snorted. 'Run? I put 'im in a flappin' race, didn't I?' He didn't joost win – he bloo-oody laps 'em. An' I had a hundred on!'

'What'll you do with 'un next, Mr Arkwright?'

'Enter 'im against fourteen-threes. They can bloo-oody gallop, can fourteen-threes. But they'll need to against 'im, I'm tellin' you!'

At last, half stunned and deafened by the noise, I levered myself out of my corner and made for the door. As I passed the bar the landlady called out to me, 'When all this lot's gone home, Tommy, coom on over to t'village hall. There's a dance on till three o'clock.'

At once and automatically I began to make excuses. Still pulling pints, pouring double whiskies and fixing 'black eyes' – cherry brandy in advocaat for the girls – the landlady fixed me with her own eye: 'Tommy,' she called, 'th'art a miserable boogger.'

Hastily backing down, I agreed to come over to the hall where she and her husband, myself and Mary, the Irish girl who brought my breakfast, danced until three next morning. But it was long after three o'clock before I got to sleep. Was she right? Was I indeed a miserable bugger? The answer came slowly, but in the end clearly. 'Yes. I *am* a miserable bugger. Why am I a miserable bugger? Because through my way of life I have lost all spontaneity and naturalness. Everything I do is thought out in advance, so that even if life were trying to be wonderful – and for all I know it may be – I don't give it even half a chance.'

After my final ride I thanked the stables and settled my account. 'The little mare can jump,' I said. He looked at me in surprise. 'If she can, you're the first that's learned it.'

I felt pleased. I must do more riding, I thought. From now on I shall go off regularly for riding holidays, and when I get back to London I shall fix up something for a day or two each week.

As for my life – in such time as I could spare to think at all during a fortnight which had been specially planned to allow me to think things out – I had resolved to stay on in my job for at least a few more years. Somewhere in the works of Arnold Bennett I had read that, in order to be free, one must have enough money saved up to live on for at least a year in case one should lose, or want to lose, one's job. I was determined I would start saving – at forty-four it was about time to begin. I would try and put together a second book of short stories – my first, *The Transitory Venus*, had been published the year before by Cyril Connolly's *Horizon* – and to complete a new short novel I had in mind. As for my marriage, I would shore it up and keep it in existence – 'for the sake of the children' was the way I expressed it to myself. The self, however, has many layers, and some layer well below the surface kept trying to inform me that 'for my own sake because I can't bear the prospect of separation from the children' would be nearer the mark. And still another layer added that a man's life cannot be built around relation-ships with small children, and that at my time of life I ought to be capable of a lasting relationship with a grown-up person.

By now, however, I had had a good deal of experience in silencing unwelcome voices and accordingly returned to Cheyne Row with everything worked out. I should stay in my job and remain married to Gerti. I should do much more riding, and was sorry to have said goodbye for the last time to my friend at the cemetery, Tom Seel.

How work and marriage eventuated will be seen; but over both the last two points I was mistaken. Tom Seel and his wife Peggy would remain friends with whom I would be in contact from time to time for the remainder of my life, and as for riding, it was already over. I should never again swing myself up on to a horse's back, not for lack of intention but because when the main pattern of one's life changes, small pieces in the pattern change as well. I would carry my riding boots and breeches around the world for the next twenty years without once using them, and when I finally handed them over to a good lady collecting jumble for a sale on behalf of old age pensioners, I should almost have qualified to benefit from her jumble sale myself.

24
Warning Voices

The winter of 1949–50 passed quietly enough, but early in 1950 I began to be bombarded with complaints, first, the familiar ones from Edward Hulton expressing anxiety over the Communist danger and his conviction that *Picture Post* was 'too left-wing'. He had, though I did not know this at the time, rejoined the Conservative Party around the time of the February general election and it did not accord with this that Labour MPs – one or two of them distinctly left of centre – should be writing in his magazine. At the same time there started to reach me from management criticism of a different kind: that the paper had lost all vitality, readers were now finding it dull and uninspiring, out of touch with the lively new spirit of the times. Some of the photographs were too large, some too small; other ought not to have appeared in any size. I was advised to study the popular weeklies, *Weekend* and *Reveille*, and told that if I would only print similar articles and pictures we could soon double our circulation.

I answered that if we were to imitate such totally different magazines we should destroy the reputation so carefully built up and be more likely to halve our readership than double it. This uncooperative attitude was put down to my always wanting to have things my own way – a failing to which I have certainly been prone. My personal interest in social conditions, I was told, was dictating the contents of the magazine and so standing in the way of the success it would enjoy if it were made more 'bright' and entertaining.

There may well have been some justice in these criticisms. Looking back, I can see a number of mistakes, and it is all too evident from the replies I wrote – and kept – that I was touchy and resented criticism. The resentment was partly due to a feeling that some of these wordy criticisms were intended more to please the proprietor than to influence the editor; also I grudged having to spend so much time defending a record which showed circulation at its highest ever, with profits of £2500 a week – a sum far greater then than it would be now. Resentment, however, is always a distraction and a waste of energy; it was round *my* head that the clouds were gathering, and if I intended to survive I should have applied myself to resolving conflicts, not to answering memoranda. Part of my difficulty arose from not knowing to whom I could speak candidly. Dickenson had now gone, and Hulton himself, though highly intelligent in an academic sense – he had at different times won eight prizes for history – was shy and diffident. He hated disagreement, would accept a proposal he disagreed with rather than engage in argument, and found it easier to dictate long memos through his secretary than to meet objections face to face. Nor did I see what concessions I could make to his changed outlook which would not involve betrayal of the paper itself – which I always thought of as an entity in its own right – of readers, staff, and of my own principles. Since I have never claimed to possess many, I clung all the more closely to the few I had.

I did not discuss these mounting difficulties with my fellow journalists, since I have always thought it an essential part of the editor's job to keep anxieties to himself and maintain as peaceful a climate as possible in which journalists and photographers can do their work. Assignments are often difficult enough in themselves, and all kinds of further problems crop up on the job which must be coped with; to interview Nehru on the future of India or to assess the political balance of post-war Poland was sufficiently exacting without a correspondent having to concern himself over the likely reactions of proprietor or management to what he wrote. Oddly enough this reticence became a cause of reproach later on from some of those who took my place, and assured me then that if they had known beforehand what problems the job involved, they would have been better placed for the experience of sitting down in a hot seat.

In the spring of 1950 two incidents took place within Hulton Press. The first had nothing to do with my difficulties, but provided one of the last agreeable interludes I would experience. I was summoned one day by Maxwell Raison and John Pearce, who had been brought in as his assistant manager, to have a look at the dummy for a new publication which had arrived by post, and they placed in front of me the paste-up of a magazine for boys quite unlike any I had ever seen. Its title at that moment, I believe, was *Dragon*, which would be changed to *Eagle* before it actually appeared. Unlike most dummies, this was not an amateurish affair with one or two pages carefully drawn and the rest hazily roughed in. It was complete from first to last with coloured drawings to scale and all the captions and articles readable and in place. But what chiefly distinguished it was the impression that the editor understood what he was doing. I knew – and still know – very little about boys aged eight to twelve, but I could see that the editor had mentally identified himself with them, and appreciated what they wanted almost without having to think.

'Well – what d'you make of it?' Raison asked.

'I've been looking at dummies on and off for the last fifteen years,' I said. 'But this is the first I've ever seen of which I'd say "Hire all the people who produced it, and start publishing it as soon as possible!"'

'We can't do that,' objected Pearce. 'He's a clergyman somewhere near Southport – the Rev. Marcus Morris.'

'Well he seems keen to become an editor,' I answered. 'So the thing is to hire him a good curate or two, and let them run the church services while he gets on with the magazine.'

Such was my first contact with Marcus Morris, who over the next few years would produce a succession of highly successful children's papers, *Eagle*, *Girl*, *Swift* and *Robin* – all precisely adapted to the age and sex of their young readers as well as to that particular decade – before moving on to wider fields and becoming managing director of the National Magazine

Company. When he turned up in our office Morris proved to be slight, fair-haired and outwardly hesitant, but soon revealed the essential streak. When I said that his plans in general looked excellent – particularly the long-running serial on the adventures of Dan Dare, that space-age pilot still remembered with enthusiasm by millions of middle-aged men – but that the adventures of St Paul at the back of the paper seemed incongruous, and that something better might surely be found to take its place, he replied, 'If that is not included than I shall not produce the magazine.'

Hastily I backed down to admit St Paul's adventures. Morris himself I nicknamed 'Father Martini', not because of any propensity to drink, for all I knew he might well be a teetotaller, but because – well-dressed, controlled, decisive – he appeared all set for publishing success and therefore for the life of high finance, good restaurants and first-class aeroplane travel which not many clergymen, I think, find themselves in a position to enjoy.

The second incident concerned me more directly. I was rung up one afternoon by a secretary who asked if I would lunch with Mrs Hulton at the Dorchester in two or three days' time. I duly arrived on the date fixed, expecting at least a small party, to learn that we were to have lunch by ourselves. Having gone quickly through the business of ordering, my hostess came to the point.

'Why don't you let Teddy do what he wants with *Picture Post*?' Not having expected anything so direct, I fenced. 'What does Teddy want to do with it?'

'He wants to run it – to decide what goes into it. After all, it's *his* magazine. He put up the money for it – you didn't.'

'That's true. But now it isn't only Teddy's magazine – it's everybody's.'

'What d'you mean?'

'It has a character of its own. Not mine, not anyone's. Really it's the character of its readers.'

'Now you're just arguing. You know quite well *you* decide what goes into the paper. Teddy doesn't. When he took you to lunch with Harold MacMillan in order for you to commission a

275

series of articles from him, you did nothing about it! But you print articles by people like Mikardo.'

'MacMillan's very clever but he writes dull articles – and they're no good for our kind of reader.'

'You haven't tried any of them, so you don't know. You never try anything different – that's why the magazine's so dull. Everyone says so! I get around and I know what people say. Stuffing away all day in the office, you haven't a clue. How could you have?'

We argued as far as the coffee, and then Nika issued her instructions.

'I've listened to all you've said. Now let me *tell* you what's to happen. Teddy will decide what goes into the paper. You can find the pictures and arrange the pages, but Teddy will make the decisions. Is that clear?'

'I realize what you want.'

'Very well then. Teddy will take charge of your weekly conferences. You can attend, but he will be in charge.'

'Anything else?'

'Yes. I'm going to be the fashion writer. You must find me an office on the editorial floor.'

'But we *have* a first-class fashion editor already, Marjorie Beckett.'

'That's your problem. I shall look after your fashion articles in future. Now – is all this clear?'

'Yes. It's clear, but it won't work. I've a great respect for Teddy – he's a most knowledgeable man. But he's not a journalist and he's not an editor. If he produces a magazine to express the views of himself and his friends, it won't sell a hundred thousand copies.'

'How d'you know? You've never let him try.'

'Look, Nika,' I said, 'I'm a professional. I make some mistakes but I know what it's all about. I can steer the ship. What you're saying to me is – "This isn't your ship, it's Teddy's. So let him do the steering."'

'Right! Why not?'

'Because he'll bump it on the rocks. He's bound to.'

'Even if that was true – which it isn't – *you* don't have to worry. We should look after you – you must know that.'

'You might look after me, but you can't look after the paper. If you do what you're proposing, it will fail.'

'You needn't worry about *that*,' said Nika with finality. 'We'd never allow *Picture Post* to fail. What should we be if we did? Just two more very rich people.'

Throughout our talk I noticed that she made use of a curious gesture as though she were snapping something in her fingers, something such as a stick of bread. But there were no breadsticks on the table.

My warning was plain enough and I felt I must be grateful for having been given one at all, but the proposal was not one which left room for compromise. Either Hulton would edit the magazine and I must content myself putting the best gloss I could on his ideas, or I could expect to go. If I stayed I would have to begin by sacking a gifted, hard-working member of the staff, since we couldn't have two fashion editors; and by telling the others to attend conferences at which the proprietor would take charge and tell them what assignments to undertake. The staff were in some ways an unpredictable, as well as a talented bunch of men and women, but I had no difficulty in predicting how they would react to this. The best of them would leave; those who stayed would be in confusion; the magazine would lose all character and I, still nominally editor, would be left carrying the can for the resulting failure.

Not long before this time I had been consulted by a friend, Gerald Barry, editor of the *News Chronicle*, whom I had known and liked since the days of the 1941 Committee. Barry explained to me that he was having great trouble in editing the paper because of constant interference from his proprietor, Lord Layton, whom I also knew. 'He wants to decide everything of importance,' Barry said, 'and a great deal that's unimportant too. I'm left as a kind of dignified office boy.'

'What shall you do about it?'

'I'm thinking of resigning. An editor who doesn't edit is nothing. He's a sham. He's worse – he's a lie!'

'*Don't!*' I burst out, surprised by my own vehemence. '*Don't* bloody well resign! We should almost never resign.'

He looked at me with astonishment. 'What d'you mean – I should go on taking his instructions?'

'Of course not! Only don't *resign*. Don't you see – that's what they count on? In any dispute we're to be gentlemen. We're to do the decent thing – retire into a backroom with a pistol and blow our brains out. Their contribution is to provide the pistol. Don't you fall for that!'

'Well, but if I *don't* resign, and *don't* do what Layton tells me – what's to happen?'

'Let him have the odium of sacking you. If that's what he wants, let him do it. Let him come down into the composing room or wherever, and say to the head printer, "Don't do what Mr Barry says. Do what I say!" Let him take responsibility for his own actions – not shovel it all off on you.'

Shortly after this our paths diverged and whether Gerald – who did in fact leave the *News Chronicle* soon afterwards to take charge of preparations for the 1951 Festival of Britain – acted on my advice I never knew, and sadly it is now too late to ask. However my advice was not destined to be wasted.

And now in June 1950 something happened which seemed at the time to have no connection with my affairs – a special number of the monthly magazine *World Review* came out devoted to George Orwell, who had died in January at the age of forty-six. The number contained extracts from Orwell's unpublished notebooks, with contributions by Bertrand Russell, Aldous Huxley, Herbert Read, Malcolm Muggeridge, Stephen Spender, John Beavan and myself, as well as a personal memoir by T. R. Fyvel, who had known Orwell better than any of us and worked with him closely. The number even then was a *tour de force* and is now a rare collector's item.

Ever since buying the magazine ten years earlier, Edward Hulton had run *World Review* as a vehicle for his own comments on the state of the world, and for the contributions of his friends and people he admired. Though he wrote large parts of it himself, he made use of a succession of part-time assistants to put the magazine together. Most of them had been content to mark up the type sizes, dig out illustrations and sub the various articles into shape without worrying themselves much about their quality. Recently, however, Hulton had taken on as his assistant someone of a very different stamp. This was a young Pole, Stefan Schimanski, short, slightly built, with a studious, bespectacled appearance and a passion for literary excellence. I had seen him occasionally around the office dodging in and out of Hulton's room, but had never said more to him than 'Good morning'. Indeed the first talk we ever had was when he told me of his plans for the Orwell issue, adding that he meant to follow this up with one devoted to short stories. I was delighted to learn that something was at last going to be made of *World Review* and said I'd be glad to help him in any way I could. But when the Orwell issue came out I noticed that Schimanski's introduction was followed by a single line:

The next issue, July, will be the last under the present editorship. S.S.

When I asked what had happened, Schimanski told me that Hulton disapproved of his efforts to make *World Review* into a serious literary magazine and was dispensing with his services. Knowing Schimanski to be a competent reporter and journalist in addition to his literary interests, I at once offered him a job on *Picture Post*. In view of my own precarious situation at the time, this can be considered as either quixotic or idiotic, or possibly both.

I was prepared for a storm over taking on my employer's reject, but I was not prepared for the reject himself proving difficult and choosy. A few days later Schimanski looked in to say that – much as he liked the idea of joining *Picture Post* – he would not be doing this for a couple of months. He had, he said, an absolute passion for airline travel and had been for some time in negotiation with an airline for a free ticket to Japan in return for writing two or three travel pieces. The opportunity had come up unexpectedly, and he meant to take it.

'Okay,' I said. 'If you prefer a visit to Japan to a job, that's all right with me. Look in when you get back, but I'm not keeping my offer open.'

Schimanski's decision appeared to have let me off the hook. I had felt impelled to make the offer, but if now for reasons of his own he turned it down, there was no more to be said. Later that evening, however, after I got home, I thought of the picture possibilities of a visit to Japan, which in 1950 had not yet moved into the tourist trap business; in addition there was a war going on in Malaya to which we had not yet given proper coverage. I talked the idea over with Ted Castle before telling Schimanski that if he could get his set of tickets doubled so as to take a cameraman with him, and if he would also stop off and cover the Malayan war – plus one or two other stories connected with it – then he might join the staff now and go out as our war correspondent and reporter.

Schimanski was delighted. He made the necessary arrangements with his airline friends, and then, in company with a staff photographer named Haywood Magee, set out to photograph cherry blossom, Mount Fujiyama, geisha girls and similar delights, following a stopover in Malaya to cover a war which has long since been forgotten. Schimanski and Magee were actually in Malaya, and I was on holiday in Austria in the attempt to piece together my dissolving marriage, when there broke out in Korea a new and far more serious war, which itself would prove to be only a rehearsal for the appalling conflict fifteen to twenty years later in Vietnam. Ted Castle phoned me that he was ordering Schimanski and Magee on to Korea as war correspondents, with which I fully agreed.

The early part of the war, it may or may not be remembered, consisted of a prolonged retreat by the South Koreans, the Americans and their United Nations allies, all down the country into a last stronghold around Pusan. At this point, having made several picture stories during the retreat, Schimanski and Magee got out from Pusan to Tokyo by air.

While they were still recuperating, an American public relations man visited their hotel to offer them places on a plane leaving at 1 a.m., next morning which would take them back to the country from which they had so recently got away. Magee, who hated air travel at any time and particularly in the direction now proposed, refused to leave. 'I told Stefan,' he said to me after he got back, 'they can sack me if they want, but I'm not going.'

'And what did Stefan say?'

'He said, "Do as you please, but I'll be on that plane."'

Schimanski never reached Korea. His plane exploded over the sea and only one survivor, an American who died within a few hours, was picked up out of the water.

Back in my office after the holiday I was sitting late one evening thinking all this over. I had believed I was doing Schimanski a good turn by offering him a job, but the result had been very different and I had just had the painful task of talking to his mother. Now, with the arrival of massive American reinforcements, the Korean war was entering a new phase and our magazine had to have effective coverage. Our best trouble-shooting cameraman was Bert Hardy, and the reporter most experienced in war coverage was undoubtedly James Cameron, who had joined us only recently from the *Daily Express*. It wasn't an agreeable assignment to offer anyone, and I was making up my mind to speak to them when there came a knock on the door. I supposed, so late, that this must be a cleaner wanting to do out the room, but it was Cameron and Hardy.

'You must be wondering who to send to Korea. We're suggesting you send us.'

25

The End of the Road

During their time in Korea Hardy and Cameron made three picture stories, the most dramatic of these being the record of General MacArthur's landing at Inchon, the port of Seoul. Seoul was not only the capital of Korea but the key centre of communications for the invading armies – North Koreans backed by Chinese – now operating far down to the south after driving the South Koreans and their allies into what Cameron called 'the toehold enclave of Pusan'. The Inchon landing effectively cut the legs from under the attackers, dramatically reversing the whole military situation. This was the second most powerful seaborne invasion ever launched – only that against Normandy five years earlier having been bigger – and our two men were the only British photo-journalists present. Hardy's photographs were worthy of the event – an impression of military might and men in mortal danger which still has power to cause a shock of silence wherever the photographs are shown, as they frequently are even today. Cameron's article sets the reader squarely down in the Inchon channel which 'on that evening of haze and filmy rain among the hills was like an Argyllshire sea-loch, somehow steam-heated and washed with pastel grey', and then '... quite suddenly we saw the floating tanks, those extraordinary sea-going hunks of amphibious hardware. They crawled awkwardly out of the hull of the mother-ship; she spawned them out in growl-ing droves, a grotesque mechanical parturition. Like a flock of rattling turtles, they lurched out of the ship and began to

crawl over the surface of the water; a spectacle utterly surrealist'.*

As I turned over Hardy's prints when they first came out of
the darkroom, I knew that I had never had a better picture story
in my hands, and decided that no one but myself should select
the photographs to be used and lay them out. I made nine pages
of them, doing the work quite rapidly though I had been
prepared to spend all day on it, and feeling as I did so that they
would surely win the most important honour then open to a
magazine cameraman – the Encyclopedia Britannica Award for
the finest picture series of the year; which indeed, a month or so
later, they did. Looking at the photographs and reading
Cameron's article, I also acquired at least some idea of what they
had both been through as a result of knocking on my office door
a few weeks earlier, and felt profoundly grateful to them.

The Inchon landing was not the only story our two men had
sent back, and one of the others posed a problem. Text and
photographs showed vividly how the South Koreans, with at
least the connivance of their American allies, were treating
their political prisoners, suspected opponents of the tyrant
Synghman Rhee. Rhee himself would in due course be ditched
as the insupportable head of an intolerable regime by the
American protectors who had kept him in power for so long;
but that was still ten years on into the future, and in the
meantime Rhee and his henchmen were our gallant allies and
the upholders of our Christian democratic way of life. By the
1980s we have all seen treatment of prisoners more openly
murderous than that revealed in Hardy's pictures, and Cameron's accompanying article would today be accounted mild.
But in the climate of that time, with British and Australian
troops involved in the fighting, any criticism of South Koreans
was certain to be regarded as criticism of 'our' side. Such
criticism, moreover, being anti–Western, must inevitably be
'pro–Eastern', and hence – with only a small distortion of
language – 'Communist propaganda', a crime of which I was
already being accused by my employer.

*Picture Post, 7 October 1950.

283

Having no wish to lay my head on any block that could decently be avoided, I waited for some days until our men got back and questioned them both closely. But there was no doubt about the pictures' authenticity, nor about the conditions which Cameron described:

They have been in jail now for indeterminate periods – long enough to have reduced their frames to skeletons, their sinews to string, their faces to a translucent terrible grey, their spirit to that of cringing dogs. They are roped and manacled. They are compelled to crouch in the classic Oriental attitude of submission in pools of garbage. They clamber, the lowest common denominator of personal degradation, into trucks with the numb air of men going to their death. Many of them *are*. The spectacle is utterly medieval. Among the crowds drifting indifferently around, a few bystanders take snapshots, grinning.

A final touch was that some of these enemies of the state, going roped together to their death, were not more than twelve years old.

Though I knew the story ought to appear immediately, I allowed myself a brief further delay while I searched all the East European magazines I could get hold of for some picture giving the opposite side of the case – ill-treatment by the North Koreans of prisoners from the South. To my surprise I actually found such a picture in a Czech magazine; it showed an American soldier dressed up by his captors in a false nose and swastika, forced to march in procession trailing the Stars and Stripes in the dust. At Ted Castle's suggestion and with Cameron's agreement, we planned the presentation as an appeal to the UN – the nominal authority over the war on the South Korean side – and sent copies to the Secretary General of UN and to the leader of the British delegation, Kenneth Younger.*

Our office routine at this period was that I would show the magazine in the form of a paste-up to Edward Hulton every Friday morning at around 12 p.m. But on this particular Friday

*We heard nothing, and never indeed did hear anything, from either the Secretary General or from Mr Younger, who presumably had more important matters on their minds than the fate of twelve-year-old enemies of Synghman Rhee.

his secretary rang to say that he had been at a party the night before and would not be in till the afternoon, so I arranged to submit the paste-up to him at 3.30. In order to allow no loopholes, I advised Hulton that there were two articles in the issue which I felt he should read carefully, his own about Greece where he had just been for a holiday, and Cameron's report on the ill-treatment of prisoners in Korea, and I left the text of both articles on his desk. His own came up an hour or so later with a number of corrections, and the proof of Cameron's article without any corrections or comment. Ted Castle, with whom I had discussed each stage in handling the article, was as relieved as I was and we spent Monday at the printers putting the issue to bed.

On the Tuesday morning, with the week's issue out of the way, I generally spent the whole morning in conference with the staff, planning what should be prepared for the following week. But in the middle of our conference I was rung up by Hulton from his home – he now had a house, Cleeve Lodge, in Hyde Park Gate – and told that the Korean story 'must on no account appear. It has to be taken out of the paper at once and something else put in its place.' I answered that I was ready to come round at any time, morning or evening, and talk the matter over with him. After a minute's delay – seemingly occupied in discussion – he replied that there was nothing to talk over; he was ordering that the article be taken out. I said that I would act on his instructions for this week, but that I should expect him to give me convincing reasons for the decision, otherwise I should put the pages back into the paper for the following week's issue. He thereupon rang off without answering, and from that moment I was never able to speak to Hulton personally either in the office or by telephone about the matter. The management, which met almost continuously in conference over the affair, finally persuaded him to see me at twelve on the Thursday, but I told them I was sure he would not keep the appointment, which in fact he did not do. In the afternoon I was sent for by the full board of directors, which included both Mr and Mrs Hulton. Edward Hulton, as chairman, then told me that though the board was unanimous in supporting the proprietor's right to put into his paper whatever he thought fit and to exclude whatever he did not like, they were prepared to allow me to make a statement.

I had, of course, thought over carefully what I would say if the opportunity occurred, and I explained why the Korean conflict seemed to me important as the first collision involving warfare between West and East, and why it was vital that 'our' side in that conflict – the side of the Western world and of the UN – should set a standard for the treatment of prisoners and captives. The propaganda victory or defeat would be as important in the long run as military victory; and if we believed in a free press it must be the duty of that press to publish the facts even when – indeed *particularly* when – they told against ourselves. I was able to add, what was in fact the case, that quite a few days earlier *The Times* had published a two-column article 'from our special correspondent in Korea' headed 'SEOUL AFTER VICTORY. REVERSE SIDE TO SOUTH KOREAN RULE', which confirmed everything Cameron had written, but was a good deal more outspoken than he had felt he could allow himself to be.*

When I ended there was no discussion. Mr Hulton said he considered I had put my case very well and they would now consider their verdict. The compliment was well-meant but cannot have been justified – or else Mr Hulton's memory played him false – for twenty-five years later, when interviewed by John Ormond for that remarkable television film 'The Life and Death of *Picture Post*', his impression of the occasion was that I had ' ... rather foolishly devoted [myself] to a rather brilliant exposé of the situation in China, which seemed to us irrelevant, and he rather implied that Europe and Britain were finished and the great thing was China'.

Whichever version of my words Mr Hulton's fellow directors took in, however, mattered little, since shortly after the meeting I received a letter in which they unanimously agreed that 'Mr Hulton's decision as Chairman and Managing Director is to be upheld,' and that no part of the Korean

*The Times, 15 October 1950, page 5.

article or pictures 'should appear in *Picture Post* at any time'.

To this I replied that I fully accepted the chairman's and the board's authority to decide who should edit the magazine, but that so long as I was editor I did not accept their authority to decide its contents. 'I take it that you will, therefore, dismiss me from my post, but want to make it clear that I do not resign.' I waited in the office until 7 p.m., but then learned that – in accordance with the mixture of farce and drama which marked the week's events throughout – they had all very sensibly gone off somewhere for a drink.

When the staff of the magazine heard what had happened they all wanted to walk out, and my last few days in the editor's chair were spent in persuading them not to do so, in urging Ted Castle to take over in my place, and in convincing the management – and through them the proprietors – that this was the only possibility for keeping the paper in existence. The staff, as was natural, were divided between determination to support their editor and reluctance to lose their jobs, a position I well understood since I was reluctant to lose my own. Ted too was divided – between the wish to become editor and in doing so save the magazine from disintegration, on the one hand, and on the other a loyal unwillingness to benefit from my expulsion. The latter was coupled with doubt about how to act over the article in dispute, since the staff were insisting on its going in and the proprietors determined to keep it out. Management too had its problems, since the Hultons had made known some time before that they would never accept Ted Castle as editor because of his direct association with the Labour Party – information which I had at once passed on to him. But I now warned the directors that, if they intended to have a magazine at all over the next months, they must persuade the Hultons to change their mind, since if they got rid of Ted and myself together, there would be no hope of keeping on the staff. And in this way, after endless arguments and discussions – one meeting with the staff lasted for the whole day – the matter was finally resolved. Ted would take over; guaranteed the editorship for six months, he was dropped as soon as the agreed period ended. The staff would stay on – except for Bert Lloyd, Marjorie

Beckett, and the science writer Derek Wragge-Morley, who resigned. Lionel Birch, who was away on holiday, gave in his resignation as soon as he got back, but was persuaded by joint representations from us all to rescind it later on.

Meantime the sound of incessant argument raging over all floors of our Shoe Lane offices* and the sight of distracted journalists rushing across the road to the Two Brewers and tottering more slowly back had attracted much interest in Fleet Street. Rumours of all kinds were flying around and newspapers started to ring up and ask for statements. I was shown one drawn up by the management which they proposed to put out via the Press Association, saying that I had 'resigned the editorship following a dispute over Korea'. I said that if they put this out I should sue them for misrepresentation, and they were still arguing over what wording to use when the matter was taken out of their hands.

Since the Tuesday morning, 24 October, when the storm broke, a full week had now elapsed, but Ted Castle did not finally agree to become editor, nor the proprietor finally accept him, until quite late on the evening of Tuesday, 31 October. By that time everyone was tired and fed up and decided that any statement could keep until next day. Late that evening, however, Ted rang me at my home to tell me that the *Daily Worker* had got the story and were running it next morning. Later still James Cameron rang through to report that the *Worker* had been on to him for comments; he said they were not only leading the front page with the heading, 'Korea Exposure Suppressed,'PICTURE POST EDITOR IS SACKED', but had got hold of and were printing his own article which had been the cause of all the trouble. I could see at once that it would be disastrous if the Communist newspaper were the only one to carry the information; for me personally it was indeed already disastrous, since such publication could only confirm rumours that I was some kind of fellow traveller. While the thought was in my mind, I was also in the same moment realizing how it had

---

*In the expressive words of Michael Middleton, the art editor, in the TV programme 'The Life and Death of *Picture Post*', ' . . . the place was rather like an antheap after it's been kicked.'

probably come about – in a big printing works there were certain to be at least a few Communists in the work-force, one or other of whom must have spoken of the row to someone on the *Daily Worker*, who would promptly have asked him to smuggle out proofs of the article in question. So now the fat, particularly my fat, was in the fire.

It was already late but I rang Pearce at his home, got him out of bed, told him what was happening and urged him to release a statement to the Press Association immediately, even if he could not remember the precise wording fixed on with his fellow directors. Accordingly *The Times* and other newspapers carried the anouncement next morning:

Mr Edward Hulton states with the deepest regret that, following a dispute about the handling of material about the Korean war, he has instructed Mr Tom Hopkinson to relinquish the position of editor of *Picture Post*. There is no personal hostility between Mr Hulton and Mr Hopkinson. Mr Ted Castle, associate editor of *Picture Post* and for six years the assistant editor of the paper, is the new editor.

This seemed to me needlessly wordy, but it made the point. 'Hopkinson,' wrote the *Observer* on the following Sunday, 'is not the first editor to find that Hulton alternates between long periods of accepting advice, and sudden irrevocable decisions of his own. In the past two years he has replaced six editors in his organization.'

Two incidents complete for me the picture of this crowded month, which would change the pattern of my life in ways which at the time I could never have visualized.

The first had already happened back at the beginning of October. The firm had recently provided me with a new car; it was not literally new, because new cars in 1950 were still unobtainable, but it was almost new and the only luxury car I had owned or would ever own. It was an Alvis, long and low and black, and had only been in my possession for a week or two. Driving from Chelsea to Shoe Lane, I used to go along Buckingham Palace Road, past the front of the palace and along the Mall, then around Trafalgar Square out into the Strand and Fleet Street. This was a drizzly morning, but there was not much traffic as I followed a taxi towards the palace, both of us travelling slowly with a reasonable distance between the two. Suddenly – for what cause I could not see – the taxi jammed on its brakes, its rear end slid towards the gutter and stopped against the kerb, pushing the bonnet out into my path. I too tried to stop and skidded, travelling with locked brakes into the taxi's rear. The taxi was unmarked, but my nearside mudguard burst, the bumpers were twisted and one of the two horns torn off. When I got home I wrote in my notebook, 'It was nobody's fault, not even mine. It just happened. I wasn't upset. Presumably it was trying to tell me something. . . .'

What it was trying to tell me was, it now appeared, that I should not expect to keep the Alvis long. At the time the row started it had only just come back from the repairers and now ten days later, having left the office for the last time, I stood looking it over outside my house in Cheyne Row. I was having a good look because I should have to hand the car back to the firm as soon as the month ended. While looking I noticed an old white shoe box on the back seat and wondered what on earth it was doing there. Then I remembered the second incident. On the day after it was known that I had been sacked, Grumpy Ainsworth had come into my office, pushed the box onto my desk, uttered some of his unintelligible grunts, and vanished. I must have carried it down to the car when I left for home that night and, in the pressure of time, forgotten all about it. I took the parcel inside, unwrapped a mass of tissue paper, and lifted out the most beautiful Tanagra figure I had ever seen – a goddess in terracotta with one breast bare, sitting on a cloud where she must have sat since at least the fourth century BC.

Upset at not having spoken to Grumpy before now, and appalled that I should have been carrying such a treasure around on the back seat of a car, I at once rang him at his home, said that his goddess was the most beautiful object I had ever seen, that I'd been happy to have it with me for a while but that now he must accept it back. From his emphatic noises it was apparent that he refused to do this, and the goddess – having travelled over much of Africa and been through two catastrophes – is sitting on her cloud in front of me as I write.

26

Who Killed Cock Robin?

My departure from the magazine I had edited for the past ten years caused a small stir in Fleet Street, more for the manner in which it happened than for the fact. It caused a much smaller one – about equivalent to a backbencher being run over – in the political world. A question was asked in the House of Commons. A few members wrote me personal letters. Herbert Morrison, then Lord President of the Council, arranged for me to be offered a public relations job which happened to be vacant; I did not in fact accept the job, but was grateful for an act of consideration coming at this moment.

The national newspapers had carried the announcement put out by the firm, but comment was mainly confined to the weeklies such as the *New Statesman* and *Spectator*. More lively was the editorial in a magazine called *Public Opinion*, then being published by the *Daily Mirror* group: 'Mr Hopkinson's abrupt dismissal may solve for the moment a highly awkward editorial situation, and although the usual diaphanous expressions of tepid friendship have been exchanged between the executioner and the decapitated, the issue at stake remains unaltered.' That, I thought, might well have been written by the *Daily Mirror* columnist Cassandra, but the writer was surely historically inaccurate in continuing: 'Many years ago the men of good-will could not be so summarily deprived of their posts as public commentators at the whim of irresponsible persons who employed them, and who profited by their talents and their integrity. That these things should occur now is a surly

291

comment on our society.'*

The choice of the word 'surly' in particular made me think of Cassandra, whom I had last seen six years earlier high up in a tree, looking like an enormous khaki-coloured hen, in the course of hostilities between the Home Guards of Turville Heath and those of Lane End. He held a pair of fieldglasses and was gazing out over the Buckinghamshire landscape, while the stout-hearted fighting men of Turville Heath were infiltrating into Lane End territory beneath his feet.

In addition to the published comments, several branches of the National Union of Journalists, to which I had always belonged, passed resolutions supporting my action and I was also invited by a few Fleet Street editors or near-editors to give them my version of events. This informal gathering took place in a handsome flat belonging to Malcolm Muggeridge, which looked out over Regent's Park. When I had said what little I had to say, one of those present asked, 'But why didn't you stop the *Daily Worker* getting hold of Cameron's article? That's done your case a great deal of harm.'

'How d'you prevent something happening which you haven't even thought of? Of course if I could have prevented it, I would.'

'We were planning to come out with an editorial in support of you,' a writer on one of the serious Sunday newspapers remarked. 'But the owner told us you were a crypto-Communist, so that of course put paid to that.'

'Where had he got *that* story?'

'How should I know. But he seemed quite confident about it.'

'Did it never *occur* to you,' asked Muggeridge, who as deputy editor of the *Daily Telegraph* was at that time less unworldly than he has since become, 'I mean to say, did you never *imagine* ... didn't it so much as even cross your *mind* ... that in sending Jimmy Cameron to Korea you could very well land yourself in *trouble*?'

'Yes.'

*Public Opinion, 3 November 1950.

'Then why on *earth*, my dear fellow, did you send *him*? Of *all* people?'

'Because he was the best man for the job I had.'

'Oh, I *see*. . . . Well, in that case, of course, there isn't *really* anything one can say. *Is* there?'

It will be convenient if I set down here what happened to the magazine, from which at this point my own life and interests diverged sharply. Its sales, which had been over 1,380,000 for the six months to June 1950, had sunk by June 1951 to 1,225,000 and to 935,000 by June 1952. They remained not far below the crucial one million mark until 1956, when they started to melt away more rapidly, and by May 1957, when the magazine folded, a printing paper reported that '*Picture Post's* average sale in recent weeks is understood to have fallen below 600,000.'*

Flattering as it would be to ascribe this publishing disaster simply to my own 'decapitation', the claim would not stand scrutiny. The truth is more complex, a number of factors being involved, any two of which could have occasioned the collapse. First place must be given, not to the absence of any particular person but to the presence of far too many – a procession of editors who at times must have been dodging in and out of offices and along corridors like husbands and lovers in a Feydeau farce. Ted Castle had been fired as soon as his six months were up, to be succeeded by an advertising man, Frank Dowling, who did not last long. Just how many people were appointed editor during the five or six succeeding years will perhaps never be known, but they included Brian Chapman, of the *Daily Mirror* and *News Chronicle*, Jack Hargraves from *Lilliput*, and Len Spooner from *Illustrated*. In addition John Pearce, as joint general manager, took the chair for a while, as did Edward Hulton himself. A Polish gentleman was said also to have sat in it, while towards the end decisions were being taken – if reports were correct – by a consortium of all surviving editors blending their talents in conference together.

Confusion spread to the boardroom, where in 1953 an almost

Printing Press and Publishing News, 23 May 1957.

entirely new set of faces had replaced those which had been there in the previous year. At one point there was something approaching a palace revolution in an attempt to unseat the chairman, but when the smoke of battle cleared, the bodies on the carpet were not those of the proprietors but of the insurrectionists. By now I was far removed from the scene, knowing only what reached me when some echo of these activities found its way into the press, usually into the business news, or on one of the rare occasions when I met someone from the office. One such meeting was with Vernon Holding, that same circulation manager who had said to me triumphantly on our first day of publication, 'It's all gone! Over the whole south and east of England you can't buy a single copy.'

Now, in answer to my query as to how things were going, he thought for a minute before replying, 'Like a football match after the goalposts have been removed. It's every man for himself – but nobody knows which way to run.'

In fairness to those editing the paper in these years, it should be recognized that the task they were attempting was impossible without more time than they were allowed. One or two were journalists with records of success in other fields who might well have succeeded here had they been able to carry through long-term plans. But when a newspaper or magazine starts to go downhill its slide must be corrected slowly; it cannot be jerked up into success, any more than someone suffering from a serious illness can be set instantly upon his feet. Declining readership means as a rule a loss of confidence by the public, which no longer feels that the paper carries a clear message and so helps them to make sense of the world about them. This is particularly true of general magazines, which are not a product of the news but of the minds of the men and women who create them and are bought as much for the magazine's character as for its content. In a time of falling sales, therefore, what is needed is a strong nerve in the editor and much patience on the proprietor's part since he has to give the chosen remedy a chance to take effect. The very worst course of action is to keep on nervously varying the formula and so adding to the readers' confusion and uncertainty. But now some issues of *Picture Post* had begun to look like copies of the *Sunday Mirror*, while others resembled an illustrated *New Statesman*. Either formula might conceivably have attracted its own kind of readership in time, but long before that could be proved or disproved some fresh remedy was being tried.

A similar indecisiveness afflicted management. Readers have became accustomed nowadays to continual price changes, but to alter the price of a publication at that time was a serious matter, demanding careful consideration and preparation of the readers' minds if they were not to feel they were being exploited. During 1951, however, Hulton Press increased the price of *Picture Post* twice within five months, from 4d. to 5d., and again from 5d. to 6d. 'These increases,' the annual report observed sombrely, 'had a very adverse effect upon circulation which in turn affected our advertising revenue.' Next year the increases were cancelled and the price put back again to fourpence. Strangest of all, in face of looming financial disaster, was the firm's decision to move into an impressive eight-storey block of offices in Fleet Street, named Hulton House, which was opened by the chairman in February 1957, the year in which *Picture Post* closed and the company's net profit totalled just over £11,000.

Perhaps the last moment when the magazine might still have been saved had come in 1953, not long after the great boardroom massacre, when Nika Hulton had the idea of visiting the United States and persuading Stefan Lorant to come back to Shoe Lane and take over the post he had left thirteen years earlier. When I heard this was happening I thought that the only possible remedy was about to be applied – and just in time. The colour might yet flow back into the corpse's cheeks. According to the *Daily Mail*,*

Dr Stefan Lorant leaves for London next week. Yesterday news agency messages said he had been offered £35,000 for a year's work on *Picture Post*. This he would neither confirm nor deny.

'If it was that sum,' he said, 'how much would be left after income tax?'

*Daily Mail, 2 March 1953.

Whether or not income tax was the snag on which negotiations foundered, certainly Lorant never arrived in London and the decline in sales continued. A final opportunity, not indeed to save the magazine but possibly to preserve something from its wreckage, came in 1957 just before the magazine folded. Negotiations had been entered into with the French picture magazine *Paris-Match* with a view to their taking over *Picture Post* and either keeping it in publication or transforming it into a British edition of their own successful paper. Early reports said that agreement had been reached, but in the end here too negotiations came to nothing, having broken down, it was said, over a last-minute increase in the demands made by one of the two parties to the deal.

Unexpected deaths generally result in inquests and there was much public interest over the death of *Picture Post*, which in its heyday had been read by some six or seven million people every week. Nobody in such circumstances likes to be thought to have wielded the knife or placed the wrong pills by the patient's bedside, and various theories were put forward to account for his demise. Rising costs had carried his usual diet of newsprint beyond what he could afford, so that he had inevitably starved to death; television, which had stolen his advertising revenue and left him naked to the blast, was denounced by others as the culprit. This was certainly Edward Hulton's view in his public announcement at the time,* and which he repeated in the television programme of 1977 already mentioned: 'The advertising agents took the view that the thing for the future was television ... they told me they would devote all their advertising either to television or to the national and Sunday press.'†

An opposite view was expressed by Gerald Barry in a letter to *The Times*: 'It is cowardly and defeatist to put the blame on competition from television; all commercial ventures have to stand up on their merits to competition with rival media.... *Picture Post* has failed over these later years because it has been

---

The Times, 16 May 1957.
†'The Life and Death of *Picture Post*', BBC1, 30 August 1977.

deprived of its initial sense of purpose, and in consequence has been forced to snatch at successive shifts and improvisations in the attempt to hang on to a circulation failing for lack of resolute direction.'*

'It's often said,' remarked Robert Kee, appearing in the same television programme as Edward Hulton, 'that it was television that killed *Picture Post*. I think this must be absolute nonsense. I know for a fact that I never saw a television set until about 1953, after I'd left *Picture Post*. People didn't watch television much in those days.' Kee might have added that until 1954, by which year *Picture Post* was already in desperate trouble, such a thing as television advertising did not exist.

In his book *Point of Departure*,† James Cameron laid the blame on the magazine's lack of character. 'In fact *Picture Post* soon painlessly surrendered all the values and purposes that had made it a journal of consideration, before the eyes of its diminishing public it drifted into the market of arch cheesecake and commonplace decoration, and by and by it died, as by then it deserved to do.'

My own view, given in the same oft-quoted television programme, was little different. 'Who really killed Cock Robin? I think the truth is that a magazine has a special character of its own, and it has to keep to that character. It is for that particular character that the readers buy it, and it is this character which keeps the staff enthusiastic and united. In its last years *Picture Post* became not one, but many different magazines. So I do not think that television is to be blamed for killing *Picture Post*. I think it just lost its sense of direction and wandered off into the fog.'

The Times, 17 May 1957.
†Arthur Barker Ltd, London, 1967.

27
Aftermath

When the storm was finally over, I realized with a kind of shock that I was no longer under the necessity of going to an office, and that this was the first time such freedom had been mine since April 1928, when I had been given my first regular job as a copywriter after the *Westminster Gazette* went down with all hands.

But did I really want this liberty – and, if so, what use should I make of it now that I had it? Offers of various kinds of work came in over the next month or two, in addition to the one Herbert Morrison had put in my way. A publisher wanted a pictorial history of the Second World War – but I was unwilling to spend a year or two on picture research, nor did it seem that on what I would receive for editing the work I should remain alive long enough to complete it. A small magazine group suggested I should plan out 'something similar but essentially different from' *Picture Post*. A film producer wanted ideas for scripts, but preferred not to commission anything. The *Daily Herald* asked me to write a column two or three times a week; but this would have meant spending most of my time going round and meeting people in order to find something to write about, and for the moment I did not much want to meet people. Also the writing of a column has always seemed to me one of the most difficult of journalistic tasks, and one for which I am by nature ill-fitted.

I went to see everyone who suggested I should do so, ate a lot of lunches at their expense, and sat in front of many imposing desks; but the more I listened, the more certain I became that I did not want to take on any of the work being proposed.

For a while a small flood of letters poured in. Those from the colleagues with whom I had worked, I valued and preserved. I had a number too from journalists and people in public life whom I knew or partially knew, sending me messages of good will, as well as others which, after a perfunctory sentence of commiseration, suggested I make use of this opportunity to obtain publicity for their own far more deserving cases. Two or three friends wrote that they had followed the affair with interest, and would have been anxious on my account had they not known very well that I must have sewn the firm up with a long-term contract, so that they had in fact no need to worry. From my father I received a most understanding letter in which he offered to lend me the little house at Aber which had been our childhood home; I was grateful for his offer but I did not want to go back to childhood.

I answered each of them as best I could, but with a feeling of hardly knowing what I was about. The truth is that I was hit on the head, partially stunned by what had happened and also full of resentment, which I had sense enough to realize was unreasonable but not detachment enough to overcome, except by slow degrees. 'Gradual by gradual, Mr Hopkinson,' a politician would say to me ten years later in another continent and in what would seem to me another life, and 'gradual by gradual' I arrived at some sort of balance sheet. From this, when I was able to assimilate the facts, I realized that I had been extremely fortunate. What I had lost was not negligible, but what I had gained was potentially far greater.

What I had lost was, first of all, money. Despite the confidence in my financial shrewdness expressed by one or two letter-writers, I had never had a contract with the firm and never asked for one, so that I had got literally nothing in writing since my original letter of employment on a monthly basis. Some months before the blow-up the management had indeed suggested that it was time a proper contract should be in force, but there had been delays over drawing it up so that it was still incompletely drafted and unsigned. After a good deal of legal squaring-up, however, I eventually received reasonable compensation for loss of office, so that I was not forced to take a job for two or three years if I did not wish. But I should never again, as it turned out, hold any position which brought me anything like so large a salary; nor would any future job provide me with a car, or produce such agreeable incidental advantages as a regular flow of theatre tickets.

Second, and this at the time mattered to me more, I had lost prestige. Ever since I had first arrived in London it had been my private dream – as no doubt of many other young men and women – to be known among the people I saw and met. I was not so extravagant in my fantasies as to expect, or even want, to be recognized up and down the place in the way actors and parliamentary figures are known, or as nowadays those who appear regularly on television find themselves recognized. What I wanted and for the past ten years had enjoyed, was not having to explain my existence to people or tell them what work I did. Now I must accustom myself again to being asked, 'What sort of work do you do?' or from those who knew me better, 'What are you up to nowadays?' Inevitable, almost always friendly, questions, but which to me in my state of touchiness and injured pride sounded like, 'Isn't it about time you did something worthwhile before you drop out of the picture altogether?'

In addition to practical advantages, I had also lost the genial companionship in which I had been living with contentment. Years before, when I first started regular work, I used to feel each morning that I was venturing into hostile territory and should be lucky if I got back unscathed. But in recent years I had looked forward to spending my working day among a company of friends almost as I had done long ago at the university – and would find myself actually expecting when I arrived at the office that something interesting and enjoyable was going to happen. Of course the company of friends still continued to exist, as I did myself, but we no longer spent time together, and – apart perhaps from an occasional celebration – I realized that we never would again. I had ceased to belong to what I had come to look on as some kind of enlarged family, but a family

I had myself largely chosen, not one provided for me. It was possibly foolish, even ridiculous, to look upon one's work companions in this way; but ridiculous or not I had come to do so, and I missed their lively and warm-hearted companionship intensely.

Lastly, I had lost that precious possession – from which we all cry to be delivered yet which few of us can contrive to live without – a routine. Any established way of life will become at times tedious and constraining, but it frees one from the burden of deciding, 'What shall I do now?' Twenty years and more before this time, at one of his crowded lectures in an Oxford hall, I had heard Robin Collingwood speak in praise of convention: 'It may be a nuisance,' he said, 'to have meals at fixed times, but what a much worse imposition it would be to have to keep thinking throughout the day, "Do I want to have something to eat?"' And from there he had gone on to an examination of convention and routine, and their value not only in the external arrangements of life, but in the complex pattern of our human relationships....

Such practical and emotional losses were inevitable and pressing. They forced themselves on my attention, making me inward-looking, unresponsive and bad-tempered. The advantages, by contrast, worked through into consciousness only slowly, but once they did so the first thing I realized was that I had been fortunate to have ended this stage of my life on a clear issue. Sydney Jacobson, in the television programme often referred to, said, 'If it hadn't been for the Korean article there would have been something else.' This was true, except that instead of being 'something' it might have been worse – a succession of near nothings. When people in the relationship of editor and proprietor no longer have confidence in one another, the editor must be grateful if the break comes on an issue which he knows is worth fighting for. A mean-minded proprietor – which Hulton certainly was not – can make an editor's position intolerable by constant pinpricks, such as the refusal to authorize necessary equipment or to pay some key man a merited increase, until at last the editor walks out over the accusation that his department has been using too many paperclips. This I had been spared.

More slowly still came the realization that I had been given an opportunity to reorganize my life. Always I had been split between the intention of being a journalist and the longing to become a writer. After a prolonged struggle I had made my way into journalism with very little knowledge of what it would be like. But now I knew, and could decide consciously whether to remain on the surface dealing with the events of everyday life, spending hours on reading newspapers and magazines and listening to radio programmes, or try to develop a more thoughtful attitude within myself. Looking critically at a short novel, *Down the Long Slide*, which I had lately written and at stories of mine that had recently appeared, I compared it and most of them unfavourably with work done earlier. In some of them, it seemed to me, there was a skilful build-up and much insight – but just at the point where the writer should penetrate to the heart of the matter, he had shied away so that the conclusion was a let-down.

Quite apart from criticism of a literary kind – and seemingly unrelated to it – I had begun to be haunted by a phrase which would come into my mind almost against my will and at times inconveniently, when I was either enjoying myself or set upon doing so. The phrase was a perfectly ordinary one: *Is there a pattern in the carpet*? What I meant by this – or rather what I took it to mean for me, since it was not a phrase I had consciously produced but rather one which had dropped into my mind like a stone into a well – was, has everything that happens to us a meaning, or is life just a casual sequence of events like a film pieced together out of fragments from the cutting-room floor? And with the phrase came a visual impression.

The impression was of a carpeted room across which some minute creature, possibly an ant, is attempting to make its way. It can see in front of it or behind, to left and right, but it cannot look up at the ceiling nor see anything more beneath itself than the floor upon which it struggles. In its progress it keeps coming across patches that are smooth and others where the pile is thick and progress difficult. At times it is surprised by tufts in unexpected colours. Having now got some way across the room, the question this ant has begun to ask itself is, 'Is there a pattern in the carpet? Because if so, and if I can work out what the pattern is, I shall know where the flat and the rough places are and be able to make progress faster. Above all I might have some idea why I am crossing the room at all, and what I shall find when I reach the other side.'

This question of a pattern, or purpose, had become acute for me because my marriage had ended, though not yet by official decree. Having no office now to go to and unwilling to be constantly about the house, I had taken a small flat for myself a mile or so away from Cheyne Row, to which I had moved a few armfuls of books and one or two of the early English watercolours I had been collecting over the past ten years. This gave me a focal point. I had long known that my marriage with Gerti would not survive, but what I had been unable hitherto to face was the breach in my relationship with our two children. What I could not face was partly the loss of their company from day to day, and partly the sense of the suffering and bewilderment they would feel; which had also its selfish aspect in that I was trying to avoid the loss of their trust and confidence in me. 'Gradual by gradual', with much distress to all, these matters would work themselves out over the next years.

Meantime I had met Dorothy, widow of the writer Hugh Kingsmill, whom I was just starting to know before his death in 1949. In two or three years' time Dorothy and I would settle down together and embark on a marriage which would last for the remainder of our lives – not without difficulties and conflicts but with increasing harmony and happiness. It would be Dorothy rather than myself who would be responsible for our spending nine years in Africa, which afforded both of us, when already in our fifties, an entirely new life without the disagreeable necessity for a new birth.

Soon after I met Dorothy, when we had already been talking for some hours, I remarked, 'Of all the people I have ever known you are the one most concerned with truth. You won't settle for anything less.'

She said nothing for a moment, but then asked, 'Well, what

about you? What's your own attitude to truth?'

I too thought for a moment, and then said, 'In the last resort I will accept the truth.'

But what is 'the last resort'? And how will any of us know when we have got there?

Postscript

I have already overrun the amount of words allotted for this book and have still only managed to reach the age of forty-five, though I ought to have arrived at my actual age of seventy-six – and had indeed undertaken to have got here. I can only say that once I started to write there turned out to have been a lot more life than I imagined. If there is still a little of it left and conditions prove favourable, I hope that the record may in due course succeed in catching up with me.

Index

Daily Dispatch, 159
Daily Express, 133, 237, 281
Daily Herald, 130, 131–3, 140, 142, 143, 145, 298
Daily Mail, 44, 122, 133, 295
Daily Mirror, 133, 157, 223, 233, 291
Daily Sketch, 133, 159, 214
Daily Telegraph, 109, 214, 292
Daily Worker, 288–9, 292
Dane, Surrey, 123, 130, 131, 134, 144
Davies, Clement, 195
Day-Lewis, Cecil, 94–5
de la Mare, Walter, 228
Delmo, 168–9
Dempsey, Canon, 39, 266
Denby, Elizabeth, 192
Deutsch, Gerti (T.H.'s second wife), 167–9, 231, 262, 264–5, 270–71, 303
Deverson, Harry, 238
Dickens, Charles, 131–2, 133, 146
Dickenson, W. J., 160, 190, 218–19, 233, 239, 260, 273
Dietrich, Marlene, 148
Dorchester Hotel, London, 254, 275
Dowling, Brian, 175n.
Dowling, Frank, 293
Down the Long Slide, 302
Drake, H. L., 85
DuBois, Dr W. E. B., 246
Dunbar, John, 144, 145–9, 159
Dunkirk, 177, 186, 187
Duval, Rev. Dr, 27

Eagle, 274–5
Earnshaw-Smith, Eric, 126, 151
Edelman, Maurice, 174, 234–5
Eden, Anthony, 254, 256
Egypt, 202
Eighth Army, 207
Encyclopedia Britannica Award, 283
England, Douglas, 119, 120
Etchells, Frederick, 118
Evening Standard, 143, 159, 190, 192
Everybody's Weekly, 240

Farmer's Weekly, 159–60
Fenby, Charles, 95, 99–100, 102–3, 104–6, 121, 174, 233
Ferguson, W. H., 49, 72–3, 74, 98
Festing Jones, 128
Finse, 257–9
First World War, 21, 36, 44–5, 116, 179–80
Foot, Michael, 192
Ford, Henry, 93–4
Foreign Press Association, 204
Forward March, 195
Fountaine, Rev. Thomas, 265
France, 126, 170, 176, 186–7, 249
Fraser, Sir Ian, 215
Fraser, Sir Robert, 146–7, 148
Freeman, Frank, 128
Freeman, John, 234
Freyn, Joe, 168, 169
Fulbright, William, 84
Fyvel, T. R., 278

General elections
   1945, 196, 216–17, 250
   1950, 261
General Strike (1926), 140
Gentleman, Tom, 119, 120
Gentleman, Winifred, 119
George VI, King of England, 206, 207
Germany, 116; Second World War, 168–71, 186–7, 188–91, 200–201, 207
Ghana, 245
Gibbons, Stella, *Cold Comfort Farm*, 121
Gibbs-Smith, Charles, 241
Gillies, Donald, 84, 162
Girl, 274
Gisburn, 266, 267
Glan Afon, Aber, 17–20
Glasgow, 221
Gloucester, Duke of, 207
Gneisenau, 204–5
Godesberg, 163
Goebbels, Joseph, 166

OF THIS OUR TIME

Goering, Hermann, 166
Goldie, Mr, 54–6, 118
Gollancz, Victor, 143, 193
Gooch Collection, 241
Good, Tom, 230
Gourmets restaurant, 229
Graham and Gillies, 162
Graves, Robert, 228
Greece, 200–201
Greene, Graham, 192
Greenheys, 59
Greenwood, Arthur, 211–12, 222
Greenwood, Walter, 188
Gridley, Sir Arnold, 215
Griffiths, Mr, 54
Grigson, Frances, 128
Grigson, Geoffrey, 128, 228
Grimble, Rosemary, 236
Gstaad, 259
Guildford, 254
Gustavus Adolphus, King of
   Sweden, 258–9

Hansard, 142
Hardy, Bert, 174–5, 236, 244, 281,
   282–3
Hargraves, Jack, 293
Harmsworth, Desmond, 137–8
Harmsworth, Esmond, 99
Harrison, Rex, 227
Hastings, Macdonald, 174, 191, 234
Havinden, Ashley, 117, 118
Havinden, Margaret, 117, 124
Healey, Denis, 234
Hellenic Society, 26
Henderson, Wyn, 137
Henson, Leslie, 228
Hepburn, Audrey, 247
Highland Division, 187
Hill, A. V., 209–10
Hinchingbrooke, Lady, 193
Hinchingbrooke, Lord, 217
Hitler, Adolf, 160, 163, 166, 169,
   170–71, 176, 185, 207, 227
Hoare, Mr, 22, 24–5, 44, 45–6
Hobman, 100, 103

Hogg, Quintin (Lord Hailsham),
   193n., 217
Holding, Vernon, 163–4, 165, 294
Holland, 170
Holloway, Balliol, 84
Holloway prison, 244
Home Guard, 176–80, 250, 292
Hopkinson (T.H.'s grandmother),
   40–41
Hopkinson, Amanda (T.H.'s
   daughter), 263, 264
Hopkinson, Austin, 27, 50, 70, 72,
   74–6, 105, 108, 138
Hopkinson, Dorothy (T.H.'s third
   wife), 303–4
Hopkinson, Esther (T.H.'s sister),
   11, 91, 122
   childhood, 29, 32
   horoscope, 42–3
   move to Burneside, 60
   works in Africa, 188
   in Second World War, 232
Hopkinson, Evelyn (T.H.'s mother),
   232, 265
   and T.H.'s childhood, 14–17
   in Colne, 30–33, 34–5, 36, 40–41
   move to Burneside, 60
Hopkinson, Henry (T.H.'s father),
   26, 266
   becomes clergyman, 11–12, 27, 91
   academic career, 13, 14
   curate in Colne, 29–31, 34–5,
   41–2
   joins Army, 44
   and T.H.'s choice of career, 45–6
   and T.H.'s schooling, 56–7
   moves to Greenheys, 59
   move to Burneside, 59
   buys car, 61
   interest in art, 70–71
   inner withdrawal, 90–91
   relations with T.H., 91–3
   sermons, 92
   objects to T.H.'s flat, 104–5
   and T.H.'s marriage, 127
   curate in Battersea, 232

310

Mikardo, Ian, 276
Miles, Bernard, 84
Miles, F. W., 193
Mills, Saxon, 117, 118–19, 124
Mim (governess), 14, 16
Ministry of Information, 185, 202–3,
    214, 220, 238, 241
Ministry of Labour, 212
Ministry of Town and Country
    Planning, 222
Ministry of Transport, 220, 224
Ministry of Works, 220–22, 224
Mist in the Tagus, 169
Mitchell, David, 256–7
Molson, Hugh, 193n.
Montgomery, Field Marshal, 208,
    211
Moody, 52
Moore, Henry, 229
Morley College, London, 193
Morning Post, 107–8, 128
Morris, Rev. Marcus, 274–5
Morrison, Herbert, 171, 200, 215,
    291, 298
Mortimer, Bishop of Exeter, 53–4
Mosley, Oswald, 245
'Mountain Madness', 149
Muggeridge, Malcolm, 278, 292
Mulready, William, 239
Münchner Illustrierte Presse, 147
Munich Agreement (1938), 193

National Front, 245
National Government, 140, 142–3
National Magazine Company,
    274–5
National Theatre, 153–4
National Union of Journalists, 292
Naughton, Bill, 228
Nawiasky, Mechthild, 228, 229
Nazarré, 167–8
Nazi Propaganda Service, 216
Nazis, 166, 176
Nehru, Jawaharlal, 273
New Republic, 153
New Scientist, 160n.

New Society, 160n.
New Statesman, 121, 143, 158, 192,
    291, 295
New Writing, 150
News Chronicle, 192, 193, 223, 277–8
1941 Committee, 191–6
Nkrumah, Kwame, 245–6, 247
Norman, Montague, 143
Norris, 49
North Africa, 201, 202–3, 207–10,
    211
Norway, 170, 205, 257–9
Nursing Mirror, 160
Nye, Leslie, 95–6, 110

Observer, 192, 223, 229, 289
Odhams Newspapers, 144, 145–8,
    157
Odham's Press, 123, 130–33, 134–7
Old Vic Theatre School, 263
Orlando, South Africa, 188
Ormond, John, 237, 286
Orwell, George, 197, 278, 279
Oslo, 259
Osterley Park, 177–80
'Over the Bridge', 153–4
Owen, David, 192
Oxford, 47–57
Oxford Mail, 121, 174
Oxford University, 73–4, 78–89,
    93–100, 121–2
Oxford University Appointments
    Committee, 98–9, 110

Padmore, George, 245
Pan-African Conference, 245–7
Paris, 253
Paris-Match, 296
Parish, Mona, 241–2
Passing Show, 159
Patrick (school friend), 71–2
Pearce, John, 274, 289, 293
Pembroke College, Oxford: T.H. at,
    73–4, 78–89, 93–100
Pembroke College Debating
    Society, 83, 84